Home Design Publishers
7737 Fair Oaks Blvd. 419
Carmichael, CA 95608

Drafting House Plans

A Whole House Drafting System for Planning and Design

Library of Congress Cataloging Card Number 90-081254

Curran, June Norris   date.
    Drafting House Plans
    A Whole House Drafting System for Planning and Design

ISBN 0-932370-04-7

*Educational consultant for this book was Marvin F.
Nunes, Architectural Drafting Instructor - board and
computer systems - Fresno City College, Fresno,
California.*

Printed in the United States of America

Published by:
Home Design Publishers
7737 Fair Oaks Blvd. no 419
Carmichael, California 95608

CONTENTS

INTRODUCTION

This book is designed to teach you how to draw a complete set of plans for a one-story house, an addition to an existing house, or a remodeling project.

It assumes that you have little or no training in the field of architectural drafting or design and walks you through the process of completing a full set of working drawings.

You will find easy to follow introductory illustrations, example plan sheets and check lists of building code requirements to guide you each step of the way.

You will learn how to visualize spatial relationships, use standard architectural scales and symbols, sketch preliminary drawings, develop a detailed floor plan and exterior elevations, and prepare a final plot plan.

Drafting House Plans is the natural outgrowth of my earlier book, **Drawing Home Plans.** It contains much of the same basic information; but goes beyond the scope of the earlier book by teaching you how to draw foundation plans, roof plans, sections and details.

Over the years, **Drawing Home Plans** has been thoroughly tested in the classroom. It has also been used by individuals working independently to draw plans for their dream homes. The book's major appeal for students, as well as instructors, is it's simplified approach to architectural drawing and the cut-out section of architectural scales and templates of furniture and fixtures.

I have retained this same unique approach to presenting architectural information in **Drafting House Plans.**

It is my sincere hope that you will enjoy working with this introductory level material and that some of you will continue on to become design professionals.

June Curran

 UNIT 1

DRAWING EQUIPMENT

Objective: *To become familiar with the Drawing Plans System components and other useful equipment.*

DRAWING PLANS SYSTEM COMPONENTS

It is much easier to get started drawing if you have the proper materials and equipment. For this reason, components consisting of scales, a grid paper guide, lettering guidelines, and drawing guides have been designed and comprise pages 177-187 of the book.

SCALES

Included on the last page of the book are scales in three different units of measurement. Cut them out carefully.

SCALES INCLUDED ARE:

One-Quarter Inch equals One Foot (1/4" = 1')
One-Eighth Inch equals One Foot (1/8" = 1')
One-Sixteenth Inch equals One Foot (1/16" = 1')

MEASURING WITH THE SCALE

Architects' scales have several different units of measurement on them and may be confusing to the person working with them for the first time. For this reason, it is suggested that you get started by using the simplified scales designed for use with this book. (See Fig. 1.1.)

DRAWING GUIDES

The drawing guide examples shown in Fig. 1.2 are reproduced in one-quarter inch scale on pages 179 - 185. Items on them represent all the component parts of a house: kitchen appliances and cabinets, plumbing fixtures, electrical outlets, fireplaces, furniture, cars, and figures of men, women, and children. These guides can be traced or cut out and placed on a plan drawn to the same scale to help you visualize space requirements and to aid in room planning and arrangement.

USING THE DRAWING GUIDES

When you are ready to use the drawing guides,

1. Check sizes and select the most appropriate items for your plan.

2. Cut out the items. The guides can be cut a little smaller or larger to fit your own size requirements where necessary. (Measure with your one-quarter-inch scale.)

3. Arrange the symbols on the plan to suit your space requirements.

4. When you are satisfied with the arrangement, simply lay a piece of tracing paper over the page and trace the layout.

5. To transfer your layout to the original drawing, slip the layout tracing under your original drawing and trace.

GRID-PAPER GUIDE

An 8 1/2 x 11 inch cut-out sheet of grid paper is reproduced on page 178. It can be used as a tracing guide for many of the projects in this book. Remove it from the book and place it under tracing paper when doing practice exercises. (See Fig. 3.2.)

LETTERING GUIDELINES

Page 177 is a sheet of ruled guidelines. Remove it from the book and place it under tracing paper for practice exercises. Practice lettering in each of the recommended lettering sizes. See Unit 2, Lettering and Lines.

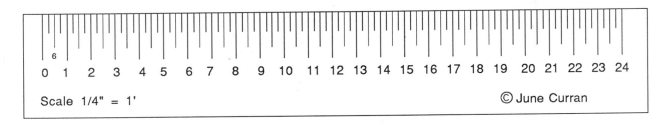

Scale 1/4" = 1'

© June Curran

Fig. 1.1 A simplified 1/4" scale. (See cut-out scales in 3 sizes on page 189.)

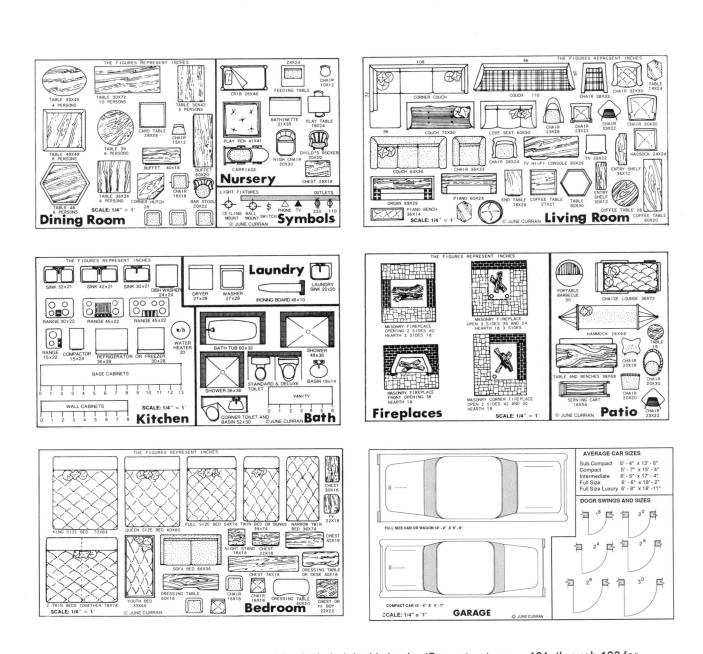

Fig. 1.2 Reduced scale examples of the drawing guides included in this book. (See cut-out pages 181 through 188 for drawing guides reproduced in 1/4" scale.)

EQUIPMENT OPTIONS

The remainder of this chapter describes equipment you may need to produce detailed and professional looking drawings.

GRID PAPER

Grid drawing paper can be purchased from stationery or artists' supply stores. Squares are printed on both translucent and opaque papers in a variety of sheet sizes and scales. When purchasing a supply for your project, ask for paper called "vellum," marked off in eight squares to the inch (sometimes written 8 x 8). For this type of work, translucent paper (paper you can see through when tracing) is preferable for two reasons: you can see through it when tracing through overlays, and it is the correct density for making prints. (See Unit 28, Making Prints.) Keep in mind that prints (sometimes called blueprints) cannot be made from opaque paper (paper you cannot see through) because light cannot pass through opaque paper.

Light-blue (drop-out) ink is used to print squares on drafting vellum. When a print is made from a drawing prepared on this type of paper, the lines do not appear on the print.

You may wish to purchase 81/2" by 11" sheets or pads of grid vellum paper. You will need to purchase larger sheets of paper when you begin drawing a complete house plan. Pads of 18" x 24" sheets are available and are adequate for drawing small homes. A variety of roll and sheet sizes is also available.

TRACING PAPER

Tracing or layout paper (sometimes called Archi-sketch) is inexpensive, thin, translucent paper made strong enough to withstand hard pencil pressure and repeated erasing. It is important for many drawing jobs. By fastening tracing paper over a drawing, you can try ideas without disturbing the original work. There are many grades readily available in stationery and artists' supply stores and it comes in rolls, sheets, and pads of various sizes. Choose the most translucent paper you can find and use it generously to sketch ideas and to conserve your supply of vellum.

PENCILS

The most readily available pencils are those numbered 2, 2 1/2 or 3. The lead in a No. 2 pencil is medium soft, No. 2 1/2 is medium, and No. 3 is medium hard. However, there are pencils and leads made especially for drafting and these are much more satisfactory for drawing house plans. Drawing leads are carefully graded and numbered according to degree of hardness.

4H-3H-2H-H-F-HB-B-2B-3B-4B
HARDEST   INTERMEDIATE   SOFTEST

Wooden pencils, Fig.1.3, item A, can be purchased in any of the above degrees of hardness. These pencils are inexpensive and can be sharpened with an ordinary pencil sharpener that grinds off the wood and points the lead simultaneously.

Most drafters use mechanical pencils made especially for drawing leads, Fig.1.3, item B. All hardnesses of leads are interchangeable in these pencils.

Lead preferences are:

4 H   Layout - Dimension Lines
2 H   Detailing - Outlining Wall Lines
F   Lettering - Outlining
H B   Sketching

If you have a tendency to apply heavy pressure on your pencil as you draw, you may need to use slightly harder leads.

The **B** grade leads are too soft for drawing architectural plans. They are primarily used for illustrating.

PENCIL SHARPENERS AND LEAD POINTERS

To sharpen wooden pencils, some drafters remove the wood with a pocketknife and rotate the lead on a piece of sandpaper or an emery board. Ordinary pencil sharpeners are often satisfactory. To sharpen the lead in a mechanical pencil, you will need a lead pointer made especially to keep a fine point on the lead. There are many kinds of lead pointers available.

ERASERS

The Ruby or Pink Pearl stick eraser is the one most suited to the type of vellum drafting paper recommended. It is made of pink rubber with an outer wrapping of paper that peels off, leaving an eraser tip narrow enough for erasing in small areas, Fig. 1.3, item C. Magic-Rub is a white vinyl eraser that peels off in the same way. This type of eraser is very useful for erasing on tracing paper and cleaning smudges from drawings.

COLORED PENCILS

A blue pencil is used to shade the lines that indicate wall thickness on floor plans. When a print is made, the blue-pencil shaded lines stand out clearly. Experiment with several different kinds until you find one that goes on the paper smoothly and sharpens easily.

NOTE: Always turn your tracing paper over and shade on the back of the drawing. This prevents smudging and makes it easy to erase if you make changes before the drawing is finished.

TRIANGLES

Drafters' triangles are transparent and come in two shapes. One can be used to draw a 45 degree angle, Fig. 1.3, item F, the other can be used to draw either a 30 degree or a 60 degree angle, depending on how it is placed on the work, Fig. 1.3, item E. Both types are available in several lengths. As a rule triangles 8 to 10 inches long are recommended. Vertical lines (up and down) are drawn by placing a triangle on a T square, moving it to the desired position and drawing along the long side, as shown in Fig. 1.3.

T SQUARES AND PARALLEL BARS

T squares or parallel bars are used for drawing horizontal lines (left to right). Figure1.3, item D, is a T square placed on a drawing board; (the board must be made with true right angles) pressed tightly against the edge. It is held in place or moved up and down along the board with the left hand, leaving the right hand free for drawing. Reverse this procedure if you are left-handed. If you are using a parallel bar, use it in the same way. When grid paper is fastened to the drawing surface, the lines of the paper must be aligned with the edge of the T square or parallel bar. The most satisfactory type of straight edge has transparent plastic edges along which a pencil glides smoothly. The transparency enables you to see through to your work.

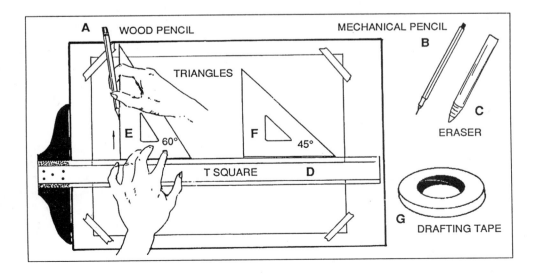

Fig. 1.3 Examples of useful equipment.

4

GENERAL-PURPOSE TEMPLATES

When drawing bathroom fixtures, kitchen fixtures, appliances and door swings on your plan, you may wish to use a general-purpose architects' template. Architects' templates are made of thin, translucent plastic. Openings or cavities in the plastic are shaped to represent the outlines of various symbols. By selecting the required shape on the template and placing it on your plan in the correct position, you can trace it's outline, thereby producing a clean and accurate symbol.

GOOD DRAWING ARRANGEMENTS

Drawing can be done much more easily and accurately if you make a few simple arrangements for comfort and convenience. A drawing board propped up on a desk or table is a tremendous help. It can be made from any smooth piece of wood, such as a breadboard or a piece of plywood. It should be thick enough to be rigid. Art stores carry lightweight, smooth boards of all sizes which are ideal for this purpose; however, a homemade board will work almost as well. Just make sure it has true right angles.

When your board is placed on a desk or table with the top edge propped up several inches, the surface is raised to a convenient working angle. You can prop the top edge of the board up with books, bricks, a piece of 2" x 6" lumber, or anything level and solid. (See Fig. 1.4.)

If your board is not smooth, fasten a flat, smooth piece of heavy, light-colored cardboard to it for a backing. Plain, smooth, light-colored linoleum makes an excellent drawing surface as well. You can also purchase standard drafting board covers from drafting supply stores. Board cover can be applied with masking tape or thumbtacks.

Fasten grid paper to your smooth drawing surface with drafting tape. It is quite similar to masking tape, but is not so sticky. It can be obtained from drafting supply stores. (See Fig. 1.3, item G.)

GOOD LIGHTING

Good lighting is another important factor in comfortable and accurate drawing. Place a table or floor lamp slightly behind you or a fluorescent desk lamp in front of the board so that light shines down on the work. Standard drafting lamps are also available.

Fig. 1.4 Example of a good drawing arrangement.

SECTION 1
UNIT 2

LETTERING AND LINES

Objective: To learn standard lettering procedures and understand architectural line weights.

HAND LETTERING

Drafters convey meaning through the use of graphics when drawing plans. These graphic lines and symbols provide much of the information needed by individuals reading the plan. However, there is some information that cannot be portrayed with graphics alone. This information must be conveyed through the use of lettering on the plans.

Though lettering is often done mechanically, by means of lettering guides, computers, etc., there will always be areas of work in which hand lettering is necessary and the person who masters this skill will be able to adapt to the variations in technique.

The vertical, single-stroke Gothic alphabet shown in Fig. 2.1 is the style most often used by drafters. Because it is legible and easy to learn, it has become accepted as a standard for technical work.

Lettering on architectural drawings is often more stylized and individual than in other technical areas. It is, however, based on the standard Gothic alphabet; therefore, one must first learn to draw the basic alphabet before architectural style variations can be developed. (See Fig. 2.2.)

STANDARDS

Select the correct size lettering from the following list, and rule guidelines accordingly.

The largest size, 1/4", is used to identify key items e.g., the project name, title of the drawing, etc.

On smaller drawings or in smaller spaces on the drawing, 3/16" lettering is also an option for identifying key items.

For general lettering and dimensions, 1/8" lettering works well.

For notes in small spaces, use 1/16" lettering.

ABCDEFGHIJKLMNOPQRSTUVWXYZ
abcdefghijklmnopqrstuvwxyz 1234567890

ABCDEFGHIJKLMNOPQRSTUVWXYZ
abcdefghijklmnopqrstuvwxyz 1234567890

Fig. 2.1 Standard single-stroke Gothic alphabet.

ABCDEFGHIJKLMNOPQRSTUVWXYZ
abcdefghijklmnopqrstuvwxyz1234567890

ABCDEFGHIJKLMNOPQRSTUVWXYZ
abcdefghijklmnopqrstuvwxyz1234567890

Fig. 2.2 An architectural variation from the standard gothic alphabet.

GUIDELINES

Always draw light guidelines before starting to letter. Use a well pointed **4H** lead for these lines. Do not erase them from the drawing when you have finished lettering. Lines drawn lightly with a well-pointed **4H** lead do not reproduce when a print is made from the drawing. (See Fig. 2.3.) A page of ruled guidelines is included among the cut-out pages at the back of the book.

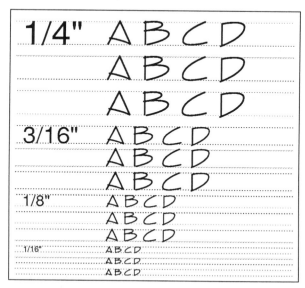

FIG. 2.3 Examples of lettering guidelines.

WEIGHTS AND TYPES OF LINES

Lines are drawn in individual, distinctive weights. Each line weight contributes definite meaning to the drawing. The American Standards Association has adopted an alphabet of lines consisting of three line weights: heavy, medium, and light. Choose the correct line weight and line type for the purpose the line will serve. Fig. 2.4 shows most of the line weights and types you will be using when drafting plans.

ACHIEVING GOOD LINE WEIGHTS

It is not difficult to achieve good line weights if you have selected the correct grades of lead. By keeping the lead consistently well pointed and by frequently rotating the pencil as you draw, you can achieve clean, precise line work.

All lines, regardless of weight, must have density. This is achieved by applying pressure on the lead as you draw. Applying slightly heavier pressure at the beginnings and endings of lines makes them start and end distinctly.

HEAVY LINE WEIGHTS

The darkest lines on the drawing are made with an F grade lead. They are used for outlining such things as wall thickness on floor plans, elevation drawings, and details. Use bold outlining to add emphasis to a drawing.

MEDIUM LINE WEIGHTS

Medium line weights are achieved with a 2H grade lead. Medium line weights are used for most of the lines on the drawing. Use them for drawing such things as cabinets and appliances, plumbing fixtures, symbols and all detailing that does not require outlining.

LIGHT LINE WEIGHTS

Light line weights are drawn with a **4H** lead. They are the lightest lines to appear on the drawing and their primary use is for drawing dimension, extension, and center lines. Light-weight lines are also used for laying out the original work. However, these original layout lines will not appear on the finished drawing.

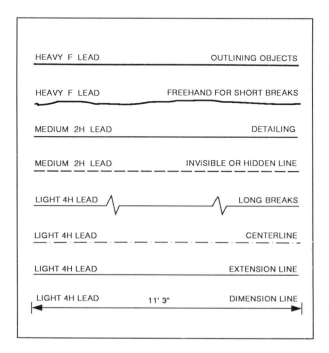

Fig. 2.4 Line weights and types.

USING A LETTERING PENCIL

For most lettering use a well-pointed **F** lead pencil. Rotate the pencil about 1/4 turn between your thumb and index finger between strokes to maintain an even point.

PLACEMENT OF LETTERING

1. Center the titles where feasible.

2. Place all notations as close to the object they describe as possible.

3. Group general notes together in a column on the most applicable sheet of the drawings. Keep a left-aligned margin.

4. Never allow any of the lettering to touch the lines of the drawing.

PRACTICE

Skillful lettering is the result of practice. One way to practice is to fasten tracing paper over the alphabet, Fig. 2.1, and trace over the letters. If you practice the basic alphabet at every opportunity, you will soon find that your lettering is legible and attractive.

TITLE BLOCKS AND BORDERS

Drawings look more professional when each sheet of the set has a border and a title block. A title block is a space set aside for the title of the drawing and other pertinent information. Use a well pointed **2H** lead and draw the border line approximately 1/2" in from the paper's edge. Title block shapes and sizes are usually flexible and can be adapted to fit the paper size and the plan size and shape. Title blocks can be placed at the bottom of the wide side of the sheet. An alternate choice for the title block location is at the end of the sheet. (See Fig. 2.5.) Once you decide on the placement and size of the title block you will use, use the same style on each sheet of the set of plans you are drawing. In most architectural offices, a uniform style is used on all plans. (See Fig. 2.6.)

Place the following information in a Title Block on each page of the set of plans:

Title of the drawing, e.g., Floor Plan
Page number of the set of drawings
Name, address, and phone no. of property owner
Address of property
Name, address, and phone no. of drafter or company preparing plans
Drafter's initials and date drawing completed
Scale to which the plan was drawn
Total square footage of the house and garage

Number and title each page as follows:

No. 1 - Plot Plan
No. 2 - Floor Plan
No. 3 - Exterior Elevation
No. 4 - Foundation Plan
No. 5 - Roof and Roof Framing Plan
No. 6 - Section and Details

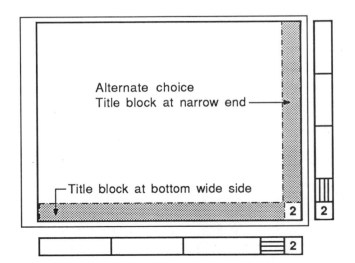

Fig. 2.5 Sheet layout and title block location.

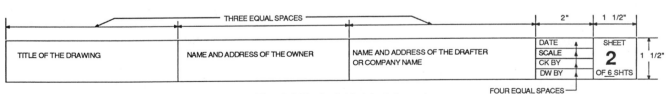

Fig. 2.6 Typical title block layout.

When you reduce something as large as a house to the size of a piece of paper, you must have some system for keeping spaces in relative proportion to each other. The method that has evolved and has been perfected over the years is called drawing to scale. Drawing to scale means reducing a house, a lot, or an individual room to a size that will fit on a sheet of paper that can be handled easily .

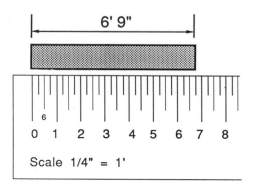

6' 9"

0 1 2 3 4 5 6 7 8

Scale 1/4" = 1'

Fig. 3.1 Measuring a line in 1/4" scale.

Though different scales are used for various types of work, the standard scale for drawing house plans is one-quarter of an inch equals one foot. The scale is written 1/4" = 1'. This means that a line is drawn one-quarter of an inch long to represent each foot of actual house space. More detailed information about this is given further along in this chapter.

MEASURING WITH SCALES

The scales that architects use have several different units of measurement on one ruler. This may be confusing to the person working with them for the first time. For this reason, it is suggested that you begin with the simplified scales designed for use with this book. They are located on page 179 and should be carefully cut out. They will enable you to work in scale very easily.

Refer to Fig. 3.1 and you will see how the 1/4" scale provides a means of working accurately in scale.

NOTE: *The zero point on the scale should be placed at the beginning of the line to be measured. Each large number represents 1'. The longer line between numbers represents 6". Each short line represents 3".*

SECTION 1
UNIT 3

DRAWING TO SCALE

Objective: To learn to read scales and to measure and draw to scale.

DRAWING A HOUSE TO SCALE

Since a house is a very large object and the paper on which it is drawn must of necessity be a convenient size, a method has been devised that makes it possible to accurately draw a representation of a house that will fit on a piece of paper.

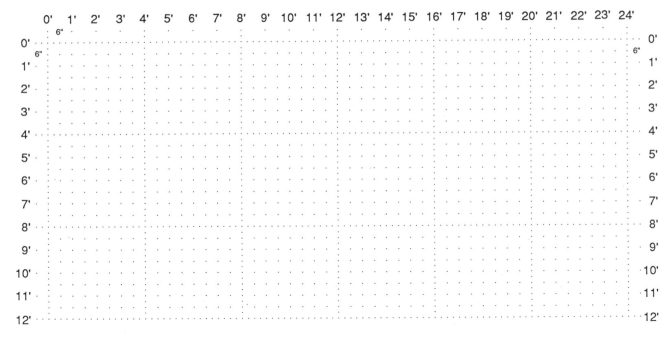

FIG. 3.2 Measuring on grid drawing paper in 1/4" scale.

MEASURING AND DRAWING ON GRID PAPER

Grid paper is often used by design professionals when drawing plans for a home. Using this type of paper will make drawing easier because the scale is already worked out. The grid squares in Fig. 3.2 , as in all the drawings throughout the book, have been reproduced in accurate scale and can be measured with your scale. They are typical of those printed on the type of paper recommended for use with this simplified drawing system. Looking closely at Fig. 3.2 you will see that there are many fine lines and a few heavier ones. Since 1/4 inch (1/4") represents one foot (1') when working in 1/4" scale, the space between the heavier lines represents four feet (4') and the space between each pair of fine lines represents six inches (6").

USING 1/8" AND 1/16" SCALES

Though most floor-plan drawings are drawn to 1/4" scale, other scales are used for special purposes. For example, in instances where the subject to be drawn is too large to fit on paper of a convenient size, smaller scales are an advantage. Plot-plan drawings (drawings of a plot of ground or a lot) are often drawn to a scale in which 1/16" is equal to 1'.

Scales in 1/8" and 1/16" have also been provided with the book to make it easy for you to measure and work in scales smaller than 1/4".

When you have learned to think and draw in 1/4" scale, you will have acquired basic knowledge that will enable you to understand other scales.

USING THE 1/4" SCALE

1. Put your 1/4" scale to work by measuring each of the lines in Fig. 3.3. Write down the length of each line.

2. Check your figures with the answers at the top of the next page.

Fig. 3.3 Measure the lines and record each length.

Correct answers to line length measurements on the preceding page:
A. 10' - 3"   B. 11' - 2"   C. 5' - 3"   D. 8' - 0"   E. 2' - 6"

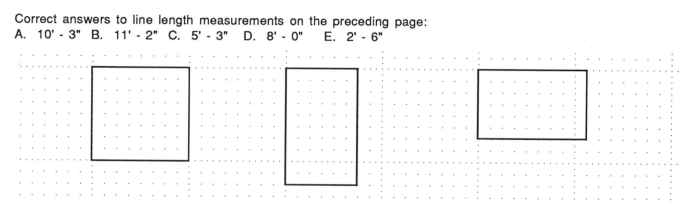

Fig. 3.4 Draw rectangles in scale.

3. Use the scale to measure on your grid paper. Draw the three rectangles shown in Fig. 3.4, and write down the dimensions of each.

COMPARING SCALES

1. Compare the rectangles in Fig. 3.5. The measurements of all three rectangles are the same; however each is drawn to a different scale. The sides of the 1/4" scale rectangle (A) are exactly twice as long as the sides of the 1/8" rectangle (B); similarly the sides of (B) are twice as long as the sides of (C).

2. Try measuring and drawing the squares in Fig. 3.6, using the 1/4", 1/8" and 1/16" scales.

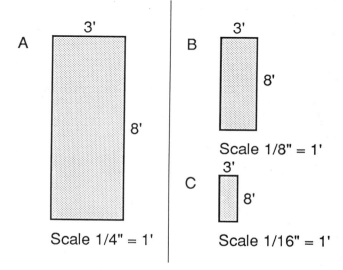

Fig. 3.5 Compare three rectangles with the same measurements drawn to different scales.

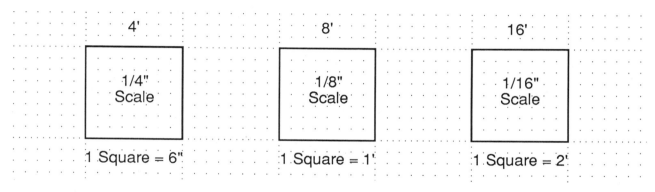

Fig. 3.6 Compare three squares of the same size measured in three different scales.

11

3. To visualize sizes in scales smaller than 1/4", compare Figs. 3.7 and 3.8 with Fig. 4.2. These three illustrations are all from the same plan. In Fig. 4.2, the plan has been drawn to a scale of 1/4" = 1'. In Fig. 3.7 the plan is shown in 1/8" scale and in Fig. 3.8 it is shown in 1/6" scale.

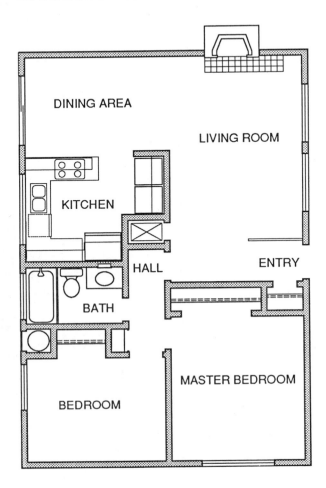

Fig. 3.7 1/8" scale drawing.

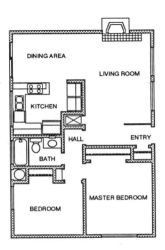

Fig. 3.8 1/16" scale drawing.

12

A procedure for portraying these details of a building has been devised which, when followed carefully, results in a drawing easily understandable to anyone working with it. This drawing is called a floor plan.

What you see when you look at or draw a floor plan is exactly like what you would see if you had a detailed scale model of a building and were looking straight down into it, as in Fig. 4.1.

THE IMPORTANCE OF A FLOOR PLAN

In planning a house, the floor-plan drawing is the starting point. It deals with such things as the size, shape and appearance of the living space in the finished house.

Before you can draw a floor plan, you must learn to visualize a house and the living space within, in scale on paper. You must also learn to draw the simple symbols and designations which represent the component parts of a house. Then you will be able to analyze space requirements in a home and translate your ideas into a scale drawing.

SECTION 2

UNIT 4

VISUALIZING A FLOOR PLAN

Objective: To clearly understand the meaning and purpose of a floor-plan drawing.

WHAT IS A FLOOR PLAN?

When you are drawing plans for a building of any kind, it is necessary to make a drawing which shows the arrangement of rooms, the placement of doors and windows, the location of closets, cabinets, plumbing fixtures, appliances, etc.

SIMPLE EXPERIMENTS

1. Compare each of the features in Fig. 4.1, used as an example to clarify the meaning of a floor plan, with the corresponding features of the actual floor plan, Fig. 4.2.

2. Observe how each part of the house is indicated on the floor plan drawing. Compare such details as windows, cabinets, and bathroom fixtures.

NOTE: *The darkest shaded lines in Fig. 4.1 indicate walls and conform to the dark shaded wall lines in the floor plan, Fig. 4.2. The floor plan is drawn to a scale of 1/4" = 1'.*

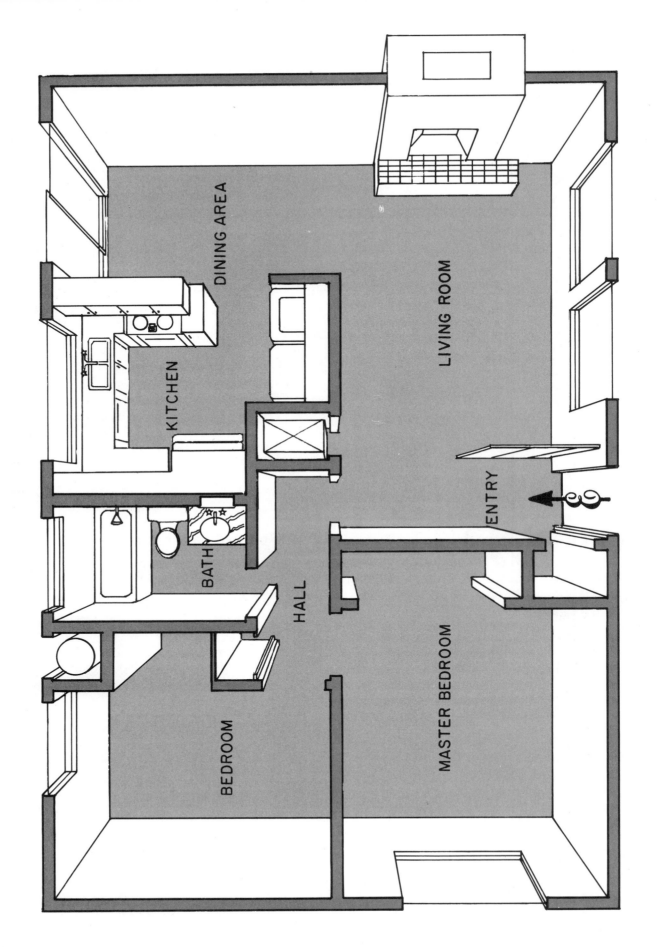

Fig. 4.1 What a floor-plan drawing portrays.

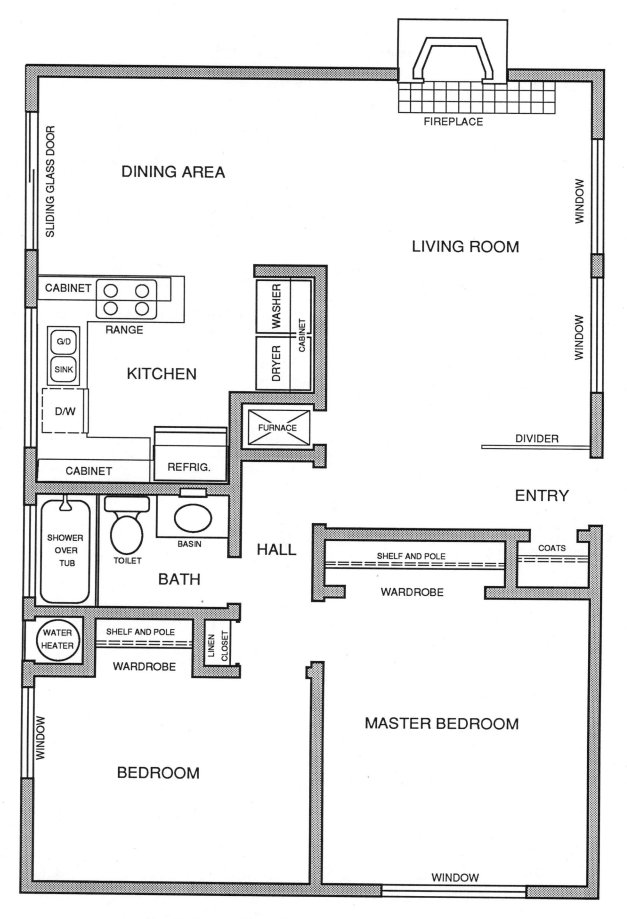

Fig. 4.2 An actual floor plan drawn to 1/4" scale.

Armed with the necessary information and knowledge of drawing, you can make room studies of your own home. By using grid drawing paper, the scale and the drawing-guide cutouts included in the book, you can make tentative room arrangements and experiment with ideas.

Begin by making a drawing of the master bedroom from the floor plan in Fig. 4.2. You will learn more from this particular project if you do not trace the room.

DRAWING A ROOM STUDY:

1. Fasten a sheet of grid paper to your drawing surface as shown in Fig. 1.4.

2. Use a well-pointed **4H** lead in your pencil for this light-line layout.

3. Lay out the length and width of the room on your paper. You can measure the plan accurately with the 1/4" scale.

4. Since a wall has thickness, two parallel lines are required to represent it. Using the intersection of two heavier blue lines on your grid paper as a starting point for the outside corner of the room, draw two parallel lines, one square apart, (6") to represent the wall thickness.

5. Measure and draw the remaining walls of the room. Your drawing will look like Fig. 5.1.

SECTION 2
UNIT **5**

STARTING TO DRAW

Objective: To learn to think in scale by measuring and drawing an accurately scaled room plan.

STARTING TO DRAW

When drawing plans for a home, one must think in terms of the complete house. However, it is easier to learn to draw in scale and to evaluate your requirements if you begin by making some individual room studies. These studies will help to define your requirements and preferences and enable you to become familiar with plan drawing techniques and space relationships on paper.

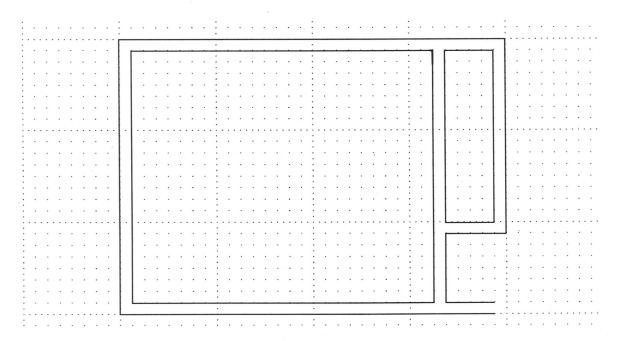

Fig. 5.1 A light-line layout of the master bedroom taken from the floor plan in Fig. 4.2.

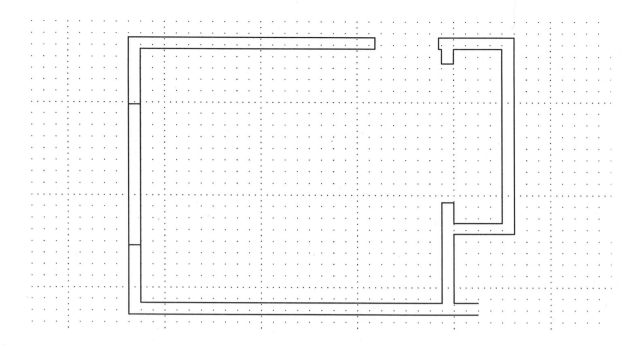

Fig. 5.2 The same room plan with an opening for a door and a closet.

6. Measure the room again to determine the location and size of the door, window, and closet openings. Erase the wall lines where door and closet openings are to appear on the drawing. Leave wall lines *in* where the window is to be located. Compare your drawing with Fig. 5.2.

7. To indicate the window, draw a fine, medium-weight line through the marked-off window-opening space, to represent glass. In the closet, draw a line to indicate a shelf. Next to it, draw two light dashed (hidden) lines to indicate a clothes pole beneath, as in Fig. 5.3.

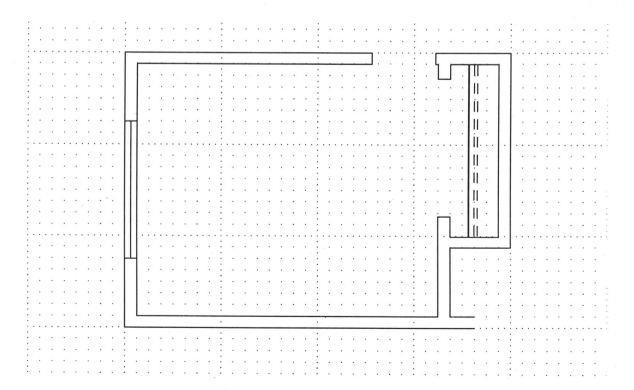

Fig. 5.3 Window and closet details have been added to the plan.

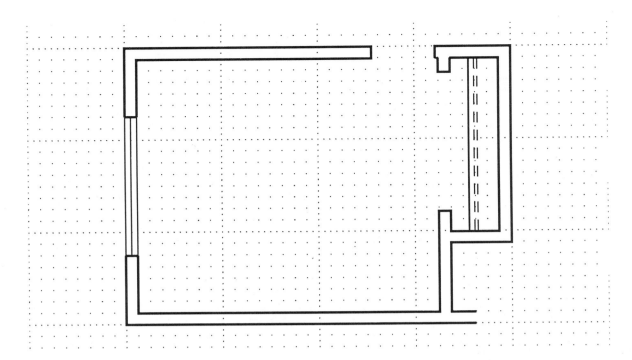

Fig. 5.4 The same room plan with wall lines darkened.

8. The lines that indicate walls are the heaviest lines on the drawing. When you are satisfied that you have them drawn correctly, trace over them with a firm pressure on a **2H** grade lead. Compare your drawing with Fig. 5.4. Turn the paper over.

9. On the back of the drawing, using a blue colored pencil, shade the lines that indicate wall thickness. Use a light, even pressure on your shading pencil; make strokes in the same direction as the wall lines. Compare your drawing with Fig. 5.5. (Note: most drawings in the book were generated on a computer.)

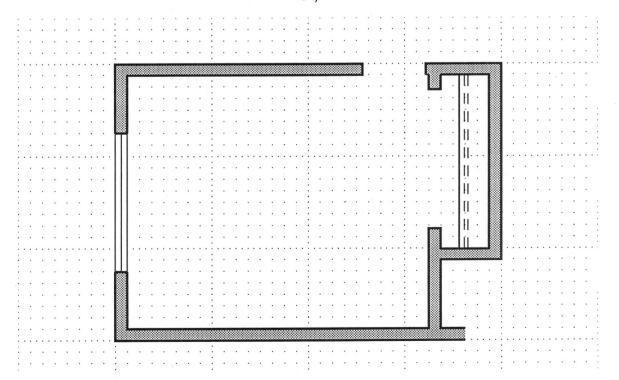

Fig. 5.5 Wall lines have been shaded. (Since the drawings in this book were generated on a computer, shading texture here is not the same as described in the text.)

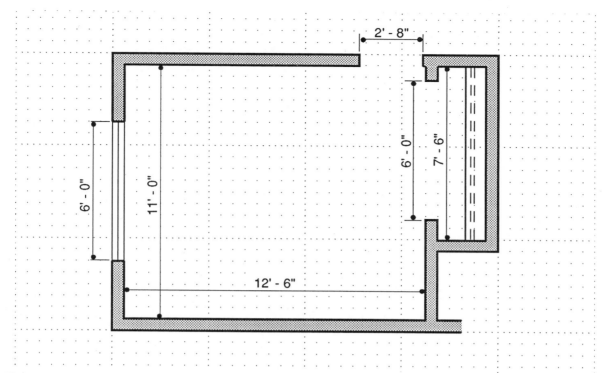

Fig. 5.6 Dimensions have been added.

10. Dimensioning your room drawing (writing down the measurements) as you work will save time and give you quick reference. For drawing dimension and extension lines, use a well-pointed **4H** lead. The lighter line weight makes dimension lines clearly distinguishable from lines indicating the walls of the structure. For writing the numbers, use an **F** lead.

PENCIL TECHNIQUES

You will notice that your lead wears down quickly. Lines made with a worn-down lead spoil the appearance of a drawing and a thick line is difficult to measure with a scale. The pencil should be sharpened frequently while you are doing finishing work. The lead wears more evenly when you rotate the pencil between your thumb and index finger as you draw a line. Also, the correct grades of lead and a good lead sharpener help to make your drawing neater and more precise. (See Unit 1, Drawing Equipment.)

As you learn to reduce a room and large objects of furniture to 1/4" scale, their relationships to each other, as they appear on paper, will become apparent. You will learn to visualize, on paper, the amount of open space around furnishings needed so that an individual can move about in a room. By drawing door and window openings and closets into the plan, you will learn how to handle them in future planning.

MEASURING AN ACTUAL ROOM

1. On a piece of scratch paper, make a fairly large, rough sketch of the room you have selected to draw. It is necessary to use only a single line, indicating the inside wall, as in Fig. 6.1.

2. Mark along the wall lines on your sketch the approximate location of each door, window, closet, and any other projections or recessed areas in the room.

SECTION 2

UNIT 6

SPATIAL RELATIONSHIPS

Objective: To learn to visualize spatial relationships on paper and to reduce a room and large objects or furniture to 1/4" scale drawings.

JUDGING SPATIAL RELATIONSHIPS

When one attempts to draw something as large as a room on a small piece of paper for the first time, the problem of judging spatial relationships becomes apparent. However, it takes surprisingly little practice with working in scale before one is almost automatically able to judge space on paper as it relates to actual room size. You can familiarize yourself with spatial relationships by drawing a room you are familiar with. Choosing the living room or bedroom will simplify the task. You will find it relatively easy to draw your own room because you have lived in the space and are completely familiar with it.

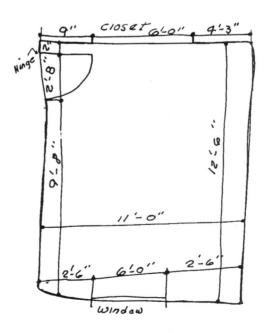

Fig 6.1 A rough measurement sketch of a room.

3. Using a yardstick or a pocket tape measure placed on the floor, start measuring in a corner. Measure from the corner to the first door, window, or other break in the wall. Write the measurement on your sketch. Then write down the sizes of the doors, windows, etc. Continue measuring around the room, writing the figures on the sketch as you go. Add total measurements to the sketch. (See Fig. 6.1.)

4. Check to see that you have included such things as projecting registers or any permanent fixtures. Note whether doors open into the room or out from it. Also note whether they are hinged on the left or on the right, as in Fig. 6.1.

NOTE: *Do not include moldings, trims, baseboards, etc. Actual wall-to-wall measurements and actual sizes of the openings are required.*

CONVERTING YOUR SKETCH TO A 1/4-INCH SCALE DRAWING

1. Fasten a sheet of grid drawing paper to your drawing surface. If the room is oblong, the widest side of the paper should be placed on the board horizontally (left to right).
Make sure that you start your drawing far enough to the left and from the top of the paper so that the entire room will fit on the sheet with space enough left for dimension lines.

NOTE: *When you are drawing an actual room in an existing house, your measurements will probably not come out exactly on the grid lines. If you get used to using a scale, you will find that the inch marks indicated on it will make accurate representation of feet and inches very easy.*

2. By using your scale, convert the actual room measurements to 1/4" scale measurements and lay out the room on your paper. Begin by drawing a light line to represent the inside of each of the four walls. Moving back one square (6") from the first lines, draw a parallel line all the way around the outside of the first to allow for the thickness of the walls. Since the measurements you made were for the inside of the room, the overall measurements of the drawing will be about 12" larger, allowing for the thickness of the two walls. (Refer to Fig. 5.1.)

3. Add the projections, offsets, or closets from your sketch to your drawing in accurate scale. You have now reached the stage of plan development shown in Fig. 5.2.

4. Referring to your sketch, determine the location of windows and doors. Using your scale, mark the placement of the openings along each wall line. Draw fine, 2H lines to represent glass where you have indicated windows. Your drawing is now in the stage of plan development shown in Fig. 5.3.

5. Go over the wall lines with an 2H lead or with more pressure on your pencil as shown in Fig. 5.4.

6. Turn your drawing over and shade the wall thickness on the back of the paper with a colored pencil. (See Fig. 5.5.)

7. Put in dimension lines with a well-pointed 2H lead as shown in Fig. 5.6. Note the measurements lightly. Making dimensions a part of the drawing at this stage gives you quick reference.

8. Make your dimensions more distinct by erasing your original notations one at a time and putting them in more carefully with a heavier pressure on your pencil. An F lead works best for lettering. Use light 4H guidelines, uniformly spaced, for all lettering and numbers. (See Fig. 5.6.)

9. Now you are ready to add furniture to the drawing. You will find, on the drawing guides, many different sizes, shapes and types of furniture. Measure each piece of furniture in the room you are drawing and make a note of its width, depth and height on your rough sketch. Choose the item of furniture from the drawing guides that is closest in size to the piece you want to draw. Trace it on the plan in the correct position. (See Fig. 6.2.) Keep in mind that the numbers on the drawing guides indicate inches.

10. Study the finished drawing and compare it with your room to become familiar with the way actual sizes and shapes appear on paper in 1/4" scale.

PENCIL TECHNIQUES

If the lead and the colored pencil smear, producing an unattractive drawing, check on the following things:

1. Are you completing your drawing with light pencil lines before going over the wall lines with heavier lines?

2. Is the lead you are using for your layout work a hard lead such as a **4H**? Is it pointed well?

3. Does your eraser do a clean and thorough job?

4. Have you used the colored shading pencil with a light, smooth stroke on the back of the paper?

5. Are your hands smearing areas you have already drawn as you work on other, clean areas? If so, try covering finished areas with a piece of tracing paper to keep them clean while you work on the rest of the drawing.

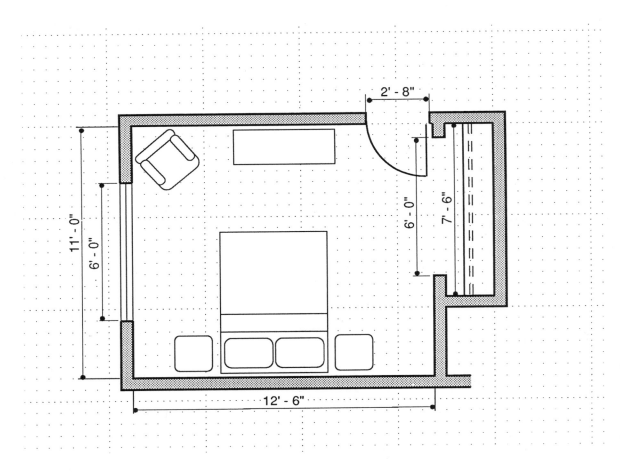

Fig. 6.2 A completed room drawing

WHAT IS A BUBBLE DIAGRAM?

A bubble diagram (also called a schematic or scheme) is a rough, freehand sketch, composed of circular shapes used to suggest the arrangement and comparative sizes of the main areas of activity.

SKETCHING A BUBBLE DIAGRAM

The floor space in every home can be divided into three major areas of activity: living, eating, and sleeping. Designers make several quick sketch-type bubble diagrams for each project to study different space arrangement possibilities. These tracing-paper sketches reveal many important facts about the project.

VALUE OF A BUBBLE DIAGRAM

Drawing several bubble diagrams gives one an opportunity to consider all the factors involved before committing to a set floor plan. It can save time and serve as a guide and a reminder when more detailed drawings are prepared. Design professionals frequently make numerous sketches and diagrams at this stage of plan development. They take into account every known factor and circumstance of the building site as well as the needs and requirements of the individuals who will live in the house.

SECTION 2
UNIT 7
SKETCHING

Objective: To learn sketching and planning techniques for developing floor-plan layouts.

SKETCHING IDEAS FOR A FLOOR PLAN

When one is beginning to draw a floor plan, there are always design parameters within which one must work. The designer must consider the needs and desires of the family who will live in the house and also the restrictions imposed by the building site. This unit will help you to learn simple procedures for analyzing space requirements and arranging living space for optimum use. By studying the sequential design procedures used in the development of the floor plan, Fig. 4.2, you can learn to draw floor plans of your own design.

PROJECT EXAMPLE

In designing the floor plan, Fig. 4.2, the project was to design a vacation house for a family of three who required a small, one-story, two-bedroom house with a two-car garage. They had purchased a 70' x 100' level lot featuring three attractive trees. Disadvantages of the site included wind from the north-west and an unattractive vacant lot adjoining the property. The budget for the project was limited.

STUDY THE PROJECT EXAMPLE

Observe the sequence of steps followed in developing the bubble diagrams and floor-plan sketches for the book plan example, Fig. 4.2.

Figure 7.1 shows several different schemes reflecting living area arrangements and stages of development of main activity areas.

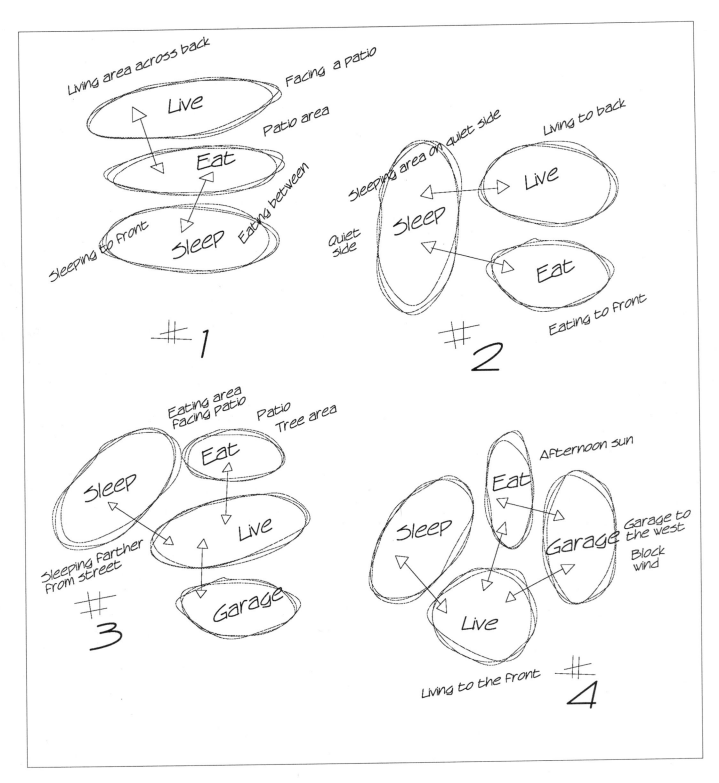

Fig. 7.1 Bubble diagrams of main activity areas.

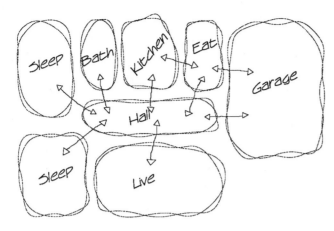

Fig. 7.2 A more fully developed scheme.

In Fig. 7.2, scheme four was selected and developed more completely. In this scheme, the correlation of each space with the other spaces was studied as indicated by the arrows used to study traffic patterns. A hall was added and access to the garage analyzed.

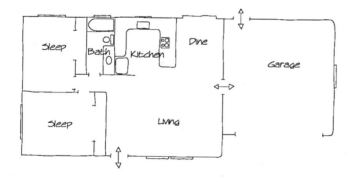

Fig. 7.3 A bubble diagram converted to a floor-plan sketch.

In Fig. 7.3, the bubble diagram was developed into a rough, single-line floor-plan sketch with appropriate room proportions in mind.

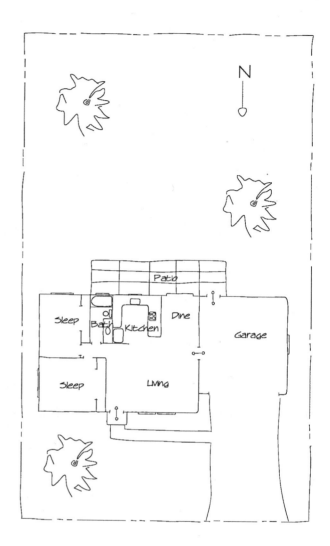

Fig. 7.4 First concept sketch of a floor plan placed on a lot.

Figure 7.4 is a study of a preliminary floor-plan sketch arranged on a lot. In this scheme, the floor plan was studied in relation to the building site.

Refer to Unit 3, Working in Scale, Fig. 3.7, a 1/8" scale drawing of this example floor plan showing the same plan with double wall lines.

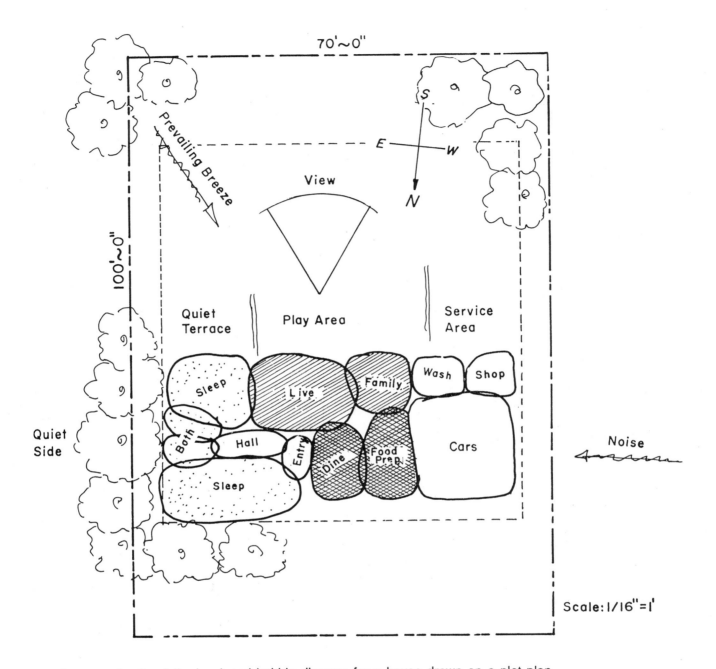

FIG. 7.5 An example of a fully developed bubble diagram for a house drawn on a plot plan.

Fig. 7.5 is an example bubble diagram for a different plan. In this sketch, the north arrow has been properly located so that the sun's effect on the project could be studied. Factors of wind, noise and view have also been studied.

PLANNING A NEW HOME ON A PLOT PLAN

The information given in Unit 26, Plot Plans, will help you formulate ideas for the arrangement of primary living areas and the most suitable shape for the house as it relates to the setting.

PLANNING AN ADDITION OR A REMODELING PROJECT

When planning a remodeling project or an addition, bubble diagrams, preliminary sketches, and plot-plan studies make it easier to visualize the effect of the changes to the original plan.

A plot plan drawing of the existing house, garage, driveway, etc., will show the available space on the lot for the addition; and the relationships of the new space to the existing space. Consider also the orientation of the windows of the addition to the sun and to the neighbors.

ORIENTING THE HOUSE TO THE LOT

The word orientation, as used here, refers to the way the sun strikes the walls and windows of the house. A house is much more comfortable if the main areas of activity are arranged so that the sun shines into the right windows at the right time of the day. Orienting a house to the best advantage is not difficult and the benefits are many. A little time invested in observing the way the sun casts its rays on the lot can reward you with amazing dividends.

NORTH-FACING WINDOWS

Although rooms facing north receive little direct sunlight, the light from north-facing windows provides excellent working light for projects that require consistent, even light throughout the day. Bedrooms with north-facing windows would be desirable for late or daytime sleepers because they would receive less direct sunlight. Rooms with north-facing windows will be cooler in the summer.

SOUTH-FACING WINDOWS

Maximum utilization of the sun to warm the house in the winter can be achieved by orienting major living areas so that windows face south. Rooms with south-facing windows will be warmer and easier to heat and they will be flooded with sunlight most of the day during the winter months. South facing windows will be shaded in the summer, when the angle of the sun is higher, if the house has a fairly wide roof overhang on the south side. Kitchens and family rooms are usually occupied in the daytime and would benefit from a southern exposure.

EAST-FACING WINDOWS

East-facing windows are suitable in rooms where early morning sunlight is desired.

WEST-FACING WINDOWS

One seldom wants large windows facing west because the summer sun is far too hot in most climates. If the plan is to have a garage, storage room, or other service facility, it is advisable to place it on the west side to serve as a buffer between the sun and the west wall of the house.

SKETCH A BUBBLE DIAGRAM OF YOUR OWN DESIGN

When you have studied the sketches in Figs. 7.1 to 7.5, you will be ready to sketch bubble diagrams for plans of your own design.

1. Begin by listing all available information about the people for whom you are designing. The size of the family, special interests of family members, number of cars in the family and the size of the budget available for the project are all factors that will give you the necessary information to begin the drawing. If you do not have a project in mind, design a house for a family you know.

2. You will also need all available information about the lot you will be working with. List the size of the lot, its orientation to the sun, where the most desirable view is, and any unsightly or undesirable features that should be screened out. For more information about building sites and orienting the house to the site, refer to Unit 26, Plot Plans. Choose any of the sample lots from Unit 26, if you do not have one for your project.

3. By drawing on tracing paper, you can experiment with and discard ideas until you find the arrangement of the main areas of activity that works best.

4. Make as many studies as necessary. Try different house shapes and main area arrangements. Keep all of your sketches for reference.

5. If you like one part of your bubble diagram but wish to change another, lay fresh tracing paper over the first sketch and copy the part you wish to use; then draw the new part.

6. Choose your best diagram, and convert it to a single wall-line sketch of a floor plan. Keep in mind the relationship of the living space to the driveway and garage access to patio and garden, privacy, and orientation to the sun. Some other factors to consider are noise, view, and the exterior appearance of the house. (See Fig. 7.3.)

7. Draw a 1/16" scale sketch of the plot plan for your project and sketch your floor plan on the lot drawing. (Refer to Fig. 7.4.)

Now, more that ever before, bathroom fixtures are available in a beautiful selection of colors, materials, and styles. There are so many new and interesting possibilities that bathroom planning is a stimulating challenge. The sizes and shapes of plumbing fixtures given on these pages are typical of the average sizes available.

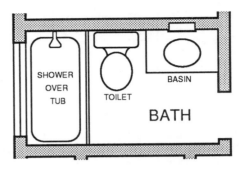

Fig. 8.1 This bathroom layout, taken from the floor- plan example, is a typical small bathroom design.

SHOWERS

The symbol for a shower is shown in Fig. 8.2 and on the drawing guides. The small circle in the center of the shower indicates the drain. The cross mark indicates the slope of the bottom of the shower to the drain. In some showers the drain is located at one end rather than in the center as shown in Fig. 8.3. This affects the plumbing and should be verified when you select the shower.

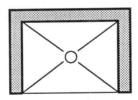

Fig. 8.2 Symbol for a shower with a center drain.

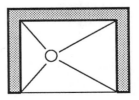

FIG. 8.3 Symbol for a shower with a drain at one end.

SECTION 3

UNIT 8

BATHROOM LAYOUT

Objective: To learn to draw bathroom layouts using correct symbols and designations.

DRAWING THE BATHROOM

The average bathroom is quite small, yet it contains several large plumbing fixtures, cabinetry, and other equipment. Drawing a plan that will accommodate all this in an efficient and convenient arrangement takes careful planning and drawing. The bathroom layout in Fig. 8.1 is taken from the floor-plan example, Fig. 4.2. It is typical of a standard bathroom used in a small home. All required space allowances have been met in this compact design.

BATHTUBS

The symbol for a bathtub is shown in Fig. 8.4 and on the drawing guide. Standard bathtubs are 30" wide by 60" long. Some special-order models, including those of fiberglass and acrylic, are 32" to 34" wide. Longer bathtubs, up to 72", are also available.

Fig. 8.4 Symbol for a bathtub with shower over.

DRAWING SHOWERS AND BATHTUBS

1. Trace from the drawing guides if you are not using a general-purpose template. (See Unit 1, Drawing Equipment.)

2. If you are using a template, select the fixture of your choice.

3. Place the template on your drawing so that the tracing opening is in the desired position.

4. If there are shaded lines around the shower and bathtub openings on your template, they indicate walls and should be placed exactly over the walls on your drawing.

DRAWING A SHOWER OVER THE BATHTUB

1. If you plan to have a shower over the bathtub, draw the symbol as shown in Fig. 8.4 and write "Shower Over."

2. Shower heads are installed at the same end of the bath tub as faucets and can be any height you specify; standard is 6 feet.

DRAWING SHOWER ENCLOSURES

There are several kinds of enclosures for showers and bathtubs. The following information will help with selections and show you how to draw the selection on the plan.

If a shower curtain is to be used as an enclosure for the shower or bathtub, the only designation needed is two parallel lines indicating the rod on which the curtain hangs. (See Fig. 8.5.)

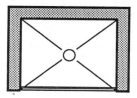

Fig.8.5 Symbol for a curtain rod.

Shower doors and bathtub enclosures such as those shown in Figs. 8.6 and 8.7 are required to be of tempered (heat-strengthened) glass, safety glass or plastic. For shower doors, half of the enclosure is fixed securely in place. The other half is hinged, and swings open.

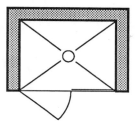

Fig. 8.6 Symbol for a hinge-type shower door.

A single line (as for glass) designates the fixed half of the opening. A door swing is drawn on the other half. Doors can swing from either the right or the left and either side can be fixed.

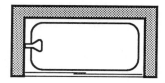

Fig. 8.7 Symbol for a sliding bathtub or shower door.

Sliding-door enclosures are made for both bathtubs and showers. In this kind of enclosure, two metal-framed panels of glass or plastic fit into tracks located at the top and bottom of the bathtub or shower. Each panel slides back its full width, permitting an opening one-half the width of the tub or shower. The correct designation for a sliding-door enclosure is shown in Fig. 8.7

Another kind of enclosure used on both bathtubs and showers is the vinyl folding door. These doors fold back (like accordion pleats) and have hardware which fits into channels at the top and bottom of the shower or bathtub. The vinyl enclosure glides along the channel when the panel is opened or closed. About 80% opening is permitted with this type of door. The designation for folding vinyl doors is shown in Fig. 8.8.

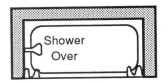

Fig. 8.8 Symbol for folding-type door.

NOTE: For safety, building codes require that doors and enclosures around showers and bathtubs be safety glass or tempered glass.

COUNTERTOPS, BASINS AND VANITIES

Manufacturers offer many choices of countertops, basins, and vanities. You may choose from a wide selection of beautiful designs. The choice of basin is dependent, in most cases, on the choice of countertop to be used. There are basins made for installation with each of the various kinds of tops.

When a plastic laminate (known under several brand names such as Formica) is used, a hole the size of the basin is cut out of the vanity top. The basin, usually round or oval, fits into the hole and is trimmed with a metal rim.

Basins are made especially for use with tile and fit into a cutout in the supporting base. The tile is usually installed with special tile trim that fits over the edge of the basin. There are other methods of installation suited to different basin designs.

For marble-like acrylics, the installation procedure and choice of basin are the same as for plastic laminate.

A self-rimmed basin is a design that can be used with any of the countertops described. The basin is designed in such a way as to eliminate the need for a metal rim.

Another choice is a one-piece acrylic unit. The basin and vanity top are molded in one piece, eliminating the joint between basin and top.

Basins are also designed for use without vanity cabinetry. Most models of this type are called wall-hung basins. There are also models with a single leg in the center which conceals the pipes. Both types are shown in the same way. (See Fig. 8.9.)

Fig. 8.9 Symbol for a wall-hung basin.

Vanity cabinet selection is not dependent on the type of countertop selected. Vanity cabinets are made to fit any of the different standard-size tops. Manufactured drawer and cabinet units come in many lengths and can be combined to fit almost any space requirement.

DRAWING VANITIES AND BASINS ON THE PLAN

1. It is only necessary to draw the simple symbols shown in Fig. 8.10 to indicate any of the preceding material selections.

2. The depth (front to back) measurement of the average vanity cabinet is 22".

3. Draw a line indicating the correct vanity cabinet depth on your plan.

4. Choose whatever length the space permits unless you will use a premanufactured unit of a specific size.

5. Select the basin from your template and place it in the desired position within the vanity lines and draw around the opening; alternatively, trace it from the drawing guide.

6. The basin can be placed at any location along the length of the countertop. Fig. 8.10 depicts a vanity, countertop, and basin.

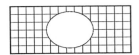

Fig. 8.10 Symbol for a vanity cabinet, basin, and countertop.

MEDICINE CABINET

Medicine cabinets are designed to fit between the studs in the framed wall. The cabinet part, which fits into the wall, is approximately 14" wide and 24" high. The mirror is slightly larger. There is also a taller model which measures approximately 30" high. Another special model is double width, approximately 28" wide. Installing the double-width type involves a little more carpentry. See Fig. 8.11, to draw a medicine cabinet on the plan.

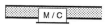

Fig. 8.11 Symbol for a built-in medicine cabinet.

TOILETS

Toilets are available in several designs and colors. Two typical shapes, designated "Standard" and "Elongated" are shown in Figure 8.12 and 13.

"Standard" indicates the design in which the oval shape of the bowl and seat are a standard size. "Elongated" describes a style in which the bowl and seat are longer than that of standard models.

Fig. 8.12 Standard toilet.

Fig. 8.13 Elongated toilet.

DRAWING TOILETS ON THE PLAN

1. To draw a toilet on the plan refer to Fig. 8.14. This drawing shows the toilet located close to the wall. If you are using a template, draw around the opening; otherwise trace from the drawing guides.

2. The minimum required distance from the center of the toilet to the nearest wall or cabinet is 15". The lines on each side of the toilet in Fig. 8.14 show the space requirements.

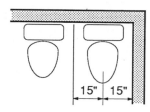

Fig. 8.14 Symbols for standard and elongated toilets showing space requirements.

3. Another important measurement is the space in front of the toilet. You must have a minimum of 2' clearance between the toilet and a wall or cabinet.

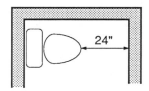

Fig. 8.15 Minimum space required in front of a toilet.

DRAWING BATHROOM HARDWARE

Towel Bars, Toilet Paper Holders, Soap Dishes, and any special hardware that is to be used in a bathroom should be shown on a wall elevation of the bathroom plan. Wall elevations are drawings that show the vertical details of the wall as in Figs. 8.16 through 18.

1. Toilet paper holders should be drawn as close to the toilet as possible and be placed conveniently. They can be recessed into a wall or surface mounted.

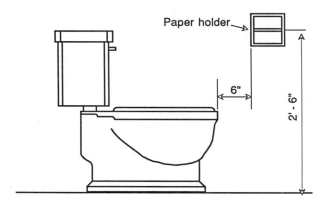

Fig. 8.16 Wall elevation showing toilet paper holder.

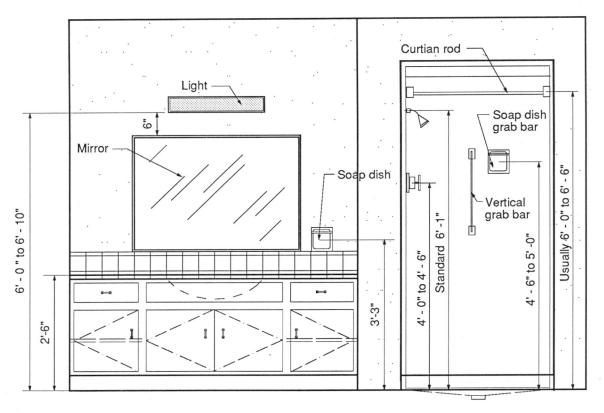

Fig. 8.17 Typical hardware measurements.

2. In the basin area, draw a soap dish, cup/toothbrush holder, and medicine cabinet. Use typical measurements as in Fig. 8.17.

3. Fig. 8.17 shows correct placement of hardware in the shower area.

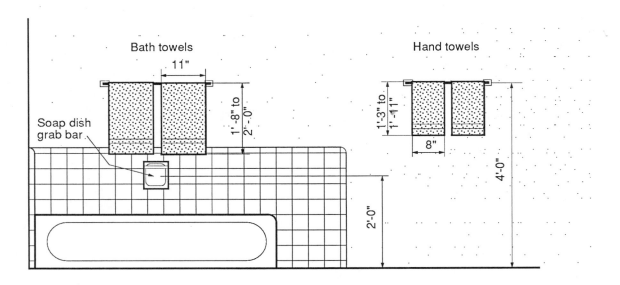

Fig. 8.18 Typical towel bar measurements.

4. Fig. 8.18 shows correct placement of a soap dish and optional towel bar in a bathtub area. When drawing a bathtub with a shower over the tub, extend the tile or other waterproof material to a height of not less than 6' from the floor. Height of the shower head is as shown in Fig. 8.17.

5. Towel bars must be conveniently placed in the most appropriate location. Note the difference in the length of hand towels as compared to bath towels. Towel bars for hand towels are usually placed in the sink area. Towel bars for bath towels should be located in the area of the bath tub or shower.

The sizes and shapes of kitchen equipment on the drawing guides are approximately the same as those of the average available equipment. Though one product varies slightly from another, sizes are so nearly standard that the information given here is adequate for most kitchen planning. When the final selection of appliances and cabinetry is made, the manufacturer will furnish literature giving exact sizes and installation procedure. Any small changes in size can be made on the plan at that time.

DRAWING THE KITCHEN PLAN

1. Begin your kitchen plan by deciding on the most convenient location for the sink, range, and refrigerator.

2. Plan the cabinet layout around these units.

3. Lay out the base (lower) cabinet line by measuring 24" from the wall into the room to show where the outer edge of each cabinet is to be located. (See Fig. 9.1.)

SECTION 3

UNIT 9

KITCHEN LAYOUTS

Objective: To learn to plan and draw a functional kitchen using architectural symbols and designations and appropriate sizes.

KITCHENS

Kitchens have been transformed by beautiful new and improved designs in appliances, cabinetry, and other equipment. However, basic sizes, shapes, and installation procedures of most of the components which make up a kitchen remain very nearly unchanged.

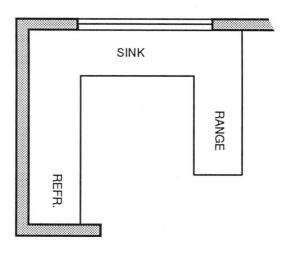

Fig. 9.1 Plan example of a kitchen layout showing a tentative arrangement of sink, range, refrigerator, and base cabinets.

SINKS

There are three sink sizes given on the drawing guides as shown in Fig. 9.2. The first, measuring 32" x 21", is a typical double sink. The second, measuring 42" x 21", is a typical large double sink. The third, measuring 30" x 21", is a typical single sink.

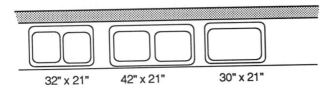

Fig. 9.2 Typical sink sizes.

DRAWING SINKS

1. If you are using a template, select the sink and decide where it is to be placed.

2. Draw around the opening.

3. If you are not using a template, trace from the drawing guides.

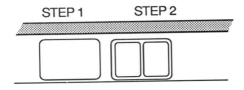

Fig. 9.3 Drawing a double sink.

RANGES

Ranges are available in many styles and a variety of combinations of cooking tops and ovens. From the standpoint of drawing ranges, however, it is necessary to consider only the following two basic types:

ONE-PIECE RANGE

A one-piece range, called a slide-in or drop-in unit, is a free-standing, conventional type of range that sits either on the floor or on a shallow, wooden base. It fits into the cabinetry to give a built-in look. The oven for this unit is usually below the range top.

There are also models with the oven above the range top and others with ovens both above and below. Fig. 9.4 shows a one-piece range with the oven below.

Fig. 9.4 One-piece range with the oven below.

SEPARATE COOKING TOPS AND BUILT-IN OVENS

A cooking top and a separate built-in oven make up another possible choice. With this arrangement, you can choose separate locations for each unit.

Fig. 9.5 Cooking top.

When a separate cooking top is used, it is installed in a cutout in the counter top with a cabinet below. Fig. 9.5 Illustrates a separate cooking top installed in a base cabinet.

When a separate built-in oven is used, it is installed in a special cabinet. It is usually located about counter height within the cabinet. Frequently, two ovens are used in this way, one above the other. Figure 9.6 shows a typical separate oven installed in a cabinet.

Fig. 9.6 Wall oven.

RANGES OR COOKING TOPS

Ranges and cooking tops are available in four typical sizes as shown in Fig. 9. 7.

The smallest cooking top has two burners and is usually 15" wide by 22" deep. It can be turned around and placed sideways in the counter if this arrangement is preferred.

An average-size four-burner range or cooking top is 30" wide by 22" deep. It is the most commonly used size.

Typical large-size ranges and cooking tops are 45" wide by 22" deep. They are available in six-burner models or with four burners and a grill or barbecue.

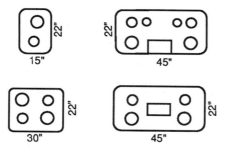

Fig. 9.7 Typical range sizes.

DRAWING THE RANGE AND COOKING TOP

1. Select the most suitable range or cooking top and oven combination for your plan and decide where the units will be placed.

2. Draw either the one-piece range or the cooking top, by selecting from the drawing guides or using a template. (See Fig. 9.8.)

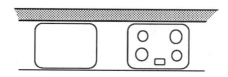

Fig. 9.8 Drawing a range.

BUILT-IN OVEN

Built-in ovens are usually designed to be built into cabinets that are 24" wide. The measurement from the top of the oven to the bottom is determined by the make, model, and size. Double-oven models or models with both conventional and microwave ovens are usually manufactured with the ovens stacked one above the other. Consult manufacturers' literature for exact measurements.

INDICATING A BUILT-IN OVEN

1. To indicate a built-in oven on a floor plan, it is only necessary to note "Built-in Oven" in the desired location.

2. When wall elevations showing cabinetry are designed and shown on a detail sheet, the built-in oven height and other details can be shown. (See Unit 25, Section and Details, Figs. 25.16 and 17.)

HOOD OR EXHAUST FAN

A hood or exhaust fan over the range is designated by writing the words "Hood" or "Exhaust Fan" over the range as in Fig. 9.13.

REFRIGERATOR AND FREEZER

The two sizes of refrigerators or freezers given on the kitchen drawing guides are average-sized equipment. The larger refrigerator or freezer requires a space 36" wide by 28" deep. The small refrigerator or freezer requires a space 30" wide by 28" deep on the kitchen floor plan.   (These sizes apply to upright-type freezers.)

When appliances are not to be included in the construction contract, they are drawn with dotted lines, and the letters N.I.C. (not included in contract) are written on the appliance. (See Figs. 10.4 and 10.5.)

DRAWING A REFRIGERATOR AND FREEZER

1. The only designations necessary on the plan for refrigerator and/or freezer are the units, their size and the line of the cabinet above. (See Fig. 9.9.)

2. Select, from the drawing guide or a template, the size required, and trace it on your plan.

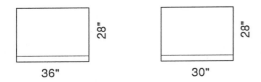

Fig. 9.9 Refrigerator and freezer sizes.

CABINETRY OVER REFRIGERATION UNITS

The refrigerator and/or freezer can simply be fitted between base and wall cabinets. In some custom-cabinet designs, this equipment is built into cabinets to match the rest of the kitchen.

There is room above the refrigerator and freezer for storage cabinets. Standard manufactured wall cabinets are 12" deep; however, they can be made the approximate depth of the equipment. Deep cabinets in this location look better, provide additional storage space and are much easier to reach. A medium-weight line above the refrigerator indicates the cabinet. (See Fig. 9.14.)

DISHWASHER

While there are many different manufacturers of dishwashers, the basic size of nearly all makes and models is 24" in width. The depth is slightly less.

Most units are designed to be built into the 24" base cabinets and fit under the countertop. (See Fig. 9.10.)

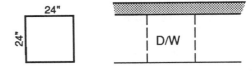

Fig. 9.10 Dishwasher size and designation.

DRAWING A DISHWASHER

1. The dishwasher is usually installed on either the right or left side of the sink and as close to it as possible. In planning the location, consider the direction from which the dishes will be picked up, rinsed off, and placed in the dishwasher.

2. When the dishwasher is located beneath the counter, it is indicated with two dashed (hidden) parallel lines 24" apart, on the countertop. The letters D/W are written between the dashed lines as in Fig. 9.10.

GARBAGE DISPOSALS

When using a double sink, choose carefully the side on which you wish to locate the garbage disposal. Take into consideration the direction from which dishes will be scraped and rinsed.

DRAWING A GARBAGE DISPOSAL

To draw a garbage disposal in either a single or double sink, write the letters G/D where the drain would be as in Fig. 9.11.

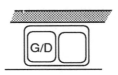

Fig. 9.11 Symbol for garbage disposal.

SPECIAL KITCHEN EQUIPMENT

If there is to be any other special equipment, such as a trash compactor in the kitchen, it is best to select it and obtain manufacturer's literature for size, space and hookup requirements.

Write the name of the special equipment on the plan in the desired location and indicate the space requirement and any special electrical outlets or plumbing connections required.

CABINETS

Cabinets can be custom-made to meet your exact requirements, or they can be purchased ready-made from one of the many cabinet manufacturers. The 24" deep cabinets beneath the counter are referred to as base cabinets (or lower cabinets). The narrower 12" cabinets above the counter are referred to as wall cabinets (or upper cabinets).

Manufactured cabinetry is available in many combinations of drawer and cabinet units which can be combined to fit your plan. Each is made in several sizes so that fitting units together to meet space requirements can be done easily. Many cabinet manufacturers have developed designs for ingenious use of interior cabinet space.

DRAWING KITCHEN CABINETS

1. In the first stages of kitchen planning, it was only necessary to indicate on the plan the area where the base and wall cabinets would be located. Wall cabinets are usually indicated with a fine solid line. Figure 9.12 shows the first layout of a plan with the cabinets indicated.

2. With the basic layout of the entire kitchen worked out satisfactorily, you can plan the details of the cabinetry more easily.

3. If you will be using manufactured cabinets, selections can be made and units planned to fit together from the detailed literature the manufacturer will supply. Many manufacturers have staff people who will help you to fit your selection of units into a plan.

KITCHEN COUNTERTOPS

When a plastic laminate (known under several brand names such a Formica) is used, a hole the size of the sink is cut out of the counter top. The sink fits into the hole and is trimmed with a metal rim.

Some sinks are made especially for use with tile. They fit into a cutout in the supporting base. The tile is usually installed with special tile trim that fits over the edge of the sink, though there are other methods of installation suited to different sink designs. Self-rimmed sinks are designed to be used with any of the described counter tops. The sink is designed in such a way as to eliminate the need for a metal rim around the edge.

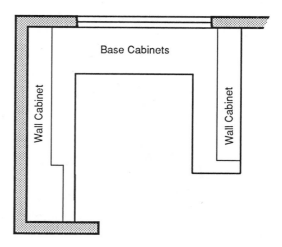

Fig. 9.12 A plan showing base and wall cabinets.

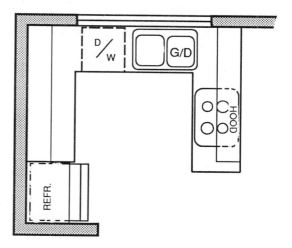

Fig. 9.13 Symbols and designations for cabinets, sink, range, refrigerator, dishwasher, garbage disposal, and exhaust fan.

The appliances vary in depth, but typically average 27" to 30". Most models project 2" to 3" beyond the 24" base cabinets.

There are also laundry appliances designed to be used beneath the counter. This type usually fits within the 24" base-cabinet depth and a continuous counter top is used. The doors open from the front.

DRAWING A WASHER AND DRYER

1. Refer to the laundry appliances on the drawing guides. (See Fig. 10.1.)

2. Trace the appliances to be used on the plan in the desired location.

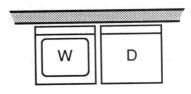

Fig10.1 Symbol for a washing machine and dryer.

SECTION 3
UNIT 10
LAUNDRY ROOM LAYOUTS

Objective: To learn appropriate symbols and sizes to lay out laundry facilities.

DRAWING THE LAUNDRY EQUIPMENT

Whether the plan is to have a separate laundry room, or to locate laundry equipment in a convenient area of the house, you will need to plan around basic laundry equipment sizes.

WASHING MACHINE AND DRYER

Washing machine and dryer sizes vary slightly. However, if the plan is to use the conventional large units (not the small portable types), a space approximately 60" wide is needed for the two units. This space allowance is a little larger than the appliances and is desirable, since it allows for moving the units in and out for servicing.

LAUNDRY SINK

The average laundry sink size is 20" x 22". Laundry sinks are usually deeper than kitchen sinks. Some are designed to be built into a base cabinet; others, called laundry trays, are hung on the wall or mounted on legs. Laundry sinks are convenient, especially if there is a separate laundry room. (See Figs. 10.3 and 10. 4.)

DRAWING A LAUNDRY SINK

Refer to the drawing guide or the laundry sink in Fig.10.2 for the correct symbol. Draw the sink on the plan.

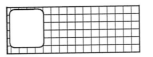

Fig. 10.2a Smbol for a laundry sink in a counter top.   **Fig. 10.2b** Symbol for a free-standing laundry tray.

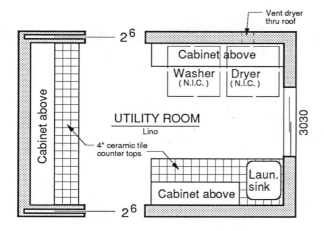

Fig. 10.3 Typical laundry facility layout.

UTILITY ROOM LAYOUTS

In the utility room layout, Fig. 10.3, the laundry sink is located in a counter top. Note the cabinets on the walls above the counter tops. A long counter has been provided in this layout for folding clothes. Because the dryer is located on an inside wall, the vent will be placed inside the wall and exhausted through the roof.

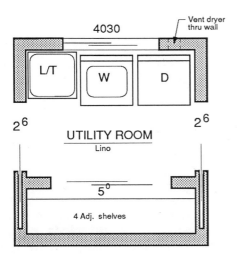

Fig. 10.4 Typical laundry facility layout.

Fig. 10.4 is a typical layout for a utility room. Note the free-standing laundry tray used in this plan. When the dryer is located on an outside wall, a vent through the wall is placed at a level near the floor, either behind or at one end of it. This utility room plan has a four shelf storage closet. When the appliances are to be part of the construction contract, they are drawn as in Fig. 10.4

BUILT-IN IRONING BOARD

When an ironing board is built in, the entire unit fits into the wall and is enclosed with a door. The board can be pulled down into correct ironing position. The symbol for an ironing board is on the drawing guide.

By tracing the symbol with a light dashed line, you can see how much space the board would take up in the room when opened into ironing position. This symbol can also be used as a guide to space requirements for a portable ironing board. (See Fig. 10.5.)

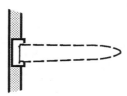

Fig. 10.5 Built-in ironing board.

Gas-burning water heaters have tall, narrow tanks. The burners are designed to burn either natural gas or liquid petroleum gas. They are available in several sizes but 30- or 40-gallon capacity models are often used in small to medium size houses.

Electric water heaters have short, wide tanks. Some types are low enough to be placed under countertops or fitted into low places.

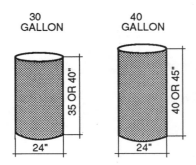

Fig. 11.2 Electric water-heater sizes.

SECTION 3
UNIT 11

MECHANICAL EQUIPMENT

Objective: To learn to plan and draw all of the necessary mechanical equipment on your plan.

DRAWING A WATER HEATER

The symbol for drawing either type of water heater is a circle the same diameter as the heater. It should be marked W/H, as shown in Fig. 11.3.

Fig. 11.3 Symbol for a water heater.

WATER HEATERS

There are two major types of water heaters used in homes: gas and electric. They are available in several size and shapes as shown in Figs. 11.1 and 11.2.

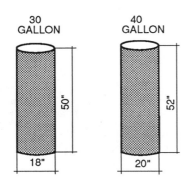

Fig. 11.1 Gas water-heater sizes.

HEATING AND COOLING EQUIPMENT

Heating and cooling equipment is available in many sizes and types. The equipment selected should supply sufficient heating and cooling so that the home is adequately warm during the coldest days and comfortably cool during the hottest.

The choice of heating and cooling equipment must be based on the type of fuel to be used. Investigate the availability and cost of fuel in your area before making selections.

Fig. 11.6 Coal- or-oil burning furnace.

GAS WALL FURNACES

There are simple and economical furnaces available which are built into the wall and do not take up floor space. These furnaces burn either natural gas or liquid petroleum gas. They are usually located in halls, so that the heat can circulate throughout the house.

The average size of a gas wall furnace and the designation for drawing it are shown in Fig. 11.4.

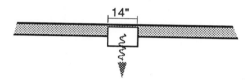

Fig. 11.4 Gas wall furnace.

LARGER FURNACES

There are many makes, models, and types of larger-sized furnaces. They are usually installed in a centrally located, especially designed closet. Heating and cooling equipment is frequently combined in one larger unit.

Figure 11.5 shows the designation for drawing larger furnaces.

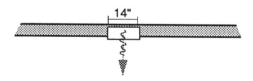

Fig. 11.5 Larger furnace.

COAL- OR OIL-BURNING FURNACES

Coal- and oil-burning furnaces are available in areas where conditions warrant their use.

Figure 11.6 shows the designation to use when indicating a coal- or oil-burning furnace.

ELECTRIC WALL HEATERS

This type of heater is sometimes called a space heater and is built into the wall. Several individual units are usually located throughout the house.

Fig. 11.7 shows the average size and designation for drawing electric wall heaters.

Fig. 11.7 Electric wall heater.

AIR CONDITIONING

Heating and air conditioning units are often combined in one piece of equipment. A dual-type installation saves floor space. Units are also made for roof and for outdoor installation .

The space allowed on the plan for a furnace and/or air conditioner will depend upon the size and type of equipment selected.

HEAT-LOSS CALCULATIONS

Because heating and cooling are complex subjects, it is advisable to consult with local heating and air conditioning equipment dealers. Heat-loss calculations which are required by most building departments are figures that determine the required size of the equipment needed for each specific house plan. These figures are based on the size of the house, window area, insulation, local weather conditions, type of equipment, etc. Heating and air conditioning contractors often supply these figures when their equipment is specified.

INSULATION

Insulation is used to hold heated air inside the house during winter months and to keep heat out during summer months. A well-insulated house is much more energy-efficient and comfortable. Insulating a new house or an addition while it is under construction is required in many states and is desirable because it can be done more efficiently and at less cost at the time of construction. However, insulation can also be installed in existing houses.

The attic ranks first in importance, but all exterior walls should be insulated as well. Heat loss is also prevented by insulating basement walls, under subflooring, and any other areas where cold air could penetrate.

SELECTING INSULATION

There are many kinds of insulation. The types and grades selected should be determined by the method of construction, local weather conditions, and building department requirements. Some states have "State Energy Conservation Regulations" with which your plan must comply. Verify requirements in your area before selecting insulation.

R Values

Certain construction materials have been tested and given a rating (R value) that indicates relatively how much resistance they offer to heat flow. The higher the R value the better the insulating value of the material. Manufacturers label their products to indicate the R value.

Determine the most suitable specifications for insulation in your area by checking with insulation manufacturers and by reading manufacturers' literature. Verify information with the local building department.

DRAWING INSULATION ON THE PLAN

Insulation is usually drawn on the section drawing with a note calling out the R value. Insulation information should also be noted along with other pertinent information as a general note on the floor-plan sheet of the set of drawings. (See Fig. 11.8)

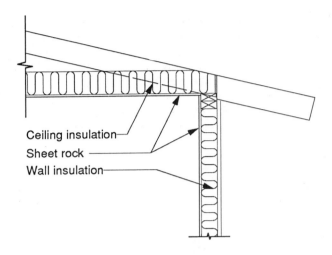

Ceiling insulation
Sheet rock
Wall insulation

Fig. 11.8 Symbol used to designate insulation.

The electrician who wires the house will perform the work according to local building code requirements, but will have no way of knowing how the rooms will be used or what the special requirements are unless all of the electrical symbols are clearly drawn on the plan. Figure 12.10 shows a completed floor plan with electrical outlets added to it. For larger jobs, a separate electrical sheet showing walls, cabinets, windows, and door swings, plus wiring details and specifications, is often used.

DRAWING ELECTRICAL SYMBOLS

Electrical symbols can be drawn freehand or traced from the drawing guides, but they are more readable when a template and a triangle are used for drawing circles, lines, and angles.

Figure 12.1 is a quick reference chart showing many of the electrical symbols typically used in residential design. (See Figs. 12.2 through 12.9 for information about each symbol.)

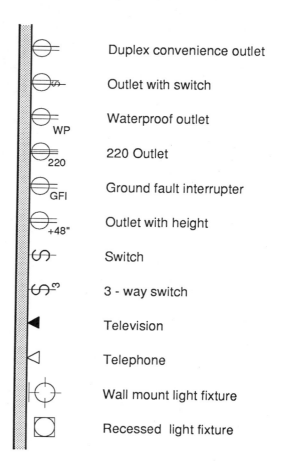

Symbol	Description
	Duplex convenience outlet
	Outlet with switch
WP	Waterproof outlet
220	220 Outlet
GFI	Ground fault interrupter
+48"	Outlet with height
	Switch
	3 - way switch
	Television
	Telephone
	Wall mount light fixture
	Recessed light fixture

Fig. 12.1 Quick reference chart showing the most commonly used electrical symbols.

SECTION 3
UNIT 12

ELECTRICAL WORK

Objective: To learn to plan and draw the required electrical work on a plan using the correct symbol to describe each item.

PLANNING ELECTRICAL WORK

When the floor-plan drawing is completed, study your room layouts for the best placement of electrical fixtures, outlets, switches, etc. After the furniture arrangement has been worked out and the swing of the doors planned, it is easy to lay out the electrical work, as you can see by referring to Unit 17, Room Studies, Fig. 17.10.

Before drawing electrical symbols on your plan, careful planning is essential. Careless planning could result in such things as outlets behind heavy furniture, none where they are needed, and possibly switches behind doors. Your local building department will require that the house be wired according to their adopted National Electrical Code. Check with them for the requirements in your area.

ELECTRICAL DUPLEX OUTLETS

When drawing outlets on the plan, use the symbols shown in Fig. 12.2. A circle with two lines through it represents the 110-volt outlet used for ordinary household current. A circle with three lines through it represents the 220-volt outlet used for items which require 220 volts, such as clothes dryers, ranges, water heaters, and air conditioners.

Outlet heights are typically 12 inches up from the floor. If a different height is required, (above the counter top in a kitchen for example) write the desired measurement from the floor to the outlet as shown in Fig. 12.2.

When outlets are placed on the outside of a building a water-proof type is specified. To indicate water proof outlets, write the letters WP beside the outlet symbol.

When the letters GFI are placed beside an outlet, they signify a "Ground Fault Interrupter". This is a safety device which is built into the outlet and is designed to shut off power when moisture penetrates the outlet. GFI's are specified for use in moisture prone areas such as bathrooms, and on exterior walls.

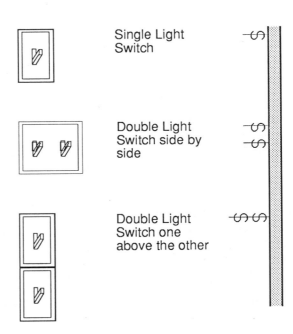

PICTORIAL · SYMBOLS

110 Volt Duplex Outlet

220 Volt Duplex Outlet — 220

Outlet with height given and switch — +48

Water Proof Outlet — wp

Fig. 12.2 Symbols for electrical outlets.

LIGHT SWITCHES

Use the light switch symbols shown in Fig.12.3 to indicate light switches on your plan. Light switches are frequently located beside doors. Refer to your preliminary studies and consider the direction of the door swing when choosing correct placement. To clarify which switch turns on which light, connect the switch to the light with a curved, dashed line as in Fig. 12.10. If the switch chosen will activate an outlet, simply dash a curved line from the switch to the outlet. Switch-activated wall outlets are useful for lighting with lamps.

A three-way switch is used when a light is to be turned on and off from two locations. Use the light switch symbol and add the numeral 3 beside it at each switch location. Draw a connecting line from the light fixture outlet to each switch.

Single Light Switch

Double Light Switch side by side

Double Light Switch one above the other

Fig. 12.3 Symbols for light switches.

LIGHT FIXTURES

Light fixtures can be mounted on the ceiling or on the wall. Select the type of fixture you wish to use and draw the symbol to represent it in the chosen location on the plan. See Fig. 12.4.

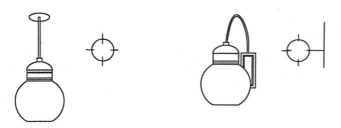

FIG. 12.4 Symbols for ceiling-mount and wall-mount light fixtures.

HEAT, LIGHT FAN UNITS

Combination heat, light and ventilation for bathrooms can be provided by installing a combination unit in the ceiling. A special switch or dial enables the user to select heat, air circulation, light, exhaust fan or any combination of two. To designate this type of fixture, use the symbol shown in Fig. 12.5 and specify "combination unit." The same symbol may be used to indicate a built-in radiant ceiling heat lamp or fan.

Fig. 12.5 Symbol for heat lights, heat fans or combination units.

FANS

The symbol shown in Fig. 12.6 is used to show the location of a ceiling fan. Ceiling fans are often required in bathrooms with inadequate ventilation, above laundry equipment, in cooking areas etc.

Fig. 12.6 Symbol for ceiling fans.

SMOKE DETECTORS

Smoke detectors are required in all new houses, additions, or remodeling projects. They must be located in all hallways providing access to rooms used for sleeping and should be mounted on the ceiling or high on the wall. In plans where the sleeping rooms are located on an upper level, the smoke detector must be located on the ceiling, directly over the center of the stairway. (See Fig. 12.7.)

Fig 12.7 Symbol for smoke detector.

TELEPHONE OUTLETS

Wiring for telephones is usually installed in the walls of a house during the course of construction. Carefully study your plan and room studies for appropriate telephone locations. Indicate them on the plan by using the symbol shown in Fig. 12.8.

Fig. 12.8 Symbol for telephone outlet.

TELEVISION OUTLETS

Television antenna lead-in wires are generally placed in the walls during the course of construction. Review your room studies and select an appropriate location for a television set. Draw the symbol for a television outlet shown in Fig. 12.9 as well as the required symbol for an electrical outlet.

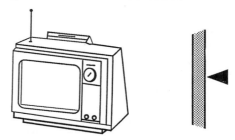

Fig. 12.9 Symbol for television outlets.

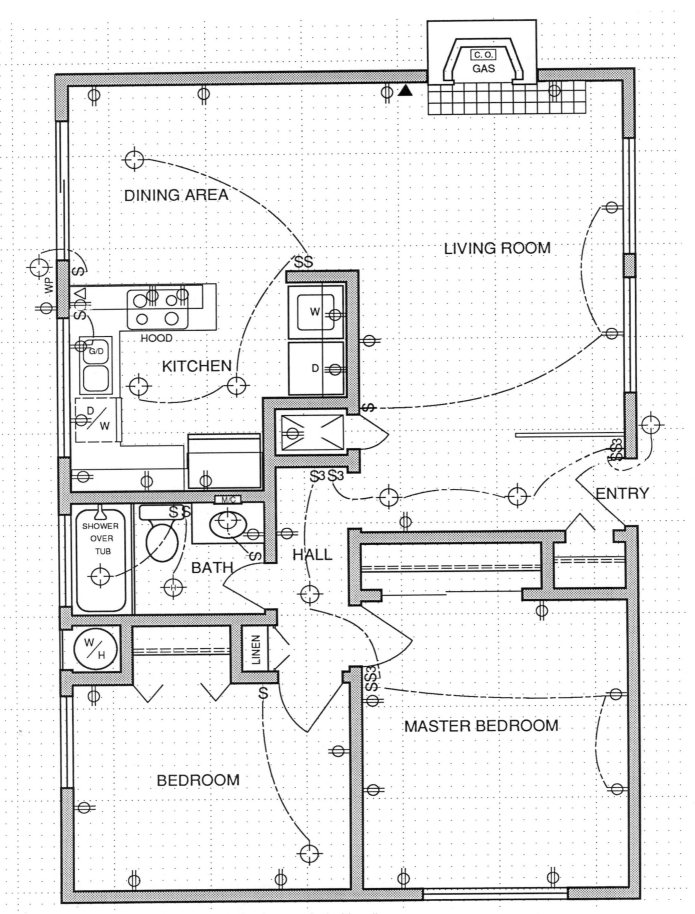

Fig. 12.10 Floor-plan example showing a typical wiring diagram.

SECTION 3
UNIT 13

DOORS

Objective: To become familiar with the various available types of doors and learn how to select and draw them on your plan.

HINGE DOORS

The most commonly used doors in a residence are the ordinary hinge-type shown in Fig. 13.1. They may be hinged to swing from either the right or left side of the opening. They can open either out of or into the room. The correct designation for drawing doors and door swings for hinge-type doors on floor plans is shown in Fig. 13.3.

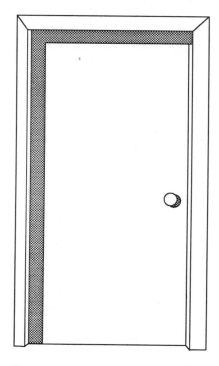

Fig. 13.1 Ordinary hinge-type door.

POCKET DOORS

A pocket door is one which slides into a pocket in the framed wall. It can be planned to slide to either the right or left, depending on the space available in the wall for the pocket. Figure 13.2 shows a pocket or sliding-type door. The pocket door is especially convenient where the swing of the door interferes with furniture or traffic paths. Fig. 13.3 shows the correct designation for drawing pocket-type doors.

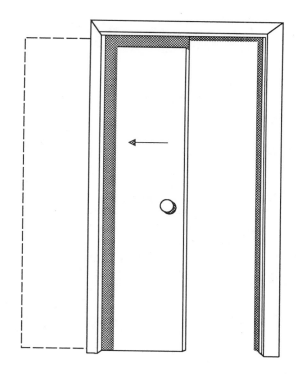

Fig. 13.2 Pocket or sliding-type door.

DOOR SIZES

Manufacturers have standardized door sizes as shown in Fig. 13.3. Standard sizes are available wherever building materials are purchased. These sizes apply to both hinge-type and pocket-type doors. The smallest opening that one can comfortably walk through is 2' - 0" wide. It is most often used in bathrooms. Most of the other doors in a house should be 2' 4", 2' 6", 2' 8", or 3' 0". Consider the size of furnishings to be moved in and out of rooms and space required for equipment such as that used by handicapped persons, when choosing door sizes. Doors leading out of the house, especially the front door, or a door to an attached garage, are typically 3' 0".

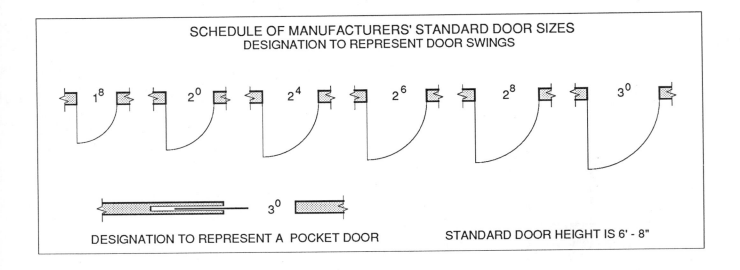

SCHEDULE OF MANUFACTURERS' STANDARD DOOR SIZES
DESIGNATION TO REPRESENT DOOR SWINGS

1^8 2^0 2^4 2^6 2^8 3^0

3^0

DESIGNATION TO REPRESENT A POCKET DOOR   STANDARD DOOR HEIGHT IS 6' - 8"

Fig. 13.3 Designation to represent pocket- and hinge-type doors.

DRAWING DOOR SWINGS

1. Door-swing designations are on the drawing guide and may be on your general-purpose template. The arc indicates the swing of the door and the straight line represents the door. (See Fig.13.3.)

2. Study your furniture plan and traffic paths when deciding on door swings or pocket doors. (See Figs. 17.5 and 6.)

3. Doors are shown on the floor plan in Fig. 20.2.

WARDROBE DOORS

Bifold and sliding doors are two commonly used types of wardrobe doors. The bifold is made from pairs of narrow folding doors as shown in Fig. 13.4. Pairs of sliding doors, sometimes called bypass doors, are depicted in Fig. 13.6.

DRAWING WARDROBE DOORS

1. Measure the width of the closet.

2. From the sizes shown in Fig. 13.5, select the pair of doors which comes closest to fitting the available opening space.

3. Find the center of the closet on your plan and mark off half the width of the pair of doors each way from the center point. Erase wall lines to make a closet-door opening.

4. Draw the pair of wardrobe doors you have selected, using the appropriate designation. See Fig. 13.5.

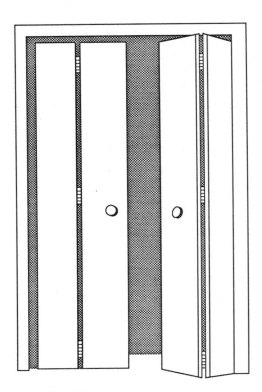

Fig. 13.4 Bifold wardrobe door.

48

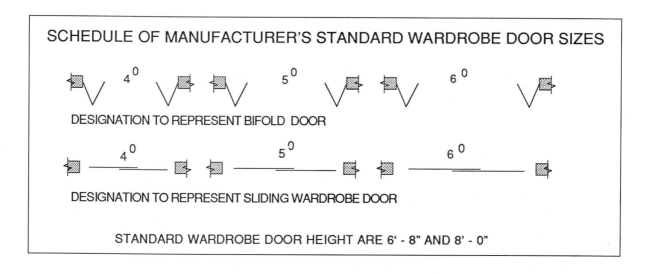

SCHEDULE OF MANUFACTURER'S STANDARD WARDROBE DOOR SIZES

DESIGNATION TO REPRESENT BIFOLD DOOR

DESIGNATION TO REPRESENT SLIDING WARDROBE DOOR

STANDARD WARDROBE DOOR HEIGHT ARE 6' - 8" AND 8' - 0"

Fig. 13.5 Wardrobe door sizes and designations.

5. For larger closet openings, use multiples of pairs of any of the standard sizes. Allow at least 6" of space between pairs for framing.

6. Fig. 12.10 shows both types of wardrobe doors drawn on the floor plan.

SLIDING GLASS DOORS

Sliding glass doors are used in instances where a large glass area, as well as access to a patio is desirable. They are sometimes referred to as patio doors. These doors are made with two or more glass panels mounted in a frame. Typically, one panel remains in a fixed position; the other panel slides back. They can be ordered with either the right or the left panel sliding. Most are interchangeable. Dual glazing (also called insulating or thermal glass) is available.

DRAWING SLIDING GLASS DOORS

The symbol for drawing sliding-glass doors is shown in Fig 13.7 and on the floor plan, Fig. 20.2

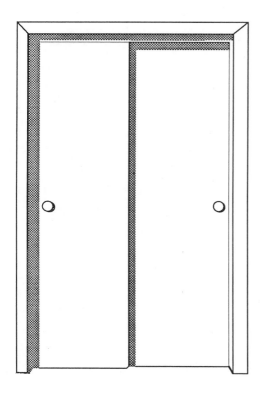

Fig. 13.6 A sliding wardrobe door

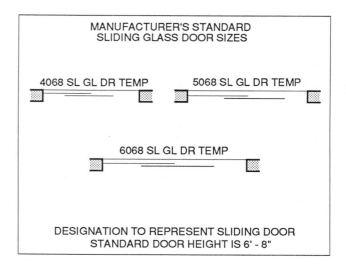

MANUFACTURER'S STANDARD
SLIDING GLASS DOOR SIZES

4068 SL GL DR TEMP   5068 SL GL DR TEMP

6068 SL GL DR TEMP

DESIGNATION TO REPRESENT SLIDING DOOR
STANDARD DOOR HEIGHT IS 6' - 8"

Fig. 13.7 Sliding-glass door designation and sizes.

49

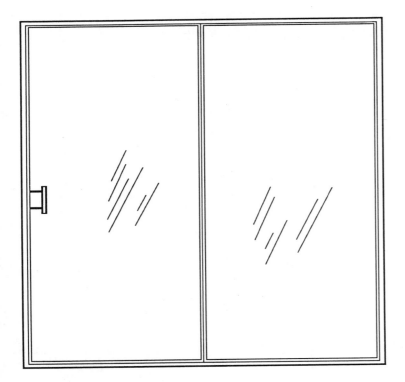

Fig. 13.8 A sliding glass door in elevation view.

NOTE: When any glass is within 18 inches of the floor it must be tempered glass (glass which has been heat strengthened) or safety glass. Check with your local building department for special requirements in your area.

HORIZONTALLY SLIDING WINDOWS

Horizontally sliding windows are shown in the pictorial view of Fig. 14.1, they slide in tracks located at the top and bottom of the frame and they are divided into two or more panels. One half is usually fixed, and the other half slides, allowing 50 percent ventilation. The screen fits on the outside of the window.

An advantage of this type is that there are no projections when the window is open. Also, large sizes are more practical in this type. They are available in wood, metal, or wood covered with either aluminum or plastic. Horizontally sliding windows are drawn on the plan as shown in the plan view, Fig. 14.1.

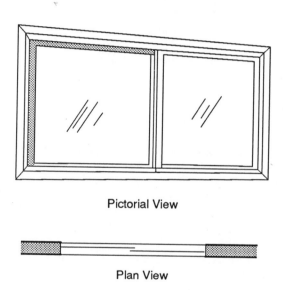

Pictorial View

Plan View

Fig. 14.1 Horizontally sliding windows.

SECTION 3
UNIT 14

WINDOWS

Objective: To become familiar with the different types of windows available and how to select and draw the most suitable windows on your plan.

SELECTING AND DRAWING WINDOWS

The suitability of a window type is determined by the special requirements inherent in the design of a home. Problems of cleaning, ventilation, and weatherproofing must be taken into consideration as well as the adaptability of the window to the design of the house. There are good window types to suit every requirement.

Windows are manufactured in a variety of sizes and materials. Window sash (the material surrounding the glass) is manufactured of both wood and metal. In one process, the insulating properties of wood are combined with the weather-resistant, maintenance-free properties of treated aluminum or plastic. In all of the following window types, insulating glass (also called thermal or double glazing) is available.

DOUBLE-HUNG WINDOWS

Double-hung windows, shown in pictorial view, Fig.14.2, are sometimes used in new construction. They are also extensively used to match existing windows in remodeling.

In this type, both halves of the window slide up and down and are held in the desired position by balanced counterweights attached to each side of the sash. Newer double-hung windows have a spring or spiral mechanism which operates the same way as the counterweight. They also have neatly fitted screens. This window is useful in extreme climates. The design assures minimum air infiltration when the window is weather-stripped. Double-hung windows come in wood, metal, or wood covered with either aluminum or plastic and are drawn as shown in the plan view, Fig. 14.2.

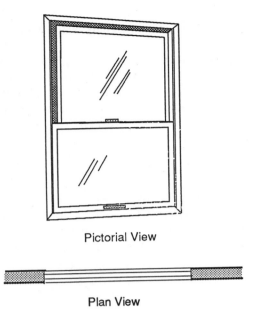

Pictorial View

Plan View

Fig. 14.2 Double-hung windows.

AWNING WINDOWS

Awning-type windows, (also called Transom windows) shown in the pictorial view, Fig. 14.3 are made to swing outward at the bottom with hinges at the top. They are constructed of both wood and metal in a variety of sizes and weights. Awning windows can be used singly or in groups.

These windows are especially adaptable for basements and above or below fixed picture windows for additional ventilation. They are utilitarian and give100 percent ventilation. Awning windows are drawn on the plan as shown in the plan view, Fig. 14.3.

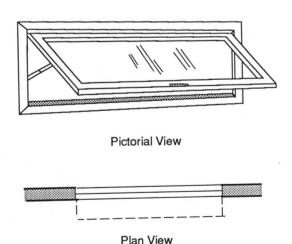

Pictorial View

Plan View

Fig. 14.3 Awning windows.

CASEMENT WINDOWS

Casement windows, shown in the pictorial view, Fig. 14.4, have panels hinged at the side of the sash. The panels usually swing outward for weathertightness. The screens and storm sash are on the inside. They are constructed of both wood and metal.

The chief advantage of this window is that it can be opened entirely, permitting 100% ventilation This may be the correct window to use in cases where maximum ventilation is important. Casement windows are drawn on the plan as shown in the plan view, Fig. 14.4.

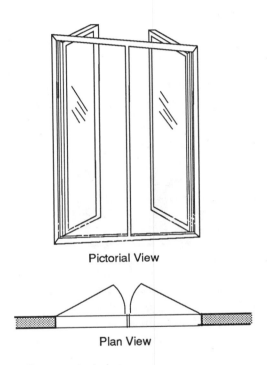

Pictorial View

Plan View

Fig. 14.4 Casement windows.

> **NOTE:** Almost all types of windows are fully assembled and glazed in the factory; they are delivered to the job ready to install.

PLANNING   WINDOW SIZES

1. When planning window widths on paper, draw them in even measurements of 12", as 2', 3', 4' etc. These window sizes are more likely to be available in any type of window chosen. Since there are so many kinds and styles on the market, it would be best to consult manufacturers' literature for exact sizes in the final stages of planning.

2. The height of the window from the floor is also a consideration. This height will not effect your drawing while you are working on the floor plan, but it is helpful to have some idea of height in mind when drawing windows into the plan. Since the tops of the windows will be at the same height as the tops of the doors, this measurement is used to determine how far from the floor the window will be.

3. For example, assume that you choose to use a standard window, 3' high. If it is installed at the usual height of 6' 8", the bottom of the window would be 3' 8" from the floor.

4. In deciding on the height of a window, consider such things as the furniture plan and the exterior appearance of the house.

NOTE: When indicating window sizes, the width is always given first, and the size is written as follows: 80 x 30.

DESIGNATING FIXED AND MOVABLE WINDOW PANELS

1. When planning horizontally sliding windows and sliding glass doors, you can specify which panels are to slide open and which are to remain fixed (not movable). Figure 14.7 shows the manufacturers' method of designating fixed and sliding panels.

2. Casement windows can be obtained with panels which open on either the right or left side, or on both sides. Fig. 14.8 is an elevation view of a casement window with a fixed glass center panel and two openable panels. The dashed-diagonal lines indicate the direction in which the two panels swing.

3. For designating windows on side-view (elevation) drawings, see Fig. 24.11

MINIMUM WINDOW REQUIREMENTS

In most areas, every room below the fourth story must have at least one openable window or exterior door approved for emergency escape or rescue. The units must be openable from the inside to provide a full, clear opening without the use of special tools. All escape or rescue windows from sleeping rooms must have a minimum net clear opening of 5.7 square feet. The minimum net clear opening height dimension is 24 inches. The minimum net clear opening width dimension is 20 inches. Where windows are provided as a means of escape or rescue they must have a finished sill height not more than 44 inches above the floor. Check with the local building department in your area for additional requirements.

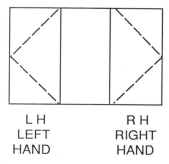

L H
LEFT
HAND

R H
RIGHT
HAND

Fig. 14.8 Manufacturers' designation for right- or left-hand opening window. (Elevation view)

X O

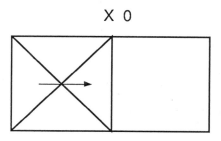

X O X

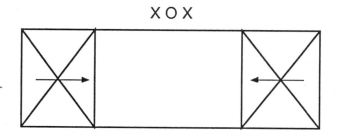

Fig. 14.7 Manufacturers' designations for fixed and movable panels in elevation view.

The preceding figures are inside wall measurements taken between framed walls or carport posts, as shown in Figs. 15.1. This garage size information meets typical building code requirements.

CAR SHELTERS

Car shelters designed according to these specifications will accommodate the number of vehicles they are designed for, but have inadequate space for storage or activities. Since car space is less expensive to build than house space, it is desirable to add two to three additional feet to your plan, either in length or width, where lot space and budget permit.

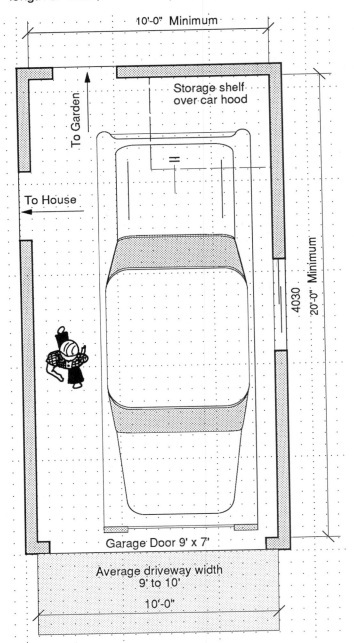

Fig. 15.1 Minimum-size one-car garage and driveway.

SECTION 3
UNIT 15
VEHICLE AREAS

Objective: To become familiar with garage and carport space requirements and learn to design a garage or carport that is appropriate for your plan.

VEHICLE AREA LAYOUTS

Accurate planning for garages, carports, driveways, and parking spaces is essential. Whether or not the plan is to build a garage or carport at the same time as the house is built, these facilities should be provided for in the original planning.

The average garage or carport is built according to the following list of minimum sizes:

Two-Car Garage or Carport

Minimum width	18' 4"
Minimum length	20' 0"

One-Car Garage or Carport

Minimum width	10' 0"
Minimum length	20' 0"

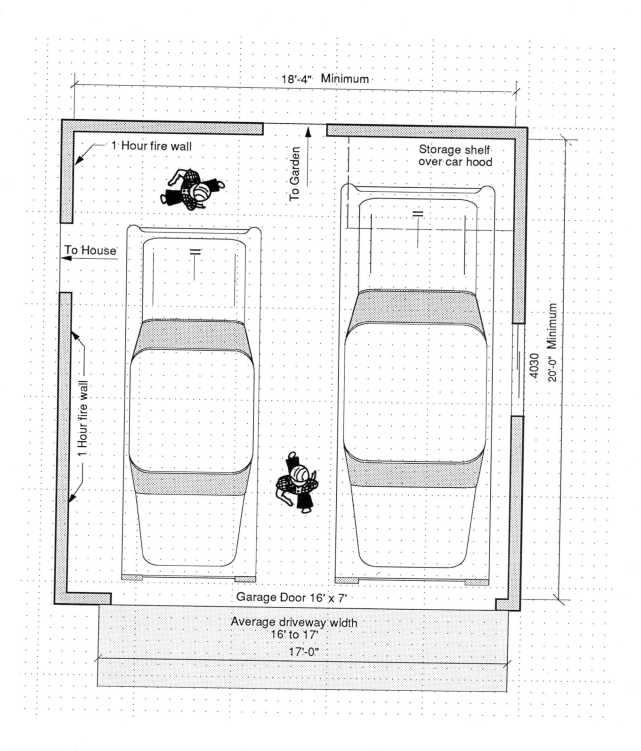

18'-4" Minimum

1 Hour fire wall

To Garden

Storage shelf
over car hood

To House

1 Hour fire wall

4030

20'-0" Minimum

Garage Door 16' x 7'

Average driveway width
16' to 17'
17'-0"

Fig. 15.2 Minimum size for a two car garage.

PLANNING THE GARAGE

1. At least one window in the garage for light and ventilation and a door leading to the service yard or garden area are required.

2. Where there is a door between the garage and the house, it must be a 1 3/8" solid-core door designed to retard the spread of a fire, should one start in the garage. Most communities require that a self-closing door be installed in this location.

3. Few codes require that the garage walls be finished inside. However, when the house and garage are attached, the common wall must be finished with plaster or gypsum board sufficient to retard a fire for one hour if it should start in the garage.

4. If an electric garage door operator is to be installed, an electric outlet will be needed in the ceiling.

5. By placing the garage door as close as 6" to the right-side corner of the garage, as in Fig. 15.2, maximum use of this minimum garage space is permitted. When a garage is planned in this way, the drivers of both cars can get out of the car on the left side.

6. A storage shelf can be placed above the hood of a vehicle when there is no other available storage space.

7. Garage floors should be sloped from the back to the front. The slope, typically 1/8" per foot, should be shown on the concrete-slab plan for the garage. (See Unit 22, Foundation Plan, Fig. 22.7 and Unit 20, Floor Plans, Fig. 20.7.)

GARAGE DOORS

There are several types of garage doors, but those designed to pull or roll up from the bottom, called overhead doors, are relatively trouble-free and when open, provide maximum space to drive into the garage. A manufactured door of metal or wood can be ordered, or a mill can make a door to match the siding on the exterior of the house.

Most manufacturers make garage doors in several sizes, but 7' in height is average and widths of 8' through 18' are available.

AVERAGE CAR SIZES

Subcompact	5' 4" x 13' 6"
Compact	5' 7" x 15' 4"
Intermediate	6' 5" x 17' 4"
Full-size	6' 6" x 18' 2"
Full-size luxury	6' 8" x 18' 11"

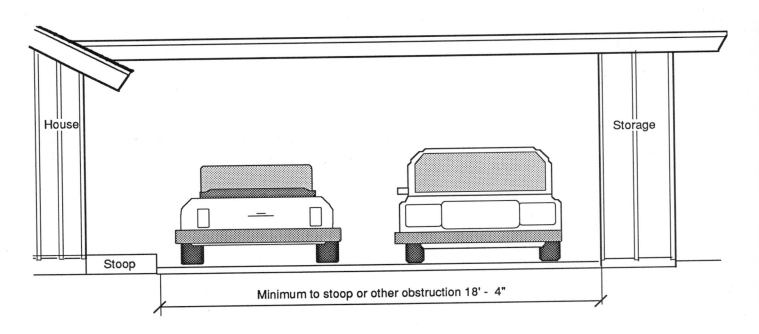

Fig. 15.3 Elevation view of a minimum-sized, two-car carport and driveway.

In selecting and planning fireplaces, there are several things that can be done to increase their efficiency and to prevent the heated air in the room from escaping up the chimney. One is to install glass doors, tightly fitted, over the firebox opening. These fit the opening in the same way as the more commonly used recessed firescreens. Another is to include an air-circulating (convection) system which draws air from the room through the bottom of the firebox, channels it around the firebox and discharges it, fully heated, back into the room. Some types of units can be installed most easily while the fireplace is under construction. Similar units are also available for installation in existing fireplaces.

Some factors to consider when selecting a fireplace design include the type and source of fuel to be used and the efficiency of the primary heating source.

If the major heating source is efficient and suitable firewood is not readily available, a fireplace loses some of it's usefulness. However if an abundant supply of wood or coal is available and is a reliable source of fuel, the more efficient types of fireplaces or stoves are a better choice.

PREFABRICATED METAL FIREPLACES

Prefabricated metal fireplaces of all types are becoming increasingly popular because most of them are slightly more efficient than the masonry types and they are easy to install and lightweight. These factors make them particularly desirable for second-floor installation.

Many of these prefabricated units are available with a built-in, air-circulating system. Moreover, when built-in prefabricated fireplaces are installed, they can be faced with any of the standard masonry, tile, or panel treatments used on masonry fireplaces.

The fireplace designs given on the drawing guides and shown in Fig. 16.1 through 4, are examples of typical shapes and sizes. The sizes are average and can vary, depending on requirements and on the local building codes.

SECTION 3
UNIT 16
FIREPLACES

Objective: To become familiar with different fireplace options and learn to select and draw the most appropriate one on your plan.

SELECTING A FIREPLACE

There are suitable fireplace designs for every floor plan. The number of styles, combined with the large selection of interesting brick, stone, and other materials suitable for fireplace construction and finish, is almost unlimited.

TYPICAL FIREPLACE DESIGNS

STANDARD

The standard fireplace design shown in Fig. 16.1 is the most commonly used fireplace style. It is a popular design for several reasons; it is economical, easy to build, and does an excellent job of heating. A 36" front opening (firebox) is typical of those used in the average home. However, the firebox is often 40" or 42" wide to allow for larger logs. If this fireplace is located on an outside wall, it takes up very little space in the room, as most of the masonry can be installed on the outside of the house. Refer to Unit 25, Sections and Details, Fig. 25.20 for a chart of standard fireplace dimensions.

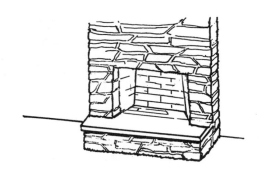

Pictorial View

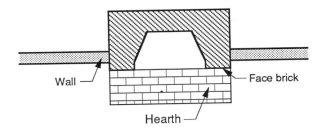

Plan view

Fig. 16.1 Pictorial drawing and plan view for a standard fireplace.

CORNER - OPEN ON TWO SIDES

The corner fireplace shown in Fig. 16.2 is a design that fits into the corner of a room. The front and one end are open, allowing a view of the fire from two sides. It is very attractive in an appropriate location. In this design, most of the fireplace and a continuous hearth on two sides project into the room. The firebox is typically 42" wide by 30" deep.

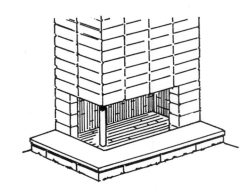

Pictorial View

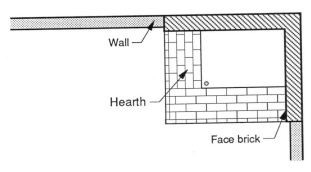

Plan View

Fig. 16.2 Perspective drawing and plan view for a corner fireplace.

OPEN ON TWO SIDES

The design shown in Fig. 16.3 is suitable for use between rooms. It is open at both the front and the back. With this design, it is necessary to build only one fire to heat two rooms. Each room appears to have its own fireplace. It takes the full width and depth of the fireplace plus two hearths out of the floor space. The firebox is typically 40" wide by 30" deep. For efficient operation, the use of tightly fitting glass doors is recommended for both openings.

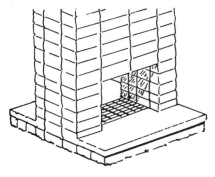

Pictorial View

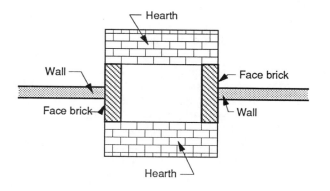

Plan View

Fig. 16.3 Pictorial drawing and plan views for a two-sided fireplace.

OPEN ON THREE SIDES

The design shown in Fig. 16.4 is open at the front and both sides. It is very effective when located properly since one can see the fire from all three sides. Almost the entire fireplace, including a continuous hearth on three sides, projects into the room. The firebox is typically 36" wide x 24" deep.

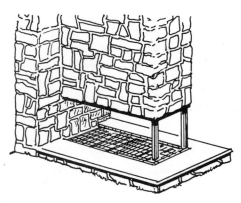

Pictorial View

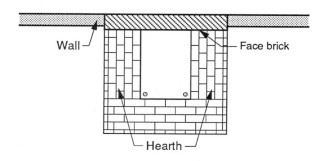

Plan view

Fig. 16.4 Pictorial drawing and plan view for a fireplace open on three sides.

DRAWING A FIREPLACE

Select from the fireplace designs and draw the fireplace on the plan according to the following instructions:

1. Decide on the fireplace fit and location in relationship to the walls. On the fireplace illustrations, the shaded lines extending from the fireplaces, represent walls.

2. Trace the selected fireplace on the plan from the drawing guide.

3. Where possible, a cleanout for ashes, as shown in Fig. 20.3, is desirable.

4. Pipe is frequently installed through the masonry to provide a gas log lighter, indicated as shown in Fig. 20.3.

> **NOTE:** A minimum of 18" in depth is required for the hearth in all fireplace designs.

For more detailed information about fireplaces, refer to Unit 25, Sections and Details, Figs. 25.16 through 18.

You may draw and discard numerous room studies before arriving at the one with which you are completely satisfied. As you continue to draw and study one room after the other, you may begin to change your mind about some of your first drawings and go back to revise them. For this reason it is only necessary to make sketches accurate enough to show details clearly. Many quick studies will prove to be more useful than one or two laboriously done drawings. Keep in mind the relationship of the room you are drawing to the other rooms in the plan.

By the time you have completed the room studies, you will have developed basic information necessary for drawing a more fully developed preliminary plan.

MAKING AN EVALUATION LIST

This is a good time to evaluate the ways in which each room will be used. This can be done by listing all of the activities that normally take place in each of the rooms.

MEASURING AND LISTING FURNISHINGS AND EQUIPMENT

Drawing furniture and any necessary equipment on the plan will help you to visualize the best way to use the available space. If presently owned furniture is to be used, obtain the measurements. It will save time if the height, width, and depth of each piece are measured and the figures kept in a notebook for handy reference. If corresponding items on the drawing guides are not exactly the same size as the pieces to be used, you can adjust the size of the items on the guide with the help of the scale.

NOTE: The living room used in this study, Fig. 17.1, was taken from the floor plan example , Fig. 4.2.

DRAWING A ROOM STUDY

Select a room from your tentative preliminary studies for your first room study; preferably an easy one to draw, like the living room. Keep your sketches, notebook of furniture measurements, and evaluation list handy for reference.

SECTION 4

UNIT 17

PRELIMINARY ROOM STUDIES

Objectives: To study each of the rooms of the plan. These studies will reveal the most suitable location for doors, windows, furniture, electrical outlets, cabinetry, etc.

MAKING ROOM STUDIES FROM PRELIMINARY SKETCHES

When your first design concepts are formulated and you have developed a preliminary sketch, the next step is to make careful studies of each of the rooms in your floor-plan sketch. The purpose of these studies is to reveal the most advantageous placement of such things as doors, windows, cabinetry, plumbing fixtures, light fixtures, and electrical outlets.

The secret of good planning is in keeping the plan flexible until you have completed studies for each room.

STEP 1

Fig. 17.1 Tentative room layout.

1. Fasten grid paper to the drawing surface. If you are planning a rectangular room, lay out the plan with the long measurement on the widest side of the paper. Draw all the walls of the room plan, then cover the drawing with tracing paper.

2. Referring to your preliminary sketches, decide on the placement for windows and door openings. Draw the windows in the desired location and erase spaces for door openings. (See Fig. 17.2.)

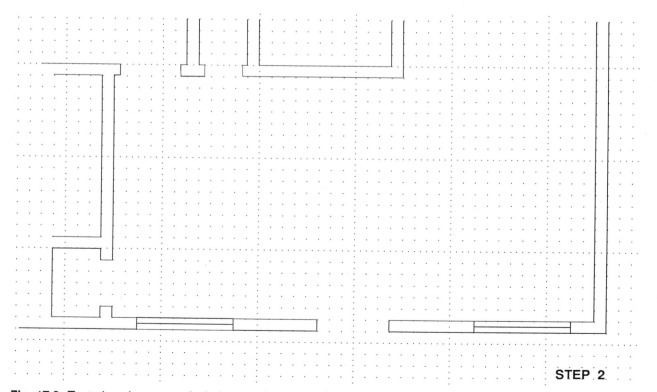

STEP 2

Fig. 17.2 Tentative placement of windows and door openings.

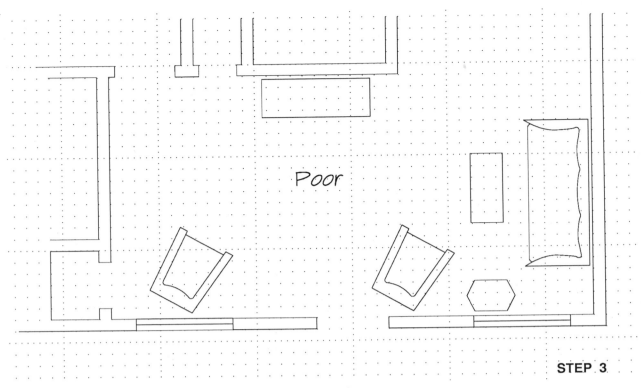

Fig. 17.3 First tentative placement of furnishings and/or equipment.

3. Tentatively plan and draw whatever furnishings or equipment the room requires. Wherever appropriate, trace from the drawing guides or cut out the required items. These cut-out pieces can be moved around on the plan until a desirable arrangement is found. If the room is to have a fireplace or other feature, keep this in mind. (See Fig. 17.3.)

4. On the grid paper drawing, relocate the door openings and windows as necessary for an improved arrangement. (See Fig. 17.4.) Then add furnishings, equipment, etc. from your sketch to the grid paper drawing.

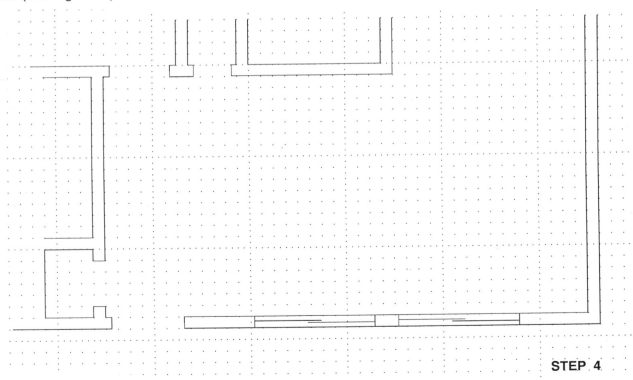

Fig. 17.4 Room plan with relocated door and window openings.

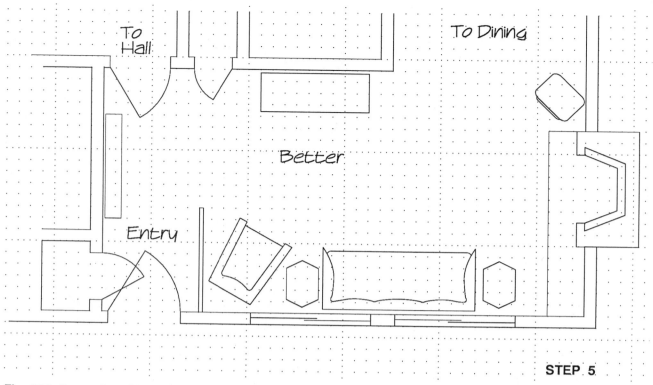

Fig. 17.5 Room plan with door swings added.

5. Draw the door swings so that you can determine whether or not open doors will conflict with each other or with other items. If a fireplace is to be added, select a design from the drawing guide and draw it in the chosen location. Keep in mind the relationship of this room to the rest of the plan.

6. Change door swing types or direction of swing where necessary. Go over lines that represent walls with a heavier pressure on your well-pointed **2 H** lead. The walls will be more clearly defined if they are shaded with a colored pencil on the back of the paper. (See Fig. 17.6.)

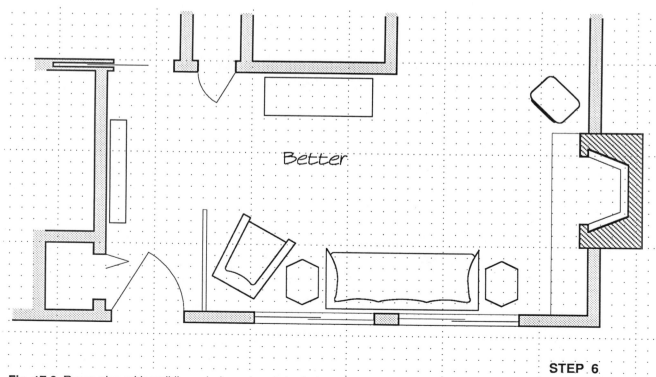

Fig. 17.6 Room plan with wall lines darkened and shaded.

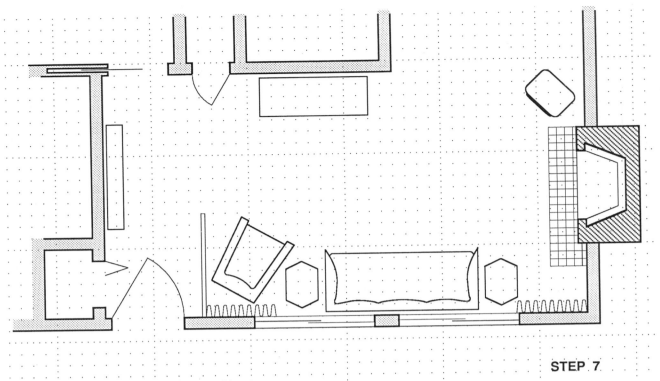

Fig. 17.7 Room plan with space allowed for drapes.

STEP 7

7. Wherever drapes will take up wall space they should be planned for. Decide on the direction the drapes will pull and draw them on the plan. Drapes that are hung on a single track will take up about 6" of floor space as shown in Fig. 17.7. At least 10" of depth is required for over drapes on a double rod. Note that the fireplace hearth has been cut back to permit the drapes to draw all the way to the corner.

8. The figure drawings in the floor plan in Fig. 17.8 are used to reveal the amount of space required for an individual to move about in a room and perform various tasks. You may trace figures on your own plan from the drawing guide or cut them out and place them on the plan.

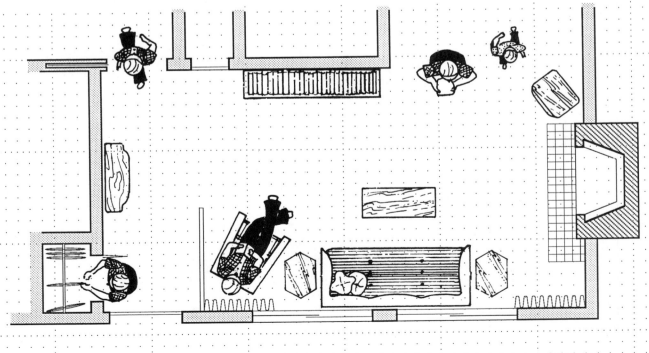

Fig. 17.8 Room plan with figures added to show space requirements.

STEP 8

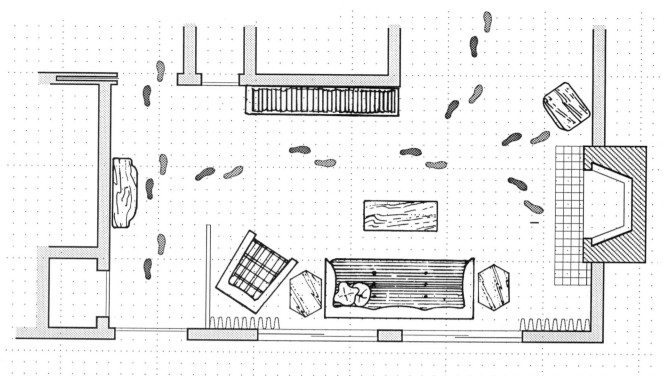

Fig. 17.9 Room plan with a traffic path study.

9. The footprints in the drawings in Fig. 17.9 show the pattern most traffic will take through the room. Consider the way people will walk through the room you are planning.

10. When all factors have been determined and you are able to visualize the room clearly, it will be easy to plan the lighting and decide on the most convenient location for the electrical outlets. (See Fig. 17.10.) Save all of your sketches. When you are drawing a floor plan, they will serve as valuable reference.

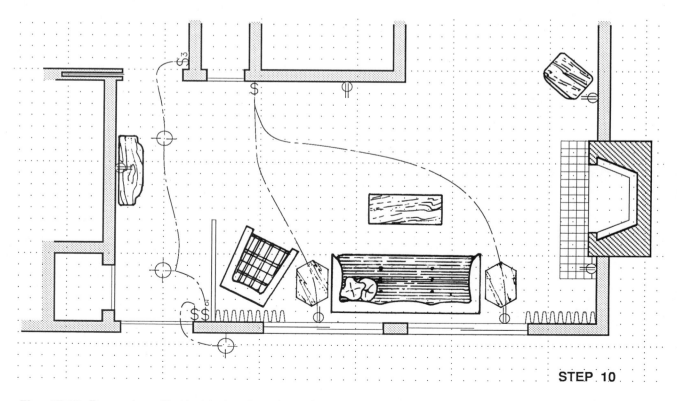

STEP 10

Fig. 17.10 Room plan with electrical outlets planned.

SECTION 4 UNIT 18

PRELIMINARY PLANS

Objective: To draw a preliminary plan to approximate scale, using all of your drawings, sketches, studies, and lists.

DEVELOPING PRELIMINARY PLANS

In Unit 7, Sketching, your initial project planning began. The second phase of floor-plan development is the preparation of the preliminary floor plan. You will need to refer to your notes, lists, bubble diagrams, room studies, site plan, and floor plan sketches. The task is to convert these sketches to a preliminary floor plan. A preliminary floor plan is a drawing that forms a link between rough sketches and detailed, finalized floor-plan drawings. It should show the size and arrangement of exterior and interior spaces. Tentative layouts for kitchens and bathrooms are also shown on this plan. Fig. 18. 1 is an example of a preliminary floor plan, developed from the plan sketch, Fig. 7.4. Although the preliminary plan is drawn to scale and shows correct space allowances, the drawing should remain loose and sketch like. It may be necessary to draw several plans, trying different arrangements, before resolving on the best use of the space and meeting all of the design requirements.

1. **Do Wants** You will find it useful to expand on your list of all the things this plan should include. List the number of bedrooms and the approximate size of each. List each of the other rooms needed and their approximate sizes. List special features the home should have, such as a family room opening to the patio as well as the kitchen, or a retreat for quiet activities.

2. **Don't Wants** A "don't want" list will serve a useful purpose also, such as "don't want" people walking through the kitchen to get to other rooms, "don't want" children using the front entrance when coming in from play, etc.

3. **Think Solar** In studying the location and arrangement of the rooms you have laid out, check your bubble diagrams and sketches and verify the direction of the sun and the effect it will have on each room. List the rooms in which morning sun is desirable and those in which morning sun is not desirable. Consider the effect afternoon sun will have on each room, in the summer and in the winter. If you live in a hot climate, consider a location for a patio that can be served from the kitchen conveniently and that is in the shade on late summer afternoons. On page 27, you will find more information about the effect the sun has on the house.

4. **Studying the lists** You have made lists of the furnishings and appliances to be used in the house and listed the size of each. This will serve to remind you of the items that must be fitted into the plan. Furniture can be laid out on the plan but it is not necessary to draw it on the final preliminary presentation drawing. (See Fig. 18.1.)

SKETCHING A PRELIMINARY PLAN

The size and shape of the house will, to some extent, be determined by the size, shape, and contour of the lot. The illustrations and accompanying information in Figs.18.2 through 5 will help you to determine the maximum buildable lot space on the building site you are working with. Consider space required for the width of the roof overhang. Local planning commissions establish minimum front, rear, and side yard setbacks. The size of the house you are designing must fit within those boundaries. Refer to UNIT 25, Plot Plans, for more information.

OVERALL PLANNING OF HOUSE AND LOT

Drawing a floor plan that seems to have suitable space arrangements for individual requirements is just one phase of home planning. A truly well-planned home is only achieved when overall planning of house and lot result in the maximum use of every square foot of lot space. The use of outdoor living space should be given equal consideration with that of indoor living space. (See Figs. 18.2 through 5.)

ADJUST THE HOUSE TO THE LOT

Since the house must fit the lot, it is logical to make a small sketch of the floor plan and study it on a preliminary plan of the building site. If you are drawing plans to remodel or add to an existing house, the plot plan, showing the size and shape of the house, garage, driveway, walks, and porches or patios will be extremely helpful.

When drawing plans for a new home or an addition, very important preliminary planning will be done on the plot plan and it will serve as a guide during construction.

DRAWING A PRELIMINARY PLAN

Preliminary plans are usually drawn to a scale in which 1/8" = 1'. However, since the final working drawing is drawn to 1/4" scale, it is suggested that you draw your preliminary plan in the scale of 1/4" = 1' - 0".

1. Fasten a sheet of vellum grid paper to your drawing surface and cover it with tracing paper taped firmly in place.

2. With the bubble diagrams, plan sketches, plot plan, and any sketched ideas you may have before you, proceed to work out a preliminary floor plan to scale.

3. Draw lines to represent the approximate location of exterior walls. Make your drawings as nearly correct in size as you are able to at this beginning stage.

4. Draw parallel lines, spaced 6" apart, to represent the thickness of the wall.

5. Lay out interior partitions tentatively, dividing the space within the boundaries of the exterior walls into rooms. Represent wall thickness with parallel lines.

6. Each time you wish to begin a new concept, fasten a fresh piece of tracing paper over the first one and redraw, copying the parts you are satisfied with and making the necessary changes.

7. You may sketch plan ideas on tracing paper many times before your drawing begins to satisfy your requirements and make the best use of interior and lot space. This stage of the drawing requires patience and perseverance. Avoid the pitfalls of clinging to your first ideas, because first ideas can always be improved upon. Keep an open mind.

8. The following details should be included on your preliminary plans:

(a) Correct closet depths: 2' - 8", including both front and back walls, is the minimum practical depth.

(b) Correct size and space allowance for bathroom and kitchen fixtures, appliances, and cabinetry. See Units 8 Bathroom Layouts, 9 Kitchen Layouts, and 10 Laundry Room Layouts.

9. During the process of working out a preliminary floor plan, it will be helpful to study the plans in this book and any others that are available to you.

10. A preliminary plan represents your first thinking, and you will make many changes before completing it. It is a creative study, made to determine the best possible use of the space available to you. Consequently, electrical and mechanical details do not appear on the preliminary plan. They will be worked out during the process of preparing working drawings. Figure 18.1 shows a preliminary plan for the example house, Fig. 4.2.

11. At this stage of plan development you should figure the square footage in the preliminary plan you have drawn. See Unit 19, Square Footage.

12. On the preliminary plan, write the total number of square feet in the house. If you have included a garage, write the square footage for the garage separately.

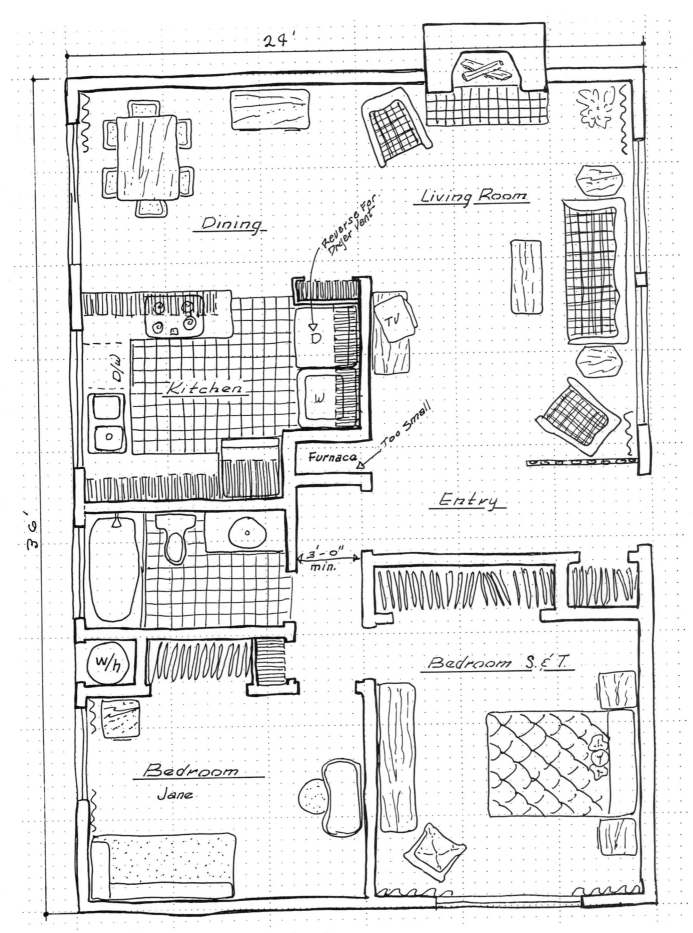

The labels visible within the floor plan:

24'

36'

Dining

Living Room

Reverse for Dryer Vent

Kitchen

D/W

D

W

TV

Too Small

Furnace

Entry

3'-0" min.

W/h

Bedroom S.É.T.

Bedroom

Jane

Fig.18.1 An example of a preliminary floor plan.

MAKING THE BEST USE OF LOT SPACE

You may feel restricted in drawing your plan because of lot limitations. However, a little experimentation will show that there are a number of ways in which the house can be placed on the lot. After you experiment by drawing the layout in several ways on the lot, the most desirable one will become evident. Figures18.2 through 18.5 show examples of the same house and car shelters placed on a lot in four different ways.

When planning the house to fit the lot, study all the things that would have an effect on its livability. Such things as the proximity of the closest neighbors, the way their windows face, and the location of their driveways can be extremely important. (See Fig. 7.5.)

By planning carefully, you can make the maximum use of the lot space. Space can be created for such things as a private patio, a children's playyard viewable from the kitchen or family room, and many other features.

MINIMUM LOT REQUIREMENTS

When both the house you are designing and the neighbor's house have roof overhangs, the minimum distance between the two outer edges is 6'. (See Fig. 18.2.)

If the neighbor's house is adjacent to the garage or carport of the house you are designing and is at least 7' from the property line, you can place the garage within 3' of the property line in most cases. The layout in Fig. 18.3 offers maximum privacy from the street. The screen connecting the house and car shelter could be a high wall. This arrangement creates a sheltered, roofed atrium.

It is usually permissible to build to the back of a lot, as long as setback requirements are observed. The arrangement in Fig. 18.4 is particularly suitable on a narrow lot.

In most cases, the minimum required space between the house and the car shelter is 10', however, when there are no windows in either facing wall, this requirement may be reduced to 5'. This regulation is for fire protection and does not apply when the house and car shelter are connected with a roof, (usually called a breezeway). In cases where a garage or carport is adjacent to the neighbor's car shelter and separate from the house, codes sometimes permit placing it within 3' of the property line. (See Fig. 18.5.)

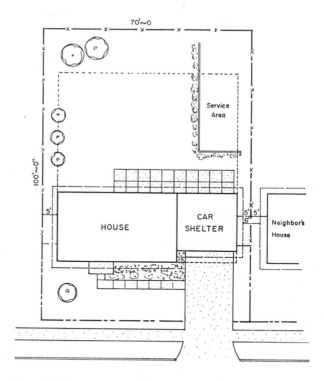

Fig. 18.2 Layout showing standard house / lot arrangement providing maximum yard space.

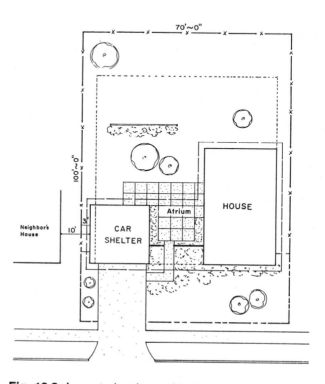

Fig. 18.3 Layout showing a detached car shelter creating an atrium.

69

MAKING A STUDY

1. Study the plot-plan example layouts in Figs. 18.2 through 18.5. They will give you some idea of the many different effects that can be achieved by carefully planning the house and garage to fit the lot.

2. Sketch the building site for your project in 1/16" scale. Use the 1/16" cut-out scale in the back of the book.

3. When you have completed a sketch of the lot, attach it to your drawing surface and cover it with tracing paper.

4. Determine the most convenient place on the lot for a driveway and car shelter in relationship to a kitchen and service area and to the neighbors' houses.

5. Be aware of unattractive features which should be screened out and of attractive features that can be incorporated into the planning.

6. Experiment with different layouts. Use a new piece of tracing paper fastened over your plot plan for each separate study.

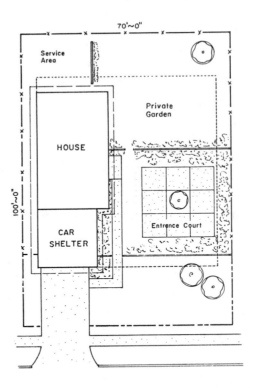

Fig. 18.4 Layout showing house placed lengthwise on the lot providing a private entrance court.

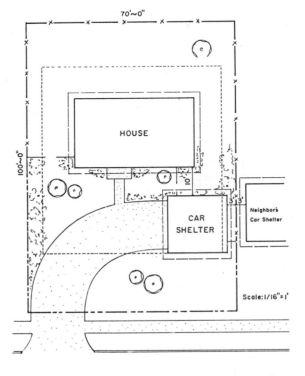

Fig. 18.5 Layout showing house placed farther back on the lot and a curved drive to the garage.

DETERMINING SQUARE FOOTAGE

When figuring square footage, always keep the figures for the house and the garage separate. There is a significant construction cost difference between the two.

1. If a house is square or rectangular, such as the plan in Fig. 20.1; which measures 24' x 36', simply multiply 24 x 36, which equals 864. Consequently there are 864 square feet of floor space in the plan.

2. If you are figuring the square footage in a house that has angles and offsets such as the plan in Fig. 19.1, mark the areas off into squares or rectangles and multiply the width times the length of each area. When you have the square footage for each area, add them all together.

> **Note:** The symbol 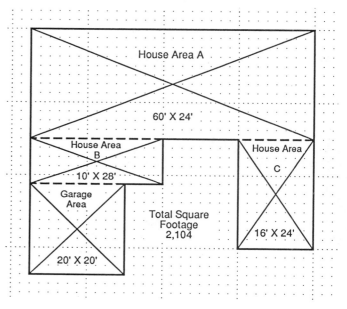 is often used to indicate square feet.

House Area:

A	60'	x	24'	=	1440	sq ft
B	10'	x	28'	=	280	
C	16'	x	24'	=	384	
					2104	sq ft

Garage Area:

20'	x	20'	=	400 sq ft

![Fig. 19.1 diagram showing House Area A 60' X 24', House Area B 10' X 28', House Area C 16' X 24', Garage Area 20' X 20', Total Square Footage 2,104]

Fig. 19.1 Figuring square footage.

SECTION 4
UNIT 19

SQUARE FOOTAGE

Objective: To learn to measure a scale drawing of a room, a house, a lot, or any given area in order to determine how many square feet it contains.

FIGURING SQUARE FOOTAGE

The cost of a house is determined by its size and the type and quality of the construction materials specified.

When your first tentative preliminary plan has been drawn, it is important for you to know the square footage of the house you have laid out. Each time you change the size and shape of an exterior wall, figure the square footage again so that you will at all times be aware of the size of the house you are drawing. These figures are necessary when determining cost, building material requirements and judging sizes of mechanical equipment such as heating and cooling units.

FLOOR
PLAN

SECTION 5

UNIT 20

FLOOR PLAN

Objective: *To learn to draw a complete floor-plan sheet. This sheet is the first of six sheets required to complete a set of working drawings.*

PREPARING A WORKING DRAWING

The final stage of floor plan development is the preparation of a working drawing. When you are satisfied with your preliminary plan, you will be ready to prepare the more complete and finalized working drawing.

WHAT ARE WORKING DRAWINGS?

A completed set of plans is referred to as a set of working drawings because these are the plans used to guide and instruct those who will work on the construction of the house. From the instructions given in this book, you will be drawing six plan sheets comprising a full set of working drawings.

Plan sheets are not necessarily assembled in the same order as they are drawn. The floor-plan sheet is to be numbered 2 because it will be the second sheet in the assembled set. See Unit 27, Assembling Working Drawings, Fig. 27.2 for an example of a completed set of working drawings.

MATERIALS REQUIRED
TO BEGIN DRAWING A FLOOR PLAN

You will need a 1/4" scale, drawing guides, a general-purpose template, all of your preliminary drawings, sketches, lists, large sheets of vellum grid paper (18" x 24" unless your drawing is quite large), tracing paper of equal size, pencils, eraser, colored pencil, and drafting tape.

FROM PRELIMINARY PLAN
TO WORKING DRAWING

1. Secure a large sheet of vellum grid paper to the drawing surface.

2. Referring to Unit 2, Lettering and Lines, lay out the borders and title block on the paper with a **2H** lead. Label this drawing floor plan. It will be sheet number 2.

3. Referring to your preliminary floor plan and room studies, lay out the exterior walls of the plan in accurate 1/4" scale. Use a light pressure on a well pointed **4H** lead. Start the drawing at the top left-hand corner of the page at the intersection of two of the heavier blue lines on the paper. The drawing should not crowd the border lines. Leave room for the later addition of dimension lines. See Unit 21, Dimensions and Notations, Fig. 21.2 for correct space requirements.

4. If you keep exterior measurements in even increments of 2' or 4' (as indicated by the heavier blue lines on the paper), framing will be simplified and there will be less material wasted. Many materials are manufactured in sheets that measure 4' x 8'.

5. Lay out the interior partitions with light lines.

6. When the plan is drawn to scale and all the walls are clearly and sharply defined, the drawing will be much easier to work with. This is a good time to re-evaluate what you have drawn. Study the details carefully and compare them with your preliminary and plot-plan studies.

7. Review your room study drawings and place the windows and door openings. (See Unit 13, Doors, and Unit 14, Windows.)

8. Compare your drawing with Fig. 20.1.

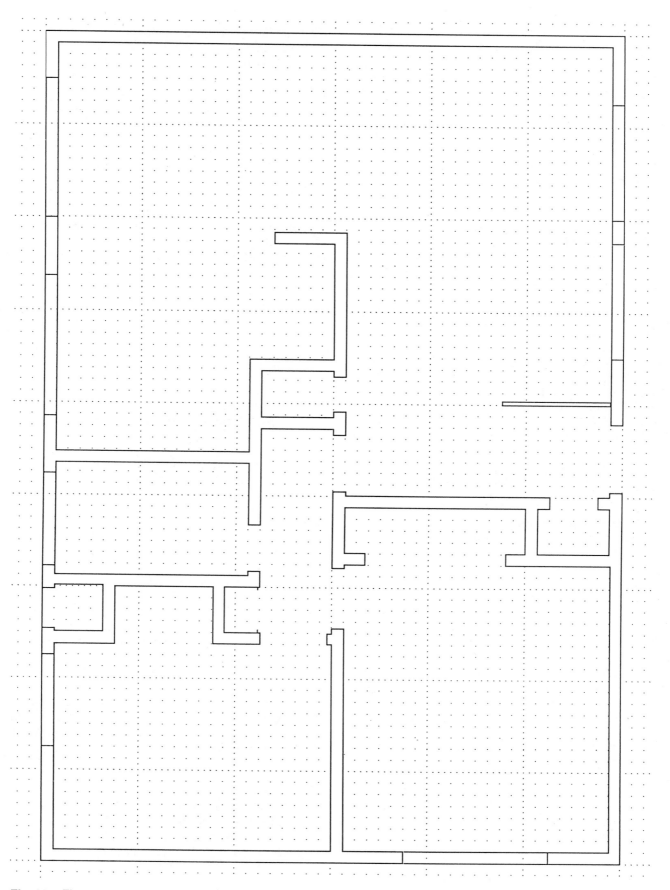

Fig. 20.1 First stage of floor-plan development. This plan shows all walls, windows, and door openings.

9. Referring to Unit 9, Kitchen Layouts, carefully measure and draw the kitchen cabinets, sink, and appliances.

10. Draw the bathroom fixtures and cabinets. Refer to Unit 8, Bathroom Layouts.

11. After reviewing the furniture arrangements in your preliminary studies, draw the doors, noting the size of each. Designate the direction of the swing or slide. (See Unit 13, Doors.)

12. Select from Unit 12, Windows, the type of window to be used and draw the correct designation in the window area of the plan.

13. If the plan is to have a fireplace, refer to Unit 16, Fireplaces, and draw the fireplace of your choice in the chosen location.

14. Compare your drawing with Fig. 20.2.

15. Referring to the furniture arrangement in your preliminary studies and the direction of the door swings on your working drawing, draw the electrical outlets, switches, and light fixtures. This can best be done by fastening a piece of tracing paper over the drawing, large enough to cover the entire plan. When you have carefully planned the electrical work on the tracing paper, transfer the symbols to the working drawing. Refer to Unit 12, Electrical Work, and Fig. 20.3.

16. Add to the plan the name of each room and of any significant items. Under the room name, write the type of floor covering. (See Fig. 20.3.)

17. Add window and door sizes to the plan. There are two ways to show window and door sizes. One is to write the sizes beside the windows and doors. Refer to the floor plan example, Fig. 20.7 and also to Unit 13, Doors and Unit 14 Windows for the correct method of showing window and door sizes. An alternate procedure is the use of door and window schedules. The symbols in Fig. 20.3 are keyed to the door and window schedules in Fig. 20.4.

18. When all of the details have been drawn on the plan, go over the wall lines with a firm pressure on a well-pointed **2H** pencil. Compare your drawing with Fig. 20.3.

19. Dimension the drawing as explained in Unit 21, Dimensions and Notations, Figs. 21.2 and 4.

20. With a colored pencil, shade the lines representing walls. Preferred procedure is to remove the drawing from the drawing surface and shade on the back side of the paper.

21. Double-check your drawing to see that you have included all necessary details by comparing it with the floor-plan check list, Fig. 20.6. Some of the items on the check list will be unfamiliar to you and some will not apply to your project; however, many of the notes and symbols will be required when seeking building permits. Because many design decisions must be made after all working-drawing sheets have been completed, some notes and other items must to be added to the floor plan at a more advanced stage of design development.

22. An example set of working drawings for a residence has been included in the book for your reference. See the floor-plan sheet from this set in Fig. 20.7. Many of the check-list notes and symbols appear on this plan. Use it for reference when deciding on appropriate notes for your own plan.

23. When the drawing is becoming crowded with too many notes, some of the explanatory information can be placed beside the plan in a "notes" column. (See Figs. 21.5 and 27.2.)

24. The plumbing, electrical, and mechanical details of the plan should be drawn after you have consulted with contractors in the respective fields; particularly if you have no prior experience in drawing plans.

25. This is an excellent time to have several prints made from your floor plan. See Unit 28, Making Prints, for information about blueprinting and whiteprinting.

26. A print of the plan can be given to each of the contractors consulted; to take and study. Most contractors will sketch their segment of the work on an individual print or on an overlay drawing.

27. Each contractor, such as electrical, plumbing, heating and cooling, etc., is knowledgeable in planning his or her segment of the work in conformance with local building codes.

Note: The prints on which mechanical, plumbing, and electrical contractors have worked out details should be stapled together with prints of your other drawings and submitted to the building department when applying for building permits.

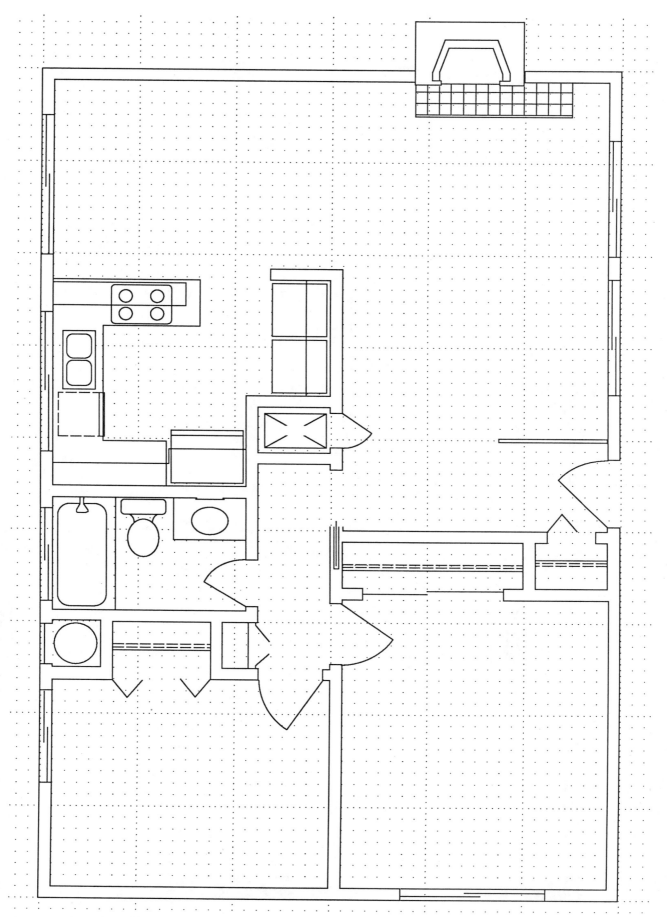

Fig. 20.2 Floor plan with windows, doors, wardrobe doors, fixtures, cabinets, and fireplace added to the plan.

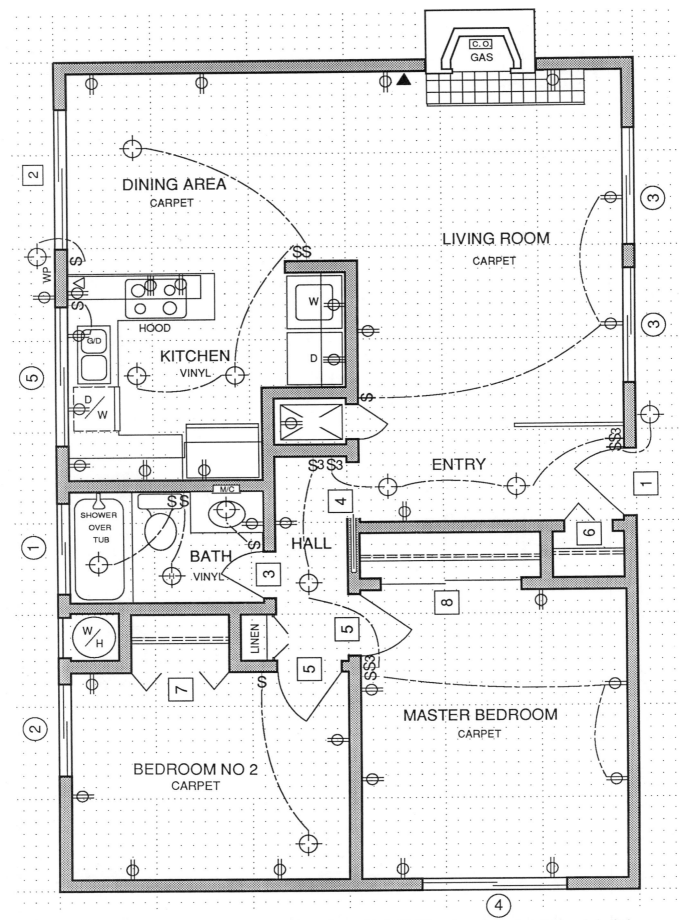

Fig. 20.3 Floor plan with electrical work, lettering and notations added. Wall lines have been darkened and shaded.

WHAT ARE SCHEDULES?

A schedule is an information list that the drafter prepares to describe the doors, windows, plumbing fixtures, electrical fixtures, and mechanical equipment shown on the plan. You can also prepare an interior finish schedule that describes wall finishes, color, and floor covering selections. Similar finish schedules describe exterior finish materials. These schedules are keyed to the relevant plan sheets through numbered symbols. (See Fig. 20.3 and 20.5.) Circles, squares, or hexagons are typical symbol shapes used on schedules and keyed to plans.

DRAWING AND COMPLETING SCHEDULES

1. Lay out ruled charts to fit available space on the floor-plan sheet. Label each column appropriately for the category of information you will be describing. Figure 20.4 is an example of typical door and window schedule headings.

2. If space permits, place each applicable schedule on the related plan sheet for easy reference.

3. Fig. 20.5 shows possible choices for window and door symbols that can be placed on the floor plan close to each window or door, and keyed to a window or door schedule.

4. The door and window schedules in Fig. 20.4 are keyed to the floor plan and describe the types of doors and windows selected for each opening shown on the floor plan.

Fig. 20.5 Symbols used on plans and schedules.

WINDOW SCHEDULE

SYM	SIZE	TYPE	MFG & CAT NO	GLAZING	MATERIAL	REMARKS
1	4'-0" x 1'-6"	HORIZ SLIDING	"INTERNATIONAL"	5/8" DUEL GLAZED	ANODIZED ALUM	SCREEN
2	4'-0" x 2'-6"	HORIZ SLIDING	"INTERNATIONAL"	5/8" DUEL GLAZED	ANODIZED ALUM	SCREEN
3	5'-0" x 3'-6"	HORIZ SLIDING	"INTERNATIONAL"	5/8" DUEL GLAZED	ANODIZED ALUM	SCREEN
4	6'-0" x 2'-6"	HORIZ SLIDING	"INTERNATIONAL"	5/8" DUEL GLAZED	ANODIZED ALUM	SCREEN
5	6'-0" x 3'-0"	HORIZ SLIDING	"INTERNATIONAL"	5/8" DUEL GLAZED	ANODIZED ALUM	SCREEN

DOOR SCHEDULE

SYM	SIZE	TYPE	MFG & CAT NO	REMARKS	MATERIAL	THK	HDWE
1	3'-0" x 6'-8"	EIGHT PANEL	"SIMPSON" 368B	3 COATS EXT. TRIM PAINT	PINE	1 3/4"	TYPE A
2	6'-0" x 6'-8"	GLASS SLIDING	"INTERNATIONAL" 36	ANODIZED ALUM	ALUM		TYPE B
3	2'-0" x 6'-8"	FLUSH H C	"WESTERN" 596	STAIN & LACQUER FINISH	BIRCH	1 3/8"	TYPE C
4	2'-6" x 6'-8"	FLUSH H C	"WESTERN" 592	STAIN & LACQUER FINISH	BIRCH	1 3/8"	TYPE D
5	2'-8" x 6'-8"	FLUSH H C	"WESTERN" 590	STAIN & LACQUER FINISH	BIRCH	1 3/8"	TYPE C
6	2'-0" x 6'-8"	FULL LOUVER	"WESTERN" 367	STAIN & LACQUER FINISH	BIRCH	1 3/8"	TYPE E
7	4'-0" x 6'-8"	FULL LOUVER	"WESTERN" 364	STAIN & LACQUER FINISH	BIRCH	1 3/8"	TYPE E
8	6'-0" x 6'-8"	FLUSH H C	"WESTERN" 594	STAIN & LACQUER FINISH	BIRCH	1 3/8"	TYPE F

Fig. 20.4 Sample window and door schedules.

FLOOR-PLAN CHECK LIST

Use this check list when preparing a final floor-plan. Many of the typical items which should be on a floor plan are listed below. Some will be applicable to your plan and some will not. Check with your building department to verify local requirements.

Check off each item on this list as follows:

√   Completed
X   Not completed
0   Doesn't apply

_____ 1. Locate and show all door and window openings
_____ 2. Show door and window sizes on plan or:
_____ 3. Complete door and window finish schedule
_____ 4. Show size of header over each openings
_____ 5. Show swing of doors
_____ 6. Show direction of door slide
_____ 7. Wall intersections drawn correctly
_____ 8. Accurate wall thickness (2x4 or 2x6 framing)
_____ 9. Interior partitions located correctly
_____ 10. All wall lines shaded on the back of the sheet
_____ 11. Show wall paper location(s)
_____ 12. Show paneling location(s)
_____ 13. Show waterproof shower wall material
_____ 14. Show one hour fire wall, house/garage
_____ 15. Accurate line weights
_____ 16. Arrow heads sized correctly
_____ 17. All walls and openings dimensioned
_____ 18. Check addition on dimensions
_____ 19. Show countertop sizes
_____ 20. Dimension toilet location (15" min. clearance)

Notes:
_____ 21. All equipment and size of each
_____ 22. All room titles
_____ 23. Floor materials
_____ 24. Countertop materials
_____ 25. Any exposed beam ceilings
_____ 26. Partial wall heights
_____ 27. Safety glass at tub/shower enclosures
_____ 28. Correctly completed title block

Detail:
_____ 29. Closet poles and shelves
_____ 30. Medicine cabinet
_____ 31. Bathroom hardware
_____ 32. Mirror size(s) and location(s)

_____ 33. Washer and dryer location
_____ 34. Range size, type and location
_____ 35. Range clearance within cabinetry
           (6" horizontal and 30" vertical)
_____ 36. Range hood and vent
_____ 37. Oven size, type and location
_____ 38. Refrigerator size and location
_____ 39. Freezer size and location
_____ 40. Garbage disposal location
_____ 41. Electric outlets - switches - fixtures
_____ 42. GFI outlets, bathrooms and garage
_____ 43. Television outlet
_____ 44. Smoke detector(s) location and type
_____ 45. Doorbell and chimes
_____ 46. Interior fans
_____ 47. Telephone outlets
_____ 48. Intercom locations
_____ 49. Electrical meter with size in amps
_____ 50. Outlets for electric and gas appliances
_____ 51. Heating equipment, size and location
_____ 52. Air conditioning equipment, size and location
_____ 53. Thermostat location and height
_____ 54. Water heater size and location
_____ 55. Dimension step tread and rise
           (rise max. 8" tread min. 9")
_____ 56. Step down area, sunken room
_____ 57. Locate all posts with metal anchor connectors
_____ 58. Exterior hose bibs
_____ 59. Hand railing height (36")
_____ 60. Fireplace size, type, and location
_____ 61. Dimension hearth, width and height
           (width min. 18")
_____ 62. Gas log lighter
_____ 63. Ash clean out

Garage area:
_____ 64. Gas-burning appliances such as water heater
           (min.18" high platform)
_____ 65. Self-closing door between house and garage
_____ 66. Note sway bracing in garage

Access:
_____ 67. Attic access (min. 22" x 24")
_____ 68. Beneath wood floor access (min. 18" x 24")
_____ 69. Tub plumbing access, concrete floor (12" x 12")

Fig. 20.6 Floor- plan check list.

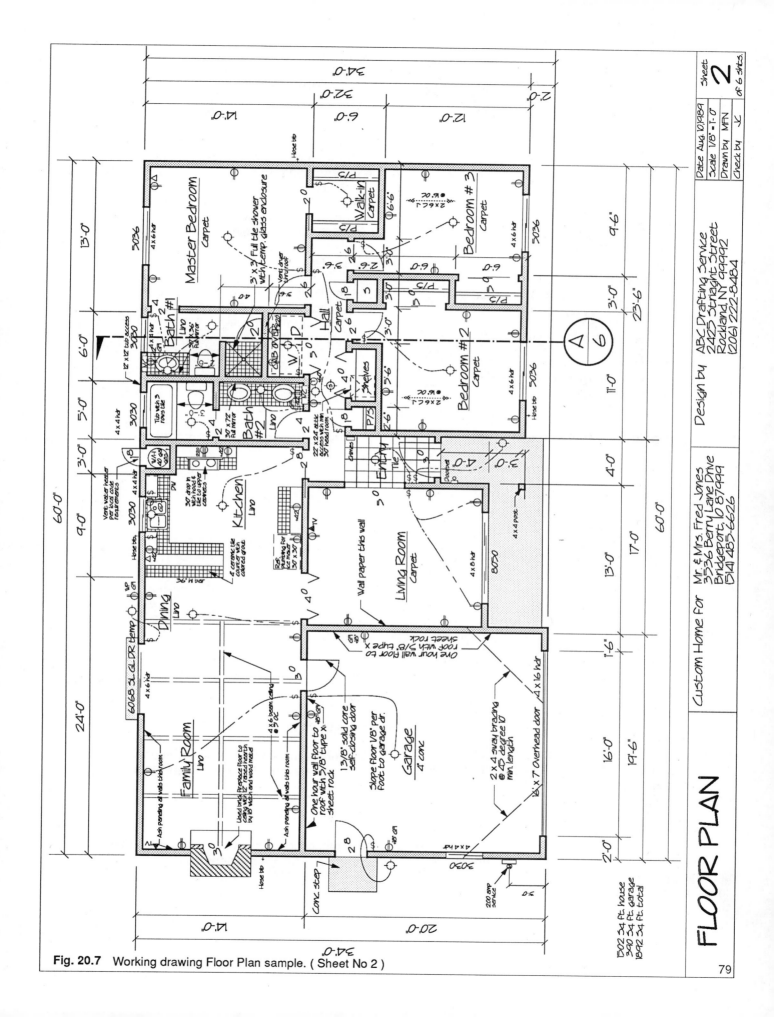

Fig. 20.7 Working drawing Floor Plan sample. (Sheet No 2)

SECTION 5 UNIT 21

DIMENSIONS AND NOTATIONS

Objective: To learn correct procedures for dimensioning drawings and adding notes.

WHAT ARE DIMENSIONS?

Dimensions are numbers which indicate actual sizes on scale drawings. Each person involved in the construction of a house will expect to find the information needed to do his or her part of the work on the prints. Consequently, the drawings must clearly show overall exterior measurements of the house, specific measurements of the interior spaces and all details. (See Fig. 21.2 and 21.4.)

WORKING DRAWINGS

Dimension Lines

Lines drawn for the purpose of showing where a measurement begins and ends are called dimension lines. All the measurements of the plan are shown on these lines. When used for dimensioning the exterior walls of the plan, they are placed around the exterior perimeter. (See Fig. 21.2.) Measurements of rooms and halls are placed within the area of the plan where necessary for clarity. (See Fig. 21.4.)

Extension Lines

Extension lines serve the purpose of showing the beginning and ending of dimension lines. Extension lines extend from all corners of the building to intersect with the dimension lines.

Centerlines

A centerline designates the center of a given area. The word centerline is often abbreviated as CL. To designate a centerline on the plan, a series of long lines and dashes is drawn through the center of any given space. The centerline symbol is placed at the end of a centerline as shown in Figures 21.2 and 4. In dimensioning a floor plan, centerlines are usually placed along perimeter dimension lines, extending through the exact center of each window, door, and interior partition. When used in this way, they serve the same purpose as extension lines.

End Marks

End marks, consisting of arrows, slashes, or dots, are placed at the point where dimension lines intersect with extension lines. When dimensioning a drawing, you have the option of using any of the three typical end-mark styles shown in Fig. 21.1.

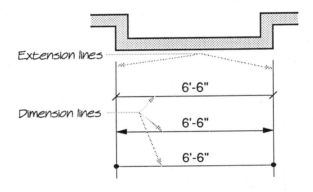

Fig. 21.1 Sample dimension line end marks.

Scale

The scale to which the plan has been drawn is always indicated in the title block in the following way: SCALE; 1/4" = 1' - 0".

Square Footage

The total square footage of the house, plus that of the garage should be placed near the drawing or in the title block.

Identifying Rooms

The name of each room should be printed on the plan. Each bedroom needs an identifying label such as: MASTER BEDROOM, BEDROOM NO 2, BEDROOM NO 3, etc. Or they could be identified as OWNER'S BEDROOM, GIRL'S BEDROOM, BOY'S BEDROOM, etc. (See Figs. 21.2 and 4.)

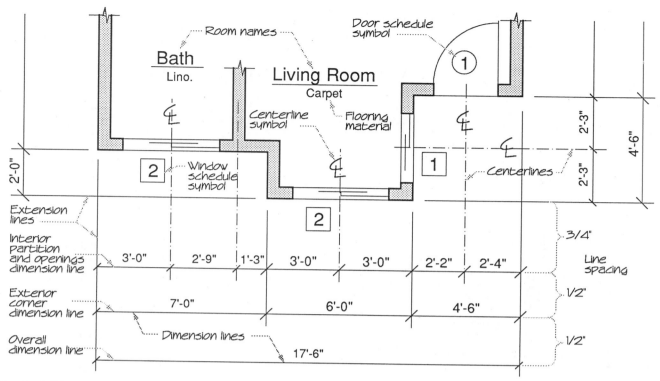

Fig. 21.2 Dimensioning procedures.

DRAWING DIMENSION LINES

1. The first dimension line around the perimeter of the house should be about 3/4" away from the wall line, leaving sufficient room to place window and door sizes; 1/2" between the first and second dimension lines is sufficient. (See Fig. 21.2.)

2. . When drawing dimension and extension lines, use a light pressure on a well-pointed, **4H** lead. They are the lightest lines to appear on the drawing. (See UNIT 2, Lettering and Lines.) When dimension and extension lines are drawn correctly, they will not be confused with the lines of the structure, but will be dark enough to reproduce when prints are made. (See UNIT 28, Making Prints.)

3. Dimensions are given in feet and inches; for example, 10' - 6". If there are no inches, the number is written 10' - 0". Numbers are always placed above the dimension lines as in Fig. 21.2.

ADDING NOTATIONS

Special notations are frequently necessary. There is not much room on the plan for these notes by the time all of the information has been drawn. Notes should be added in small legible printing and placed as close to the object they describe as possible. Use a small arrow to connect the note to the object it denotes.

GENERAL NOTES

Information in the form of notes must be given about various parts of the plan. When there are too many notes for clarity, arrange some in a GENERAL NOTES column, beside the drawing, on the floor-plan sheet if space permits. Fig. 21.5 is an example of GENERAL NOTES. Units 20 through 26 contain check lists relating to each of the plan sheets. They will supply you with additional standard notes and notes applicable to each plan sheet.

SECTION CUT-SYMBOLS

See Unit 25, Sections and Details, Figs. 25.7 and 12 for examples of section-cut symbols and how they are used.

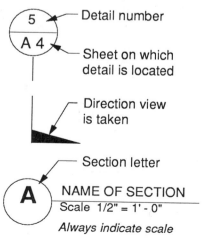

Fig. 21.3 Section-cut conventions. (Symbols)

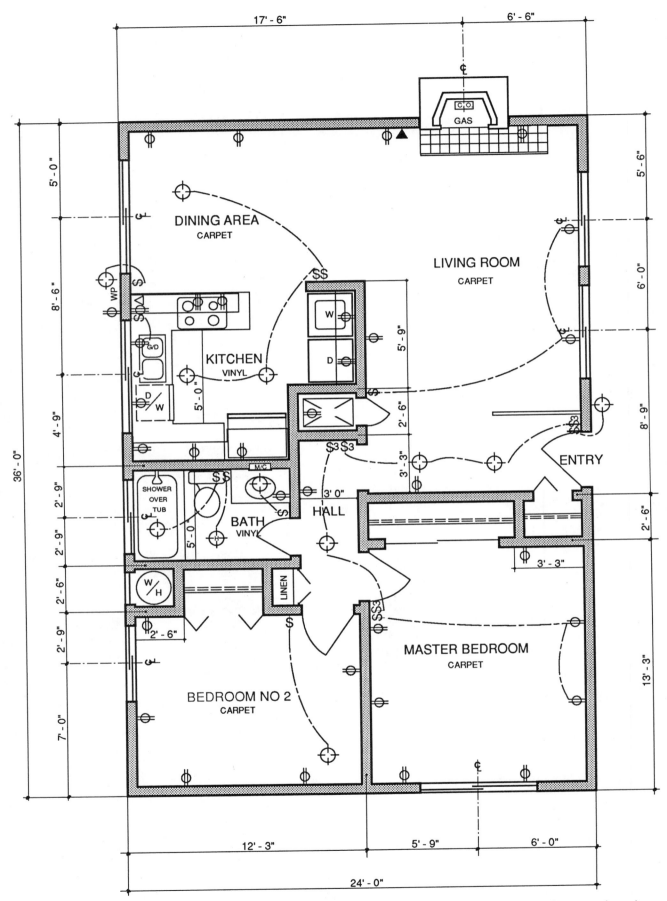

Fig. 21.4 A working drawing with dimensions added. (Not to scale; reduced to show dimensioning procedures.)

GENERAL NOTES

1. All contractors are responsible for compliance with codes applicable to their work. All contractors shall comply with the "Occupational Safety and Health Act" (OSHA) and the safety and health regulation for construction.

2. Contractor shall verify all pertinent dimensions, grades, and any other site conditions prior to commencing with the work. If any discrepancy exists, the person preparing the plans is to be notified.

3. Where special makes or brands are called for, they are intended to represent the standard of quality required. Substitutions of equal quality may be used provided that approval is first obtained in writing. Requests for substitutions shall be submitted promptly to allow ample time for review. Contractor proposing substitutions assumes responsibility for providing full information for review and for the satisfactory operation of the substituted items.

4. Contractor shall provide temporary sanitary facilities as required by governing laws and regulations. Contractor shall provide temporary power, heating and lighting services for the duration of construction. Contractor shall provide pipes, taps, and hoses to distribute water from the service on the site. All utilities are to be brought to the site by others; not a part of this contract.

5. The contractor shall secure and pay for general building permits and services or licenses required for the work. Electrical, plumbing, and mechanical subcontractors shall secure and pay for permits pertaining to their work.

6. When not particularly specified, materials will be of good quality. All work shall be of good quality in comparison with current construction standards; free from faults and defects and in conformance with the construction documents.

7. Contractor shall guarantee materials, equipment, and workmanship for a period of one year from the date of occupancy.

SHEET

A2

OF 6 SHTS.

Fig. 21.5 Example of a column containing general notes.

CONCRETE SLAB

A concrete slab is a level surface of concrete poured on top of footings. In deciding on the thickness of the concrete slab, check with your local building department for typical requirements. Average thicknesses are 3 1/2" to 6". Depending on soil conditions and loading factors, the concrete slab could require reinforcing with either weld-wire fabric or reinforcing bars. Slabs are underlain with a fill of gravel or sand to improve supporting capacity. A plastic membrane (called a vapor barrier) is typically placed over the fill to eliminate moisture penetration. (See Figs. 22.1 through 22.4.)

FOOTINGS

To construct footings, concrete is poured into continuous forms which have been dug into undisturbed earth a minimum of 12" deep around the perimeter of a building. Footings serve the purpose of transferring the load from the structure to the soil. When circumstances warrant, reinforcing rods are required and are embedded in the concrete. The size of the footing depends on the structure it is supporting, the soil conditions, and prevailing weather. Footings are drawn in plan view in Fig. 22.5 and in section views in Figs. 22.1 through 22.4.

A section view is a side view at an imaginary "cut" through a building or any part thereof.

FOUNDATION BOLTS

Typically, bolts (steel rods 1/2" x 10") are placed along the the perimeter of the foundation, 12" from the corners and spaced at intervals not to exceed 6' OC (on center). Their purpose is to attach the mudsill to the foundation. The placement of foundation bolts should be shown on the plan view of the foundation plan, as shown in Fig. 22.5.

MUDSILLS

Mudsills are the bottom horizontal piece of a wood-framed wall. Typically they are required to be redwood or pressure-treated lumber. Holes are drilled in the sill at intervals located to fit over the foundation bolts. When framed walls are erected, they are secured in place with washers and nuts. This is shown in Figs. 22.1 through 22.4.

SECTION 6
UNIT 22

FOUNDATION PLAN

Objective: Learn to draw a foundation plan and the required details, and to complete a sheet of your set of working drawings.

WHAT IS A FOUNDATION?

A foundation is that part of a building which is in contact with the earth. It transfers the weight of the structure to the earth.

There are many variations in methods of constructing foundations, but the basic principles are the same. The construction material used is most often concrete.

The foundation for the sample house plan in this book is called a concrete-slab foundation. With this method of foundation construction, the footing and also the surface of the floor is constructed of concrete. (See Fig. 22.5.)

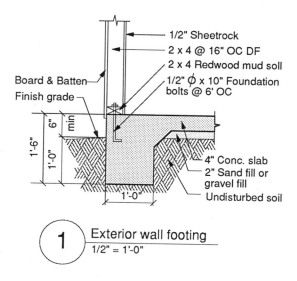

Fig. 22.1 Exterior footing detail.

Figure 22.1 is a section view of the footing at the exterior corner of a house. A portion of the concrete slab floor is shown plus 2" of sand or gravel fill under the floor. The shaded area represents concrete. Above the concrete is the framed exterior wall with the mudsill bolted to the concrete.

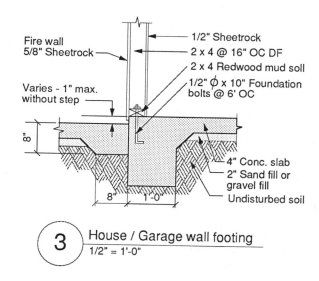

Fig. 22.3 House / garage footing detail.

Figure 22.3 is a section view of a typical footing supporting a wall between a garage and a house. Note that if the garage slab is more than 1" below the level of the floor of the house, a step must be used.

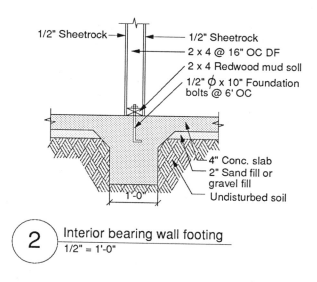

Fig. 22.2 Interior bearing footing detail.

Figure 22.2 is a section view of a typical bearing wall footing placed directly beneath the bearing wall for the purpose of supporting the roof load.

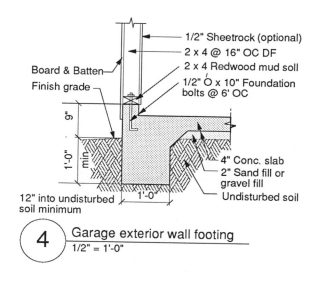

Fig. 22.4 Garage stem wall footing detail.

Garages have stem walls on each of the two sides. Figure 22.4 shows a section view of a typical stem wall footing supporting the exterior walls of the garage. Its purpose is to raise the framed wall up off the garage floor allowing the concrete slab to slope to the front.

DRAWING A FOUNDATION PLAN

1. Secure your floor-plan drawing to the drawing surface. Cover it with grid vellum drawing paper. Allow enough room on the paper, beside the floor plan, to draw the applicable footing details from the examples in Figs. 22.1 through 22.4. It will be the fourth page in the bound set of working drawings.

2. Lay out the border line and the title block and label the sheet Foundation Plan. Number the page 4.

3. Trace the perimeter of the floor plan exterior wall, using your **4H** layout pencil.

4. Refer to the exterior footing detail, Fig. 22.1. Note that the typical thickness of an exterior footing is 1'. In 1/4" scale, dash a line 1' in from the exterior perimeter line. This is a dashed line (hidden line), because it indicates that the footing is beneath the floor slab.

5. Referring to Fig. 22.2, note the shape and size of the footing used to support an interior bearing wall. The footing is represented on the foundation plan by two dashed lines 1' apart centered beneath the bearing wall.

6. Show the placement and spacing of the foundation bolts as in Fig. 22.5.

7. Show the required strength test for concrete by listing the typical pounds per square inch (psi) test strength given in Fig. 22.5.

8. The top half of the section-cut symbols marked 1 and 2 are keyed to the footing details marked 1 and 2. The space in the bottom half is for the plan-sheet number. In this instance, the book page number was used. Draw a section-cut symbol for each different type of footing detail used on your plan. Key them to the footing details as shown in Figs. 22.1 through 22. 4.

9. Dimension the foundation plan as shown in Fig. 22.5.

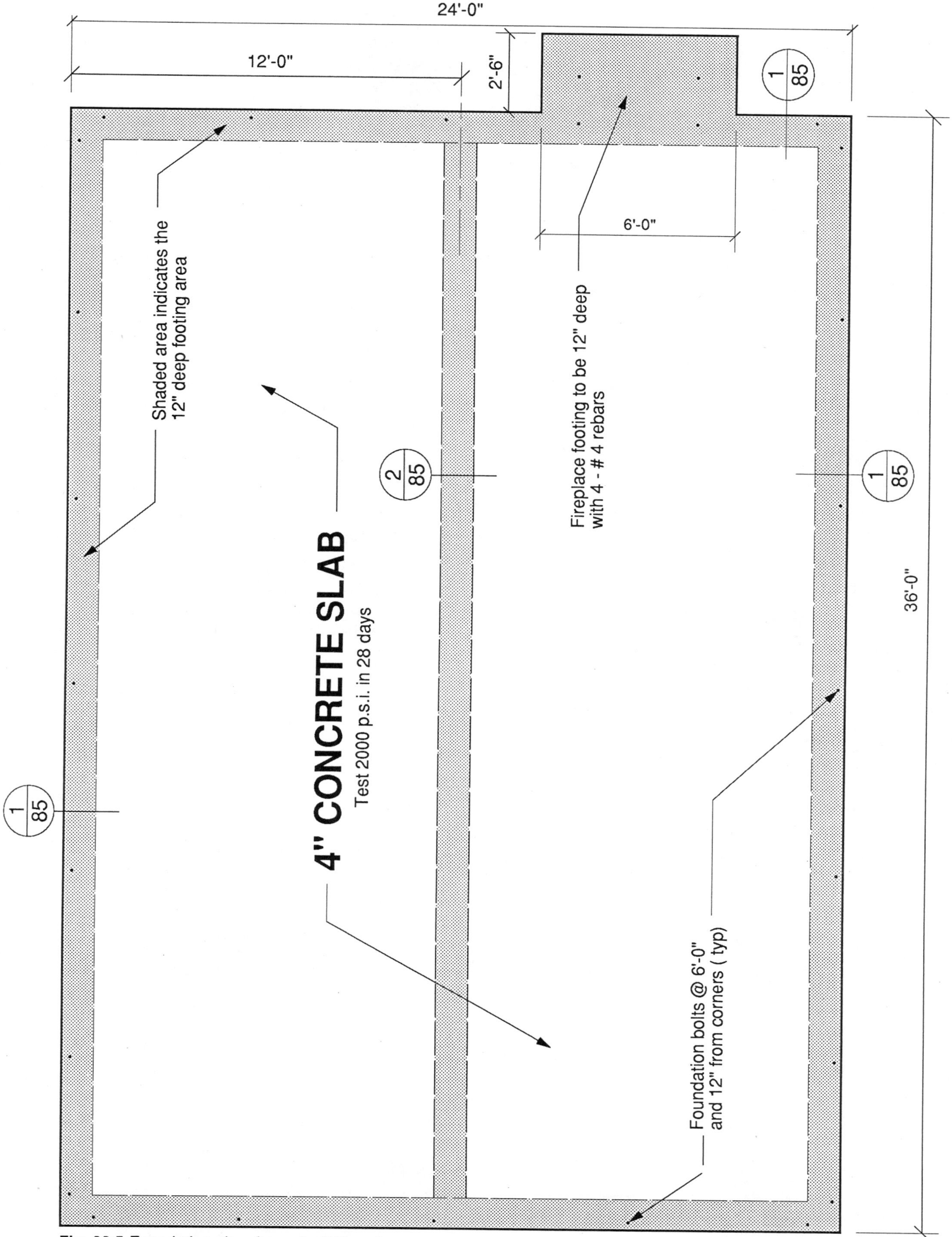

Fig. 22.5 Foundation plan drawn to 1/4" scale.

24'-0"

12'-0"

2'-6"

1/85

6'-0"

36'-0"

2/85

1/85

1/85

Shaded area indicates the 12" deep footing area

4" CONCRETE SLAB

Test 2000 p.s.i. in 28 days

Fireplace footing to be 12" deep with 4 - # 4 rebars

Foundation bolts @ 6'-0" and 12" from corners (typ)

FOUNDATION-PLAN CHECK LIST

Use this check list when preparing a final foundation plan. Many of the typical items which should be on a foundation plan are listed below. Some will be applicable to your plan and some will not. Check with your building department to verify local requirements.

Check off each item on this list as follows:

√____ Completed
_X___ Not completed
_0___ Doesn't apply

____ 1. Concrete foundation slab
____ 2. Concrete type, thickness, and location
____ 3. Footing size and depth (hidden line)
____ 4. Interior bearing wall (hidden line)
____ 5. Bearing wall, size and location
____ 6. Thickness of special walls
____ 7. Garage wall thickness
____ 8. Garage floor slope (1/8" per ft)
____ 9. Foundation bolts, size and location
____ 10. Fireplace footing, size and thickness
____ 11. Finish floor elevation
         (min. 6" above finish grade)
____ 12. Footing detail references
____ 13. Cross-section detail references
____ 14. Show bearing and nonbearing footings

____ 15. Depressed slabs for tile and sunken areas
____ 16. Verify all dimensions with floor plan
____ 17. Dimension and size of post(s)
____ 18. Post connector size, type and, location
____ 19. Note type of mudsill lumber
____ 20. Reinforcing bar in footing
____ 21. Reinforcing mesh in concrete slab
____ 22. Shade all concrete footings on back of sheet
____ 23. General concrete notes

Items applicable to wood floor-joist system:
____ 24. Foundation wall for wood floor
____ 25. Wood floor girders, size and spacing
____ 26. Wood floor pier, size and spacing
____ 27. Subfloor, material and size
____ 28. Correctly completed title block

NOTES

The following typical notes can be added either to working drawings or to specifications.

1. All concrete to test minimum 2000 p.s.i. at 28 days.

2. Top of finished concrete slab to be a minimum of 6" above finished grade and above the street center line.

3. Shading indicates concrete bearing footings 12" wide to extend a minimum of 12" into undisturbed soil.

4. Concrete slab to be a min. of 3 1/2" thick, 5 sack mix concrete, over 2" sand fill, over visquene vapor barrier.

5. Garage to have stem wall of 3 1/2"

6. Provide at all exterior doors - foundation grade redwood sill set into edge of concrete footing with 20 penny nails at 8" on center at bottom side. (galvanized s.m. wrapped)

7. Pressure treated fir sills may be used in lieu of foundation grade redwood sills.

8. Nailing as per uniform building code table No 25p

9. All framing members to be marked No 1 or better. (unless otherwise noted)

10. Weatherstrip all exterior doors.

11. All window headers to be 4" members with 1" depth per lineal foot of span min. (unless otherwise noted)

Fig. 22.6 Foundation-plan check list.

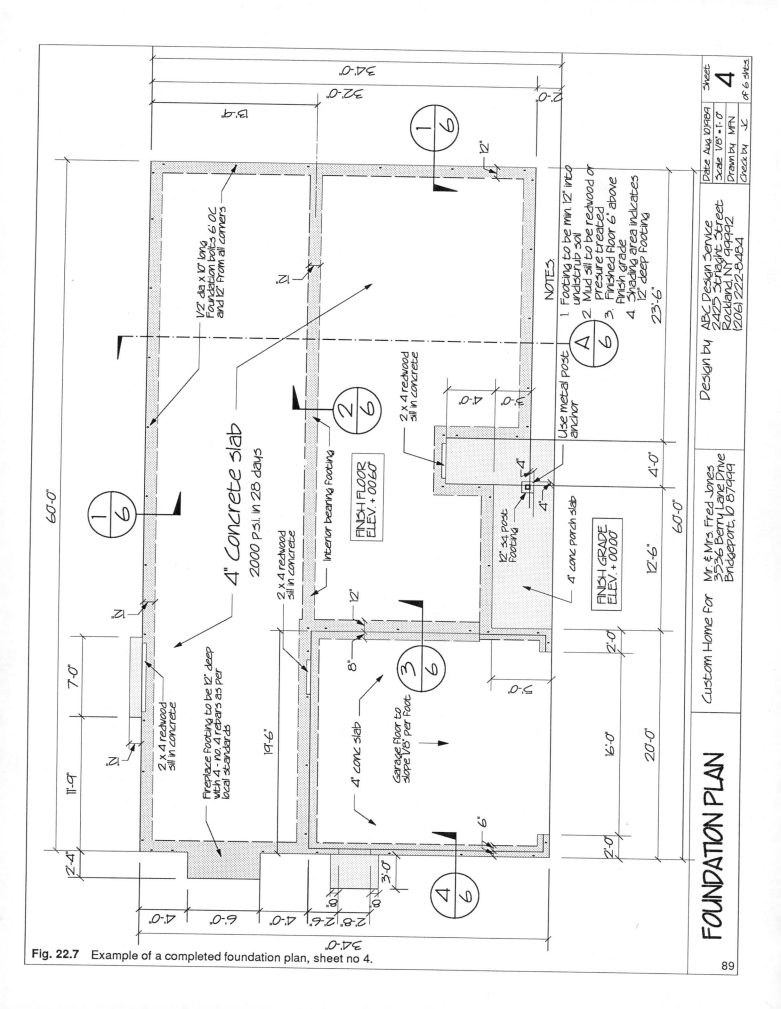

Fig. 22.7 Example of a completed foundation plan, sheet no 4.

89

ROOF
FRAMING
PLAN

SECTION 7
UNIT **23**

ROOF PLAN

Objective: To draw the Roof Plan sheet from the floor plan, showing all necessary details.

DESIGNING A ROOF

The roof is a major element in the overall design concept. The style and materials you select should coordinate with and enhance the appearance of the house. Study the illustrations in Unit 24, Fig. 24.19 through 23. Choose a style that is suited to the shape and design of the house plan you are drawing. Figure 23.1 shows four different roof designs and how to draw them.

RIDGE LAYOUT

When using a gable or hip roof, the ridge can run parallel with the front of the house as in Fig. 23.2, or it can run from front to back as in Fig. 23.3. When the house is rectangular in shape, rafters are usually placed so that they span the two narrow sides of the rectangle.

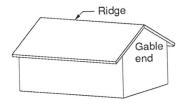

Fig. 23.2 A view of a gable roof with the ridge running parallel to the wide side of the house.

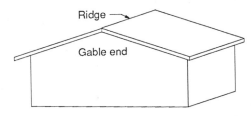

Fig. 23.3 A view of a gable roof with the ridge running parallel to the narrow side of the house.

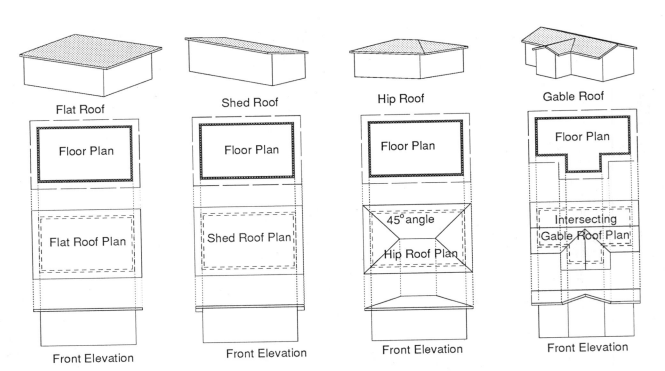

Fig. 23.1 How to draw four different styles of roof designs.

SELECTING ROOFING MATERIALS

New materials and methods are continually increasing the flexibility of roof designing. It is best to check manufacturer's specifications for the roofing material you select before deciding on the exact slope of the roof.

If the house is to be located in an area of high fire risk, consider flammability of material when making selections and the increased insurance rates applied to homes with roofs that are not fire-retardant.

The roofing materials most frequently used are listed below.

ROLL ROOFING

Roll roofing is a term used to describe a roofing material manufactured by saturating dry felt with asphalt and then coating the saturated felt with a harder asphalt mixed with a fine mineral, glass fiber, or other organic substance; available in the form of rolls. It is applied over 15# felt to the plywood sheathing in overlapping layers, as shown in Fig. 23.4. This roof treatment is most often used on flat or shed type roofs. Several color selections are available. It has excellent fire-retardant properties.

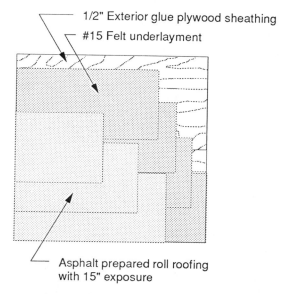

1/2" Exterior glue plywood sheathing

#15 Felt underlayment

Asphalt prepared roll roofing with 15" exposure

Fig. 23.4 An example of roll roofing.

ASPHALT SHINGLES

Asphalt shingles are frequently chosen for their fire-retardant properties. They are also a good choice for low-budget homes and are frequently used for remodeling projects and for additions to homes.

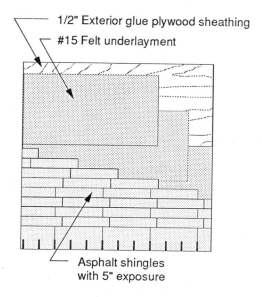

1/2" Exterior glue plywood sheathing

#15 Felt underlayment

Asphalt shingles with 5" exposure

Fig. 23.5 An example of an asphalt shingle roof.

WOOD SHAKES OR SHINGLES

Shakes and shingles are typically made from cedar wood. They add depth, texture, and character to the overall design. Shakes are thicker than shingles and have a more rustic appearance.

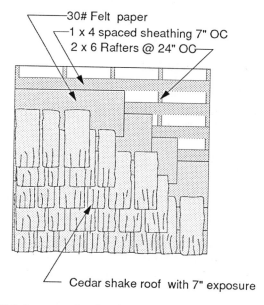

30# Felt paper

1 x 4 spaced sheathing 7" OC

2 x 6 Rafters @ 24" OC

Cedar shake roof with 7" exposure

Fig. 23.6 An example of a shake or shingle roof.

ROOF PITCH

When deciding on the roof pitch (slope of the roof), the roofing materials selected and factors of appearance, cost, and weather should all influence your decision. It is suggested that you observe the roofs on houses in your area. In most cases, they have been designed to withstand local weather conditions and to utilize roofing materials that are readily available in the area. For extreme climates, research may be necessary to verify that the roof pitch is adequate to withstand maximum anticipated snow loads. Refer to Unit 24, Fig. 24.7 for a simplified method of laying out and drawing the roof pitch.

DRAWING A ROOF PLAN

A plan of a roof defines, for construction people interpreting it, the location of the ridge and the spacing and placement of the rafters or trusses. It shows the amount of roof overhang and describes plywood or other surfacing material to be applied over the rafters and beneath the finish roofing materials. Select the most appropriate roof design and materials and refer to the manufacturer's specifications pertaining to the roofing material you select.

1. Lay grid paper over your floor plan and draw the borders and title block. Number the sheet 5.

2. Using a **2H** lead pencil draw a dashed (hidden) line around the outside perimeter of the building to represent the exterior wall line.

3. From the dashed line, measure the desired amount of overhang and draw a solid line around the perimeter of the building to represent the roof overhang.

4. Select the ridge layout to be used from Figs. 23.2 and 23.3.

5. Find the center point on the roof plan that represents the top of the ridge and draw the ridge line as in Fig. 23.9.

6. When drawing a hip roof, or when two gables intersect to create a valley, draw a line from the outer edge of the roof overhang to the ridge, to show the hips and/or valleys. The line is typically drawn at a 45 degree angle. Refer to Fig. 23.1 and 23.11.

7. Draw the rafters, spaced at 2' intervals, as shown in Fig. 23.9.

8. Add a small portion of the plywood sheathing and/or other surfacing material, as specified by the manufacturer of the roofing material you plan to use. (See Fig. 23.9.) It is not necessary for you to draw as much detail as shown in this illustration. The information can also be provided in the form of notes.

9. Draw bracing where required. (See Fig. 23.8.)

10. Eave details, such as those shown in Fig. 23.7, can be placed either on the roof-plan sheet or on the sections and details sheet.

ATTIC VENTILATION

All attics require ventilation. Ventilation can be achieved in several ways. An example showing a typical continuous eave vent is shown in the eave vent detail, Fig. 23.7.

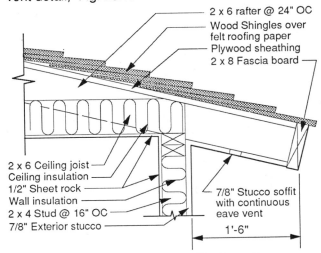

Fig. 23.7 Detail showing stucco soffit with continuous eave vent, insulation, and roof framing.

DIAGONAL SWAY BRACING

For some roof designs, diagonal sway bracing is necessary. The roof plans in Fig. 23.8 are examples of correct placement for bracing. The roof plan in Fig. 23.11 is a hip roof design. Hip roofs are framed in such a way as to eliminate the need for diagonal sway bracing.

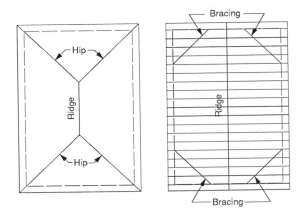

Fig. 23.8 A hip roof design in which no diagonal sway bracing is required and a gable roof plan showing the necessary bracing.

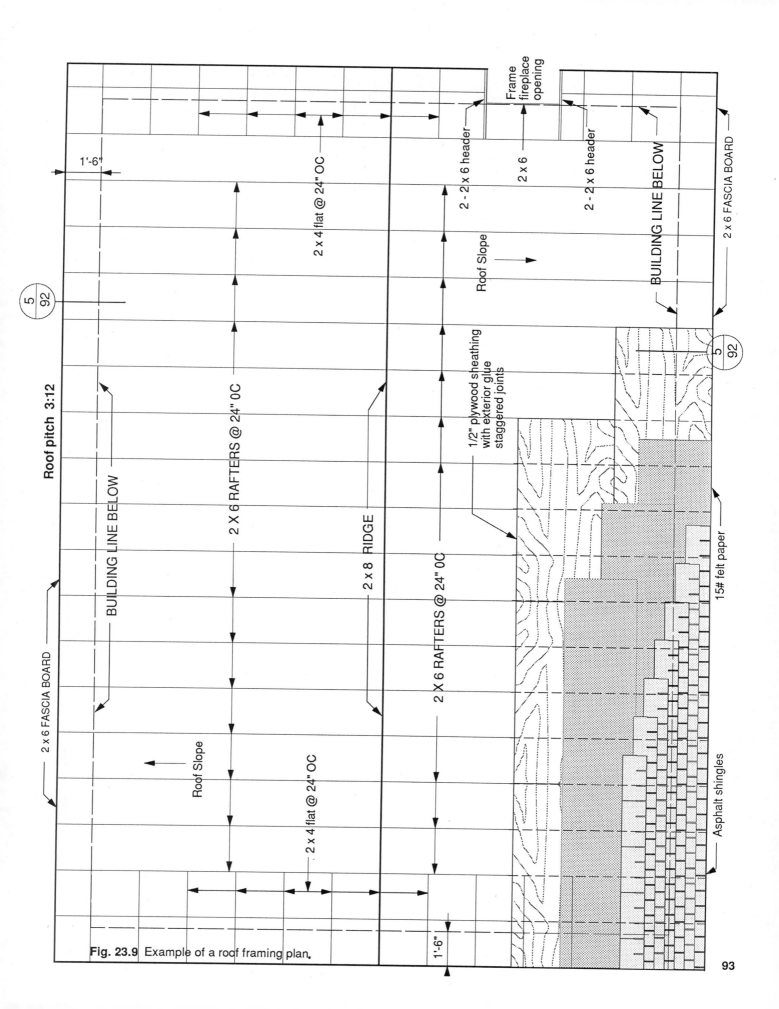

Fig. 23.9 Example of a roof framing plan.

Roof pitch 3:12

1'-6"

2 x 4 flat @ 24" OC

2 X 6 RAFTERS @ 24" 0C

2 X 8 RIDGE

BUILDING LINE BELOW

2 x 6 FASCIA BOARD

Roof Slope

2 x 4 flat @ 24" OC

Frame fireplace opening

2 - 2 x 6 header

2 x 6

2 - 2 x 6 header

BUILDING LINE BELOW

2 x 6 FASCIA BOARD

Roof Slope

1/2" plywood sheathing with exterior glue staggered joints

2 X 6 RAFTERS @ 24" 0C

15# felt paper

Asphalt shingles

1'-6"

93

ROOF-PLAN CHECK LIST

Use this check list when preparing a final roof plan. Many of the typical items which should be on a roof plan are listed below. Some will be applicable to your plan and some will not. Check with your building department to verify local requirements.

Check off each item on this list as follows:

√___ Completed
_X___ Not completed
_0___ Doesn't apply

____ 1. Roof overhang (solid line)
____ 2. Building line below roof (hidden line)
____ 3. Roof slope, with arrow
____ 4. Patio roof
____ 5. Projection beams
____ 6. Roofing material, size and type
____ 7. Show all ridges, hips, and valleys
____ 8. Dimension roof overhang
____ 9. Roof jacks for plumbing, electrical
____10. Fascia material and size
____11. Type of framing members, size and location
____12. Roof sheathing material, size and type
____13. Attic ventilation
____14. Note draft stop if attic is over 3,000 sq. ft.
____15. Sky lights, size and location
____16. Garage square foot area
____17. Roof gutters and downspouts or:
____18. Rain diverters
____19. Note drawing scale

Fig. 23.10 Roof- and roof-framing plan check list.

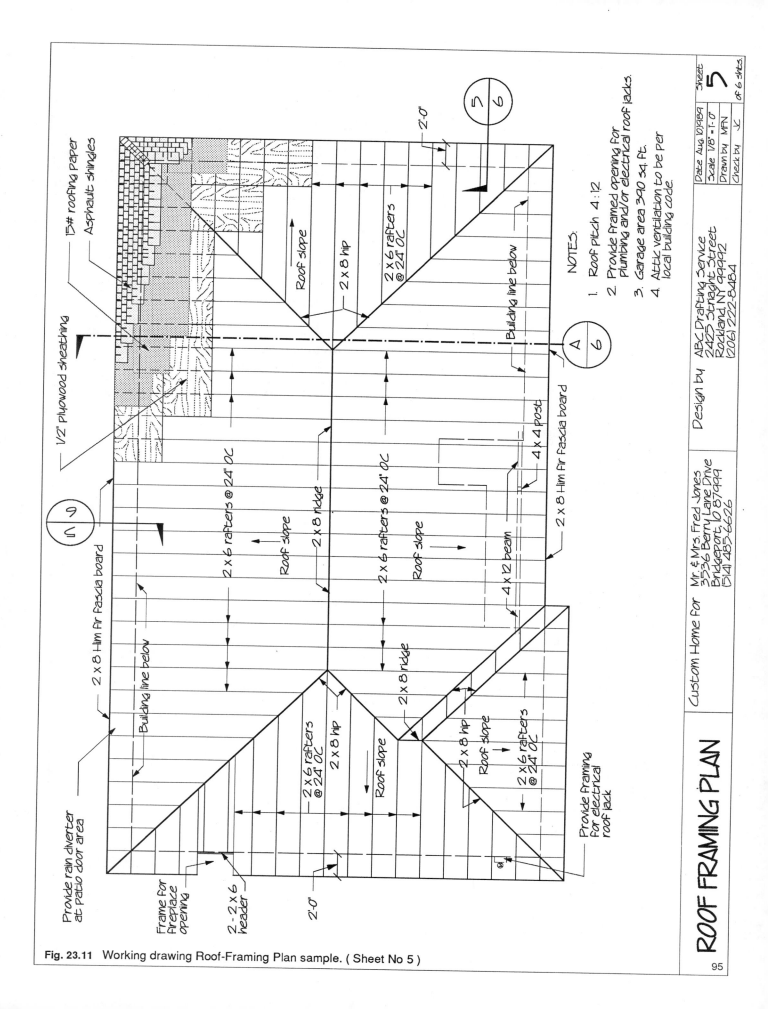

Fig. 23.11 Working drawing Roof-Framing Plan sample. (Sheet No 5)

95

SECTION 8

UNIT 24

EXTERIOR ELEVATIONS

Objective: To construct drawings of the four sides of the house that will show the roof design, window type, and trim materials to be used and also reveal the general style and appearance of the house; sheet 3 of the set of working drawings.

WHAT ARE ELEVATION DRAWINGS ?

Exterior elevations of a house are drawings that show the vertical details of the exterior. From them, one can learn what the proposed house would look like. A separate drawing is made for each side of the house.

The following information should be conveyed by, or noted on, elevation drawings:

Roof: Shape, style, pitch, and roofing materials to be used

Height: One story, two stories, split level, etc.

Windows and doors: Appearance, type, placement, width, and height.

Wall treatment: Stucco, siding, brick, cement block, stone, or combined materials

Trim: Placement, design, and materials to be used

Floor system: Height of the finished floor from the ground line, depending on the floor system used. (See Fig. 24.5.)

Before starting to draw the elevation views, you should have a mental picture of what the house will look like. The perspective drawing and front elevation views, Figs. 24.20 through 23, show exterior treatments and roof styles. They may serve as a guide in deciding on the exterior treatment to be used.

DRAWING ELEVATION VIEWS

In Fig. 24.1, each of the four sides of a house is shown pictorially. The A,B,C, and D portions of the drawings are elevation views. The following instructions are given for drawing elevation views of a house with a simple gable-roof design as shown in Fig. 24.1.

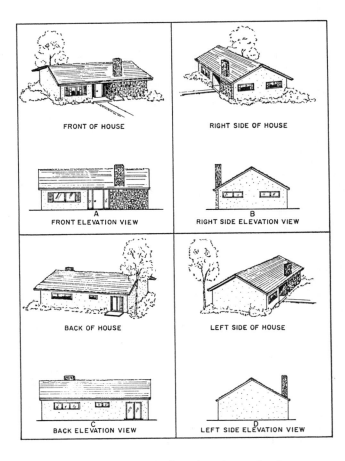

Fig. 24.1 Perspective and elevation views of a house.

STARTING TO DRAW AN ELEVATION VIEW

1. Turn the floor-plan drawing so that one of the sides, where the gable end is to be, is facing you.

2. Place it on your drawing surface so that the exterior wall line of the floor plan, which is facing you, is about halfway down on your drawing surface; then fasten it securely. The back half of the floor-plan drawing will probably hang over the back of your drawing surface. (See Fig. 24.2.)

3. Fasten tracing paper on the lower half of the board, covering the floor-plan exterior wall lines. Proceed with the steps given on the following pages to draw your selected view of the house.

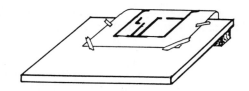

Fig. 24.2 Set up the drawing.

DRAW THE BOTTOM PLATE

Start by drawing a light line on your tracing paper to represent the bottom plate. Place it about 6" below the wall line on your floor plan. (See Fig. 24.3.)

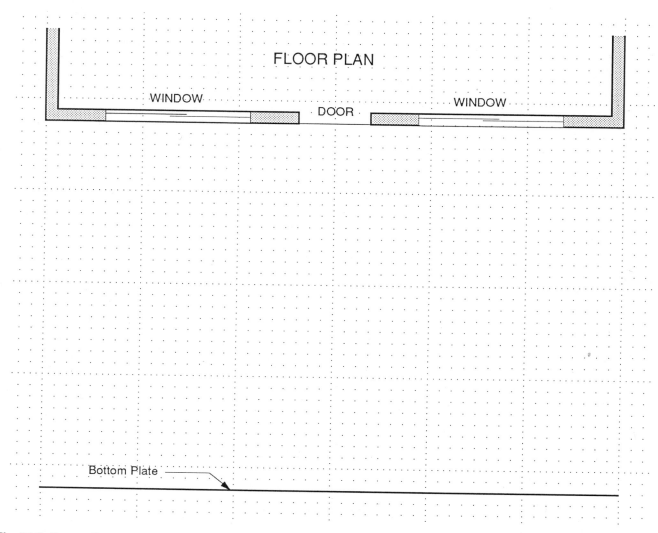

Fig. 24.3 Draw a line to represent the bottom of the bottom plate (mudsill).

DRAW THE CAP PLATE

1. Draw light projection (connecting) lines *down* from the outside corners of the floor plan, allowing them to intersect with the bottom-plate line. (See Fig. 24.4.)

2. Measure *up* from the bottom plate line 8' - 1" in 1/4" scale and draw a line to represent the top of the wall (cap plate) as shown in Fig. 24.4.

3. Go over the portion of the line that represents the outside corners of the wall with a heavier pressure on your pencil.

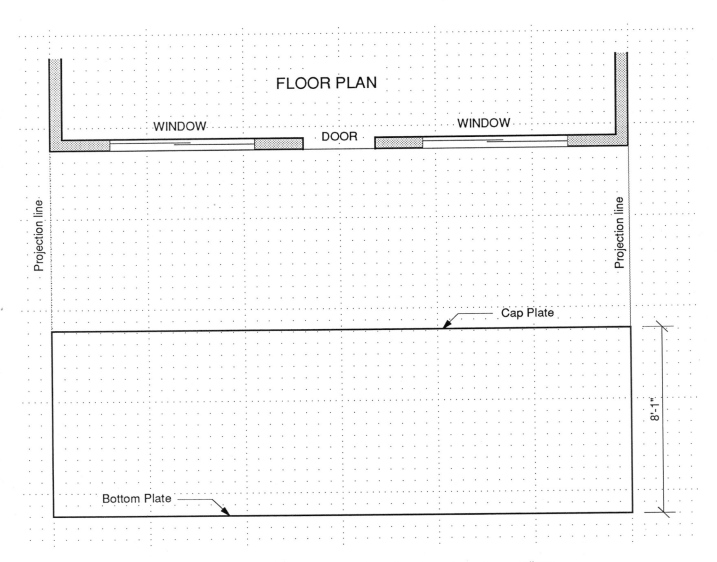

Fig. 24.4 Measure the wall height and draw the top of the cap plate; then draw the wall corner lines.

CHOOSE A FLOOR SYSTEM

CONCRETE SLAB FLOOR SYSTEM

1. If the house is to have a concrete slab floor system, as shown in the **a** portion of Fig. 24.5, measure *down* 8" (in 1/4" scale) from the bottom-plate line and make a mark.

2. Draw a line that indicates the ground (called ground line).

3. Draw the symbol representing earth as shown in Fig. 24.5.

FLOOR JOIST SYSTEM

1. If the house is to have a wood frame floor joist system, as shown in the **b** portion of Fig. 24.5, measure *down* approximately 2' - 3" from the bottom-plate line and make a mark.

2. Draw the ground line, as in Fig. 24.5.

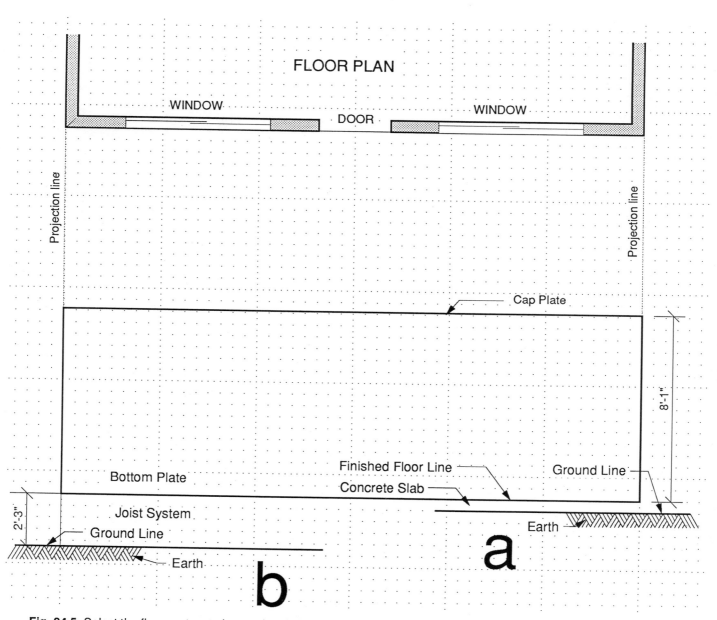

Fig. 24.5 Select the floor system to be used and draw the ground line.

DRAW THE DOORS AND WINDOWS

1. Measure *up* from the bottom-plate line 6' - 8" in 1/4" scale and draw a light horizontal line across the drawing to indicate the top of the doors and windows. (See Fig. 24.6.)

2. Extend light projection lines from the outer edge of each window and door on the floor plan, through your elevation drawing, as shown in Fig. 24.6.

3. Check your floor plan for the height of each window. Measure *down*, from the line indicating the top of the window, the predetermined distance. Draw a line indicating the bottom of each window.

4. With a slightly heavier pressure on your pencil, or a heavier lead, draw around each window and door so that it is clearly distinguishable, as shown in Fig. 24.6.

5. When drawing elevation views, it is often necessary to rearrange windows and sometimes change sizes in order to improve the overall appearance of the house. Be sure that any changes you make do not interfere with your interior space arrangements.

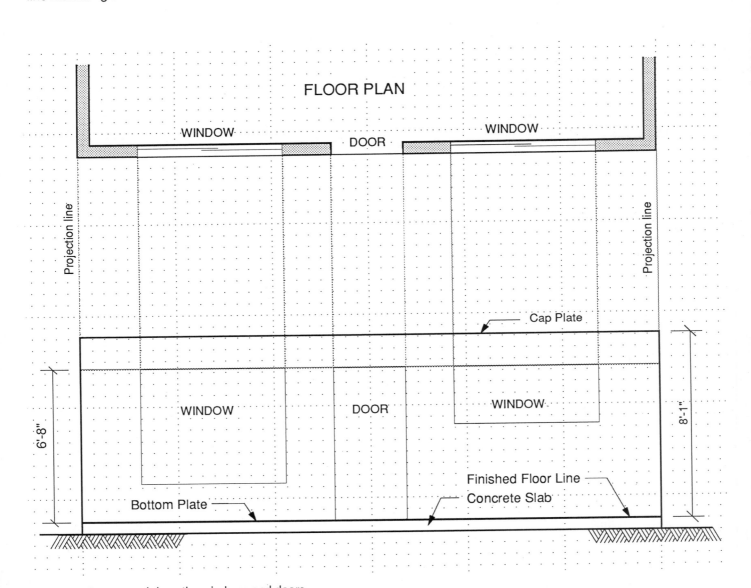

Fig. 24.6 Locate and draw the windows and doors.

DESIGNING A GABLE ROOF

PITCH

The word pitch means the angle of incline of a roof, or its slope. The degree of pitch is figured by increasing the angle of rise (or slope) 1 ft, for every 12 ft of run. This is illustrated in Fig. 24.7.

The pitch of a roof is expressed as:
1 in 12, 2 in 12, 3 in 12 ,etc.

The symbol for roof pitch is a triangle showing the number of feet of rise for each foot of run. The symbol is shown in Fig. 24.7a. It is placed on the drawing as shown in Fig.24.7.

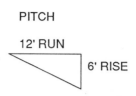

Fig. 24.7a Symbol to show the roof pitch.

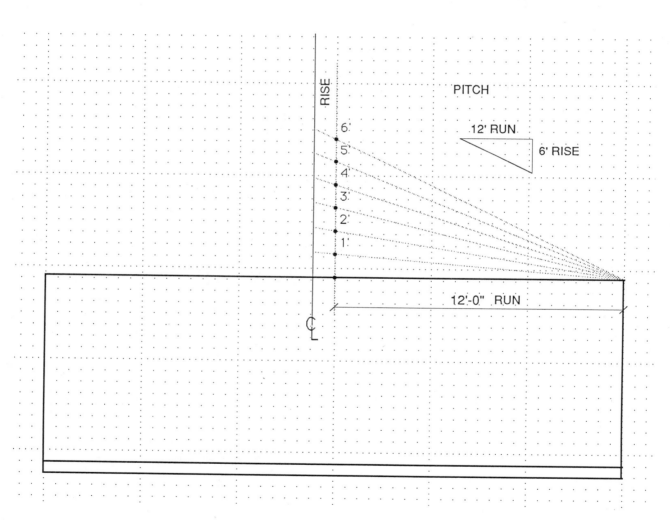

Fig. 24.7 How to figure the roof pitch.

MEASURING FOR THE ROOF PITCH

1. To construct a gable-roof design, begin by measuring *in* 12' from one of the corner walls on your drawing, along the top of the cap plate. Draw a light, vertical line, as shown in Fig. 24.8.

2. Measure *up* 1' for each foot of rise, depending on the roof pitch selected. Make dots on the vertical line at intervals of 1'. (See Fig. 24.8.)

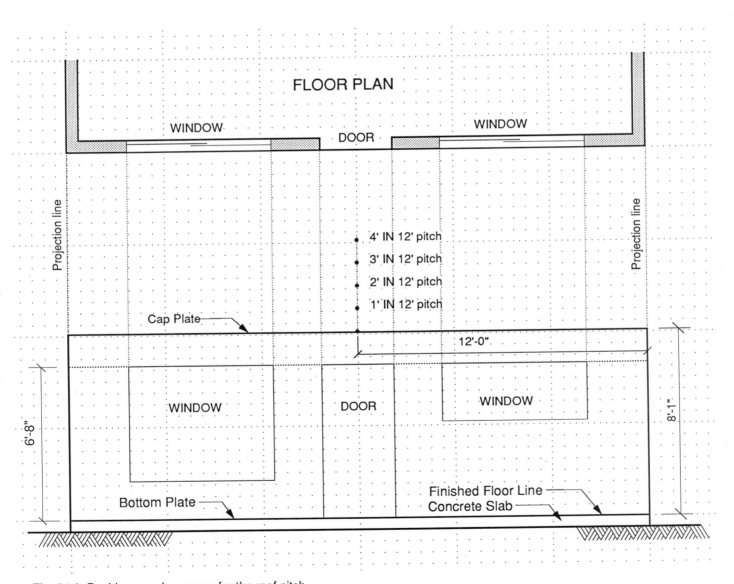

Fig. 24.8 Decide on and measure for the roof pitch.

DRAW THE ROOF PITCH

1. Measure to locate the center of the wall.

2. Draw a light centerline up from the cap plate, as shown in Fig. 24.9.

3. Lay your triangle or straight edge on the drawing and connect the top corner of the wall with the dot on the 12' line as in Fig. 24.9.

4. If your drawing is wider than 24', as shown in Fig. 24.7, extend the line at the same angle to intersect with the centerline of the building.

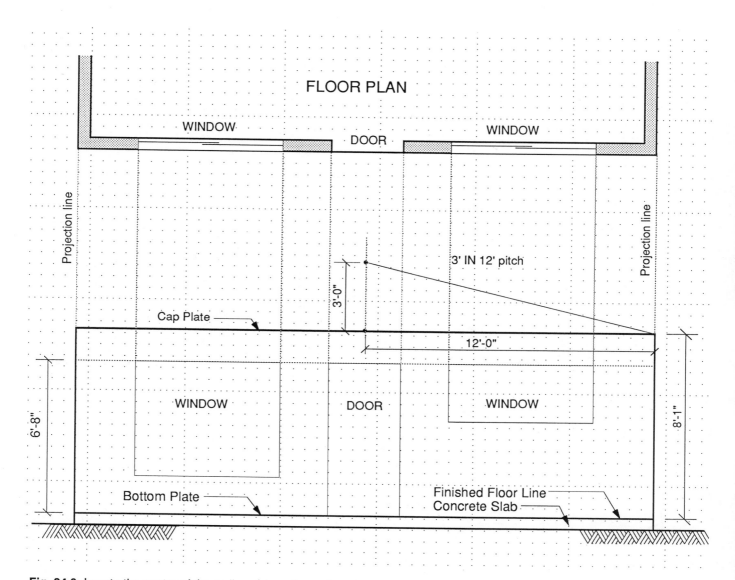

Fig. 24.9 Locate the center of the wall and draw the roof angle.

COMPLETE THE GABLE END:

1. Draw a line from the top of the opposite outside wall to the established top of the gable, completing the gable end. In Unit 25, Sections and Details, Fig. 25.2 shows the way roof rafters rest on the top plates. Notice, on the same drawing, the way the eaves, or overhanging ends of rafters, appear on a drawing.

2. Referring to your Roof Plan, measure *out* from the wall corners, on both sides of the elevation, for the correct amount of overhang and extend the lines of the roof accordingly. (See Fig. 24.10.)

3. Draw the roof-pitch symbol designating the rise and the run of the roof pitch.

DRAW THE FINISHING DETAILS

1. Fascia board is typically applied to rafter ends. Draw it as shown in Fig. 24.12. Fascia boards are usually 2" thick by 6", 8", or 10" wide, depending on the desired appearance. The minimum width required is one size larger than the rafters.

2. Plan and draw details of exterior finishing materials such as wood siding, stone or brick facing, or stucco. See Fig. 24.11. Figs. 24.20 through 23 are examples of the use of various exterior finishing materials and interesting ways of combining materials.

3. Draw details of trim such as frames around windows and doors, porches and steps, and exterior light fixtures,

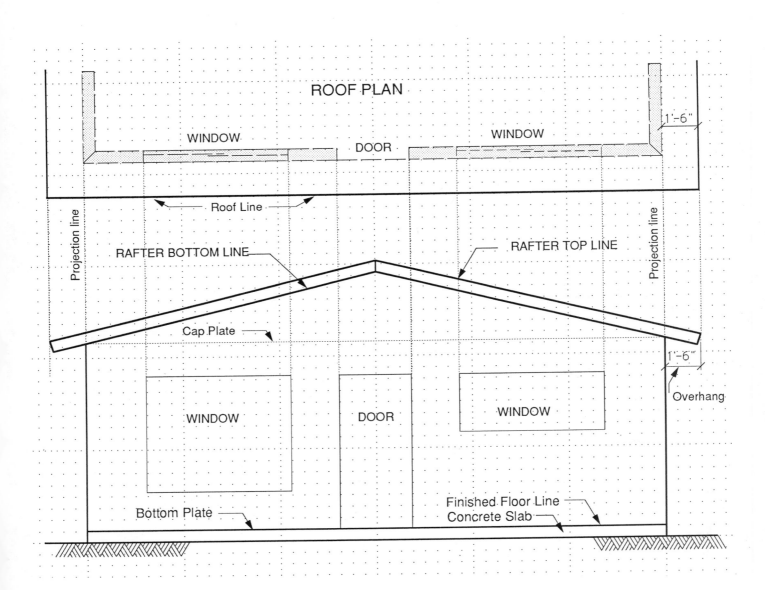

Fig. 24.10 Complete the gable end and the roof overhang.

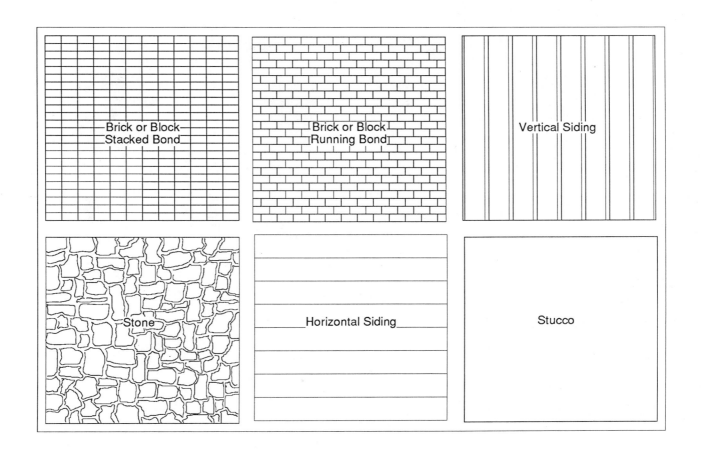

24.11 Symbols to represent exterior wall finishing materials.

Brick or Block—Stacked Bond

Brick or Block—Running Bond

Vertical Siding

Stone

Horizontal Siding

Stucco

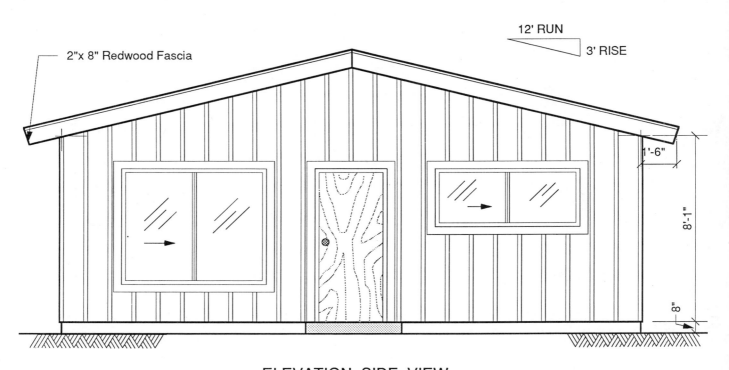

2"x 8" Redwood Fascia

12' RUN

3' RISE

1'-6"

8'-1"

8"

ELEVATION SIDE VIEW

Fig. 24.12 Draw the finishing details.

DRAWING VIEWS OF ALL FOUR SIDES

1. Place the floor plan on your working surface, as in Fig. 24.2, with the side to be drawn facing you.

2. Draw the elevation view, using the vertical measurements already established on your first elevation view. (See steps 1 and 2 in Fig. 24.13.)

3. Continue to turn the floor plan around and draw an elevation view for each of the other two sides of the house as in steps 3 and 4 in Fig. 24.13.

NOTE: *When drawing a simple gable-roof design, the highest point of the gable, as established in your first drawing, will be the height of the ridge in all views.*

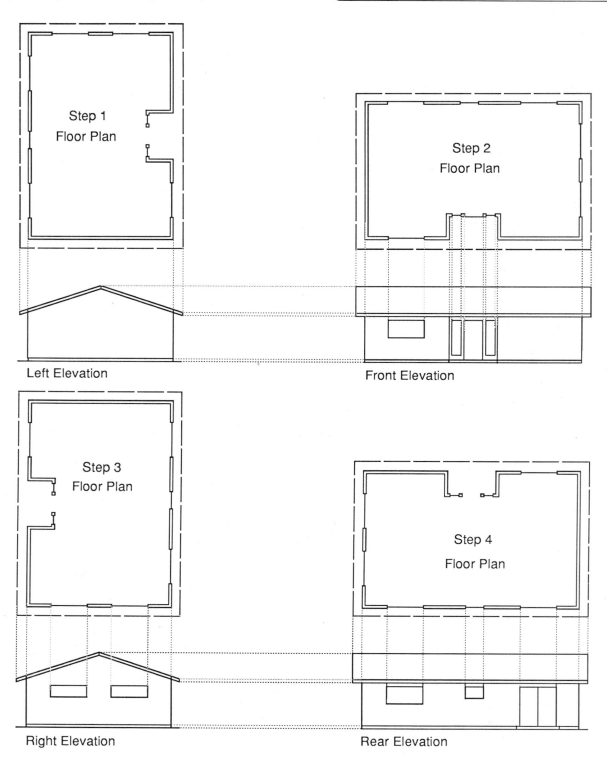

Fig. 24.13 Construct each of the other elevation views.

FINAL STEPS

When all four views have been drawn individually on tracing paper, you will be ready to make a finished drawing.

1. With scissors, trim the surplus tracing paper, then align and fasten the four elevation views to your working surface in a neat arrangement that will fit on your large sheet of paper, as shown in Fig. 24.14.

2. Place a large sheet of paper over the elevation views and fasten it securely to your working surface.

3. Draw a border and title block and number the sheet 3.

4. Trace each view sharply and neatly and draw in all the details.

5. Fig. 24.18 is a check list of notes and information that should appear on an elevation drawing. Check your drawing with it and add any necessary notes and dimensions. Figure 24.19 is an example of a completed elevation plan sheet. By studying it, you can see how notes, dimensions, and other details are added to the plan. (See also Figs. 24.20 through 23)

6. If your plan has a fireplace, draw and dimension the chimney on the appropriate view as in Fig. 24.15. The elevations in Fig. 24. 16 are for the book example plan. Note the fireplace chimney in all four elevation views.

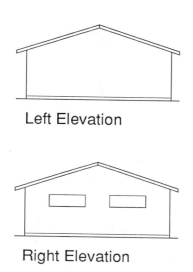

Left Elevation

Right Elevation

Fig. 24.14 Arrangement of elevation views.

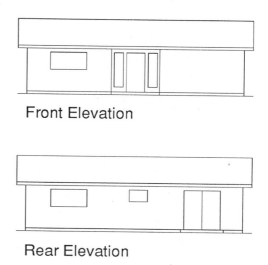

Front Elevation

Rear Elevation

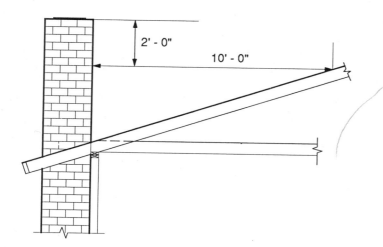

Fig. 24.15 Fireplace chimney distance requirements from roof.

FIREPLACE CHIMNEY HEIGHT

To calculate the height of the fireplace chimney, find the point on the slope of the roof where the horizontal measurement, from the chimney to the roof is 10' -0". (See Fig. 24.15.) Measure up from that point an additional 2' - 0". This is the correct chimney height. Write these measurements on your elevation-plan sheet as shown in Fig. 24.15. See Figs. 25.17 and 18 for additional fireplace chimney information.

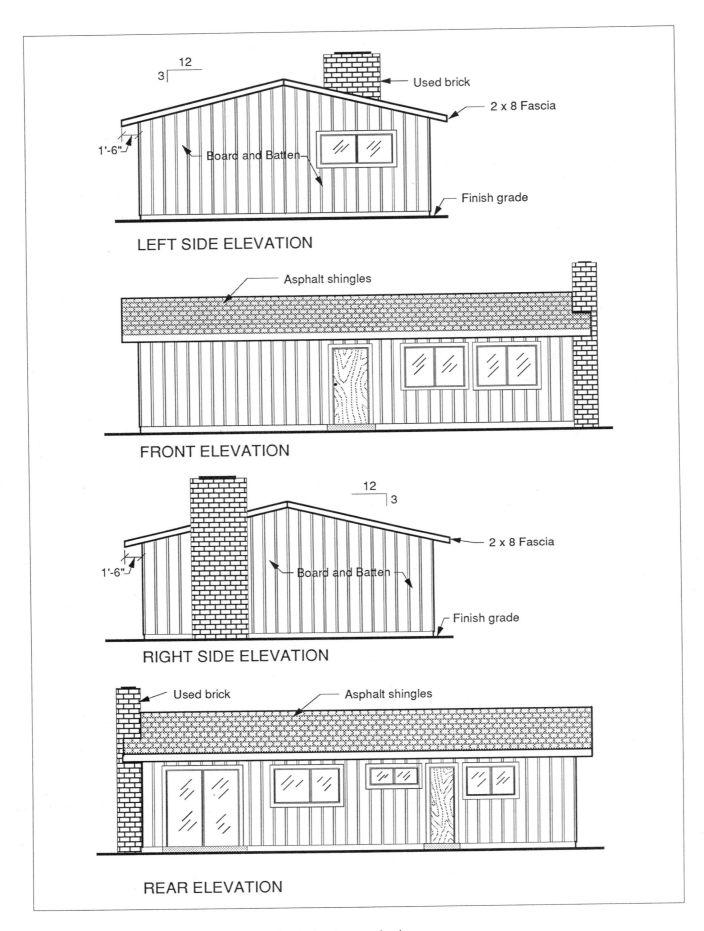

Fig. 24.16 Completed elevation sheet for the book example plan.

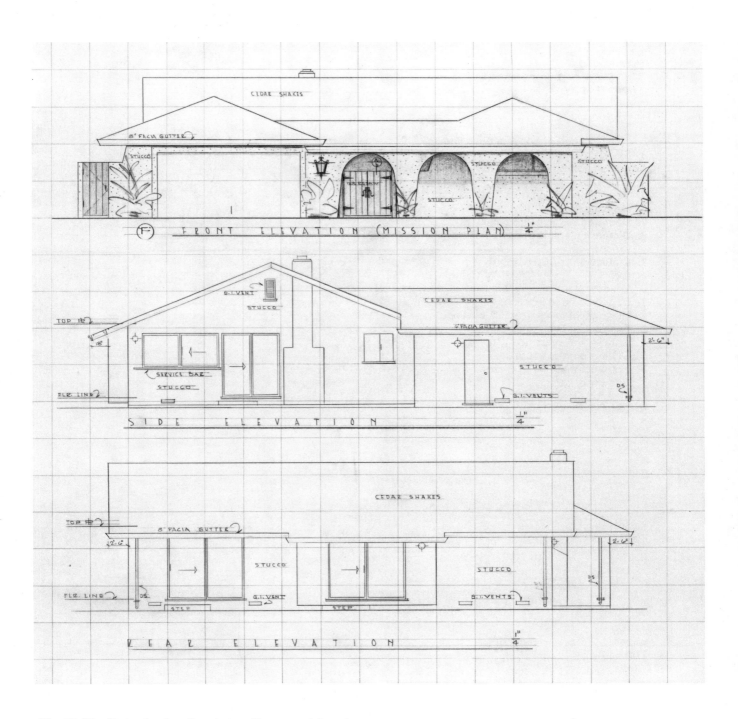

Fig. 24.17 Example elevation views with appropriate notes.

ELEVATION-PLAN CHECK LIST

Use this check list when preparing a final elevation plan. Many of the typical items which should be on an elevation plan are listed below. Some will be applicable to your plan and some will not. Check with your building department to verify local requirements.

Check off each item on this list as follows:

__✓__   Completed
__X__   Not completed
__0__   Doesn't apply

____ 1. Ground line
____ 2. Finish grade - 6" above ground line
____ 3. Floor elevation
____ 4. Foundation wall (hidden line)
____ 5. Finish floor line (min. 6")
____ 6. Vertical dimension from floor to top of top plate
____ 7. Door and window locations
____ 8. Dimension height of all doors and windows
____ 9. Dimension fireplace with reference to roof
____ 10. Window types and materials
____ 11. Door types and locations
____ 12. Diagonal bracing size and location
____ 13. Fascia size and material
____ 14. Note all wall materials
____ 15. Dimension roof overhang
____ 16. Note roof material
____ 17. Show roof pitch
____ 18. Gauge of roof flashing
____ 19. Gutters and downspouts

Fig. 24.18 Elevation-plan check list.

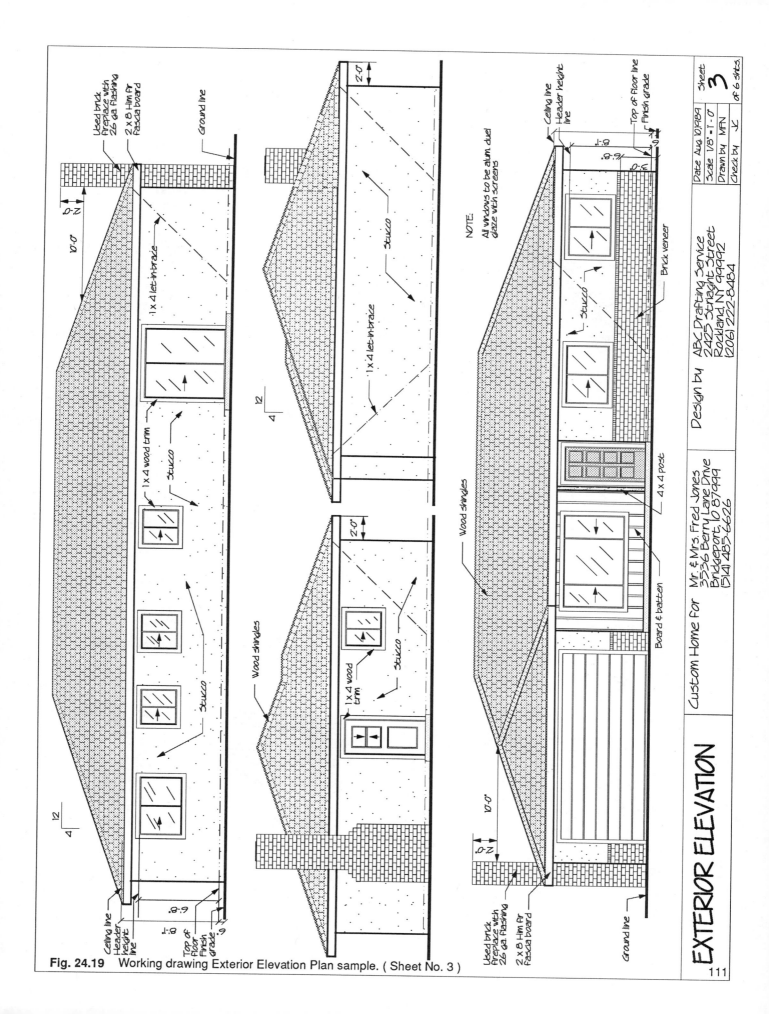

Fig. 24.19 Working drawing Exterior Elevation Plan sample. (Sheet No. 3)

EXTERIOR ELEVATION

Custom Home For   Mr. & Mrs. Fred Jones
3536 Berry Lane Drive
Bridgeport, Io 87999
(514) 485-6626

Design by   ABC Drafting Service
2425 Straight Street
Rockland, NY 99992
(206) 222-8484

Date Aug 10,1989	Sheet
Scale 1/8"=1'-0"	**3**
Drawn by MFN	
Check by JC	of 6 shts.

111

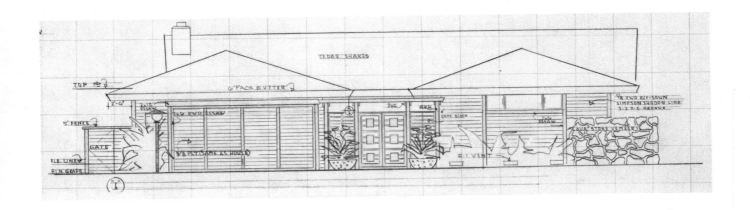

Fig. 24.20 A perspective drawing and an exterior elevation view of a house.

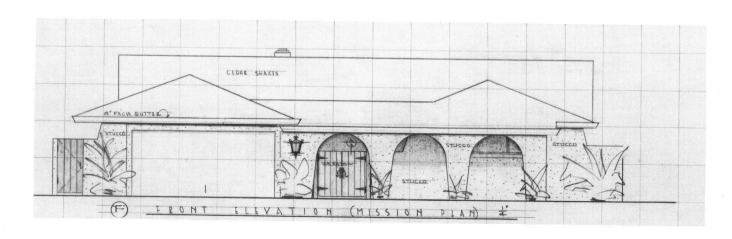

Fig. 24.21 A perspective drawing and an exterior elevation view of a house.

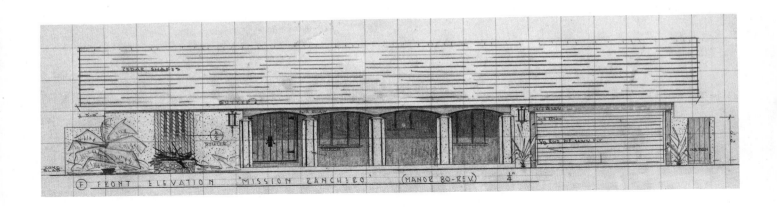

Fig. 24.22 A perspective drawing and an exterior elevation view of a house.

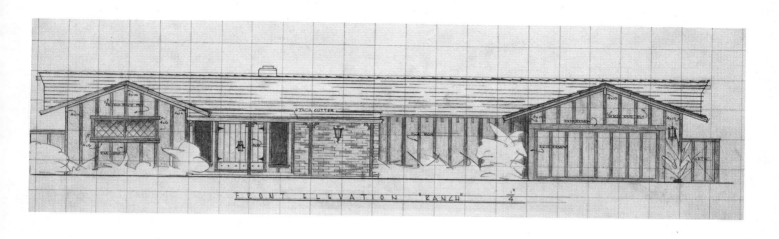

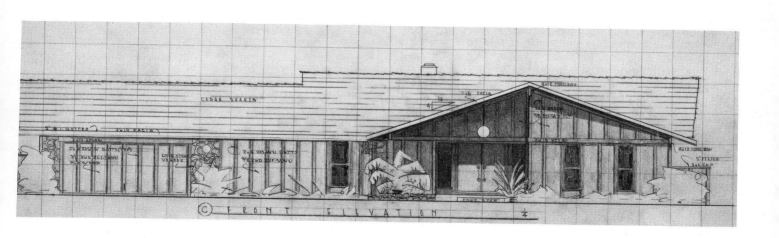

Fig. 24.23 Front exterior elevation views of two different houses.

SECTION &
DETAILS
PLAN

SECTION 9
UNIT 25

SECTIONS AND DETAILS

Objective: To learn to draw sections and details and prepare the sheet labeled 6, of the set of working drawings.

SECTIONS AND DETAILS

A house is composed of many parts, and each one must be drawn in such a way as to be understandable to individuals reading the plans. There are parts of a drawing that are not clearly visible from floor-plan or elevation views. So that construction people may understand all the intricate parts, certain items must be drawn, either in section view (cut through vertically) or in enlarged plan or elevation views called details.

Detail and section views of miscellaneous parts of a building are grouped together on one page of the set of plans. This page is referred to as a detail sheet. Fig. 25.1 is an example detail sheet in reduced size.

Before starting to draw Sheet 6, Sections and Details, study the information in this unit to familiarize yourself with the types of drawings required to sufficiently describe each part.

When you select details to be included on a detail sheet, consider whether or not sufficient information has already been given, either in drawing or note form, to make the part clearly understandable. Following is a list of some of the types of details and sections that may be required to complete a set of working drawings.

Framing Sections and Details Figures 25.3 through 5 are examples of wood framing methods and the types of drawings that may be required on your detail sheet. Figure 25.2 is a pictorial type of framing section which has been prepared for your information only. On it, each framing member is defined.

Gutters and Downspouts Miscellaneous items such as gutters and downspouts should be shown on the detail sheet. (See Fig. 25.6.)

Window and Door Sections and Details Figures 25.8 through 11 are drawings prepared to show typical finish framing around doors and windows. Note that the section-cut symbols on these drawings are keyed to the exterior wall elevation in Fig. 25.12.

Cabinet Sections and Details Figures 25.14 and 15, which are interior wall elevations showing kitchen cabinets, are typical of the type of cabinet drawings required. Similar details should be drawn for any other cabinets in the plan. Fig. 25.13 is a section view of the kitchen cabinets, showing construction methods and materials.

Fireplace Sections and Details You will need to provide details of the fireplace that show the design and materials to be used, the size requirements, and how the fireplace is to be built. Figures 25.16 through 18 are examples of elevation, section, and plan views for a typical, standard fireplace.

Roof Sections and Details Roof details such as those in Unit 23, Roof Plan, Figs. 23.7 and 8 can appear on either the roof plan sheet or on the detail sheet.

Foundation Sections and Details You have the option of placing foundation sections and details on either the foundation plan as in Unit 22, Foundation Plan, Figs. 22.1 through 4, or on the detail sheet.

WHAT IS A SECTION?

Visualize a house cut through from the top of the roof to the bottom of the foundation footing as shown in Fig. 25.7. Imagine that the dotted half of the building in that drawing has been removed. When drawing sections, what you will be drawing is the imaginary exposed area at the selected point of the cut.

Symbols are used to key sections and details to plan and elevation drawings. They show the exact place where the section view is taken. The top half of the symbol gives the section-cut number and the bottom half gives the plan-sheet number on which the keyed drawing appears. This system helps one to quickly locate keyed information.

Some of the drawings in the book are keyed to the appropriate sections and details. On the bottom half of the symbol, relevant book page numbers have been used for your reference. When drawing your own plan, use the page number, of your set of plans, which the detail describes.

DRAWING IN LARGER SCALES

The drafter is given some latitude in selecting the scale in which to draw details. The choice you make should depend on the space you have on the drawing and the clarity of portrayal required. Details are typically drawn to larger scales, ranging from 1/2" = 1' to 3" = 1' or larger.

PREPARING SHEET NUMBER 6 SECTIONS AND DETAILS

It is not possible for the drafter to draw details of the entire building, therefore parts that show the most detail are selected and details drawn of them. These parts reveal such things as nailing, bolt connections, metal straps, shear panels, etc. Figure 25.1 is an example of a detail sheet.

1. Plan your Sections and Details sheet by deciding which of the sample types of details is applicable to your project. List them for your own reference. Add to your list any additional details specific to your project. Refer to the check list in Fig. 25.19.

2. Lay out your working drawing sheet on vellum grid drawing paper, adding the border and title block. Label the sheet Sections and Details, number 6.

3. Referring to your list of items to be included on this sheet, lay out blocks of space for each of the details you have listed, using light pressure on a **4H** lead. Judge the size of the space required by checking Figs. 25.1 through 20. Choose larger or smaller scales as necessary to fit space allowances. Allow room for any necessary notes.

4. Experiment by drawing each of the details on tracing paper to familiarize yourself with them.

5. On the master sheet, draw and dimension each detail in the space allowed on your layout.

6. Add any necessary notes to clarify the information drawn and show the scale to which each section or detail was drawn.

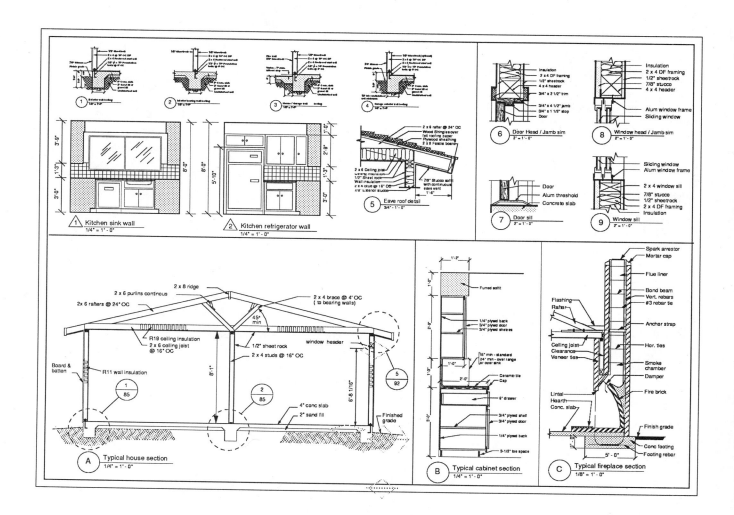

Fig. 25.1 An example of a typical detail sheet. (Reproduced in reduced scale.)

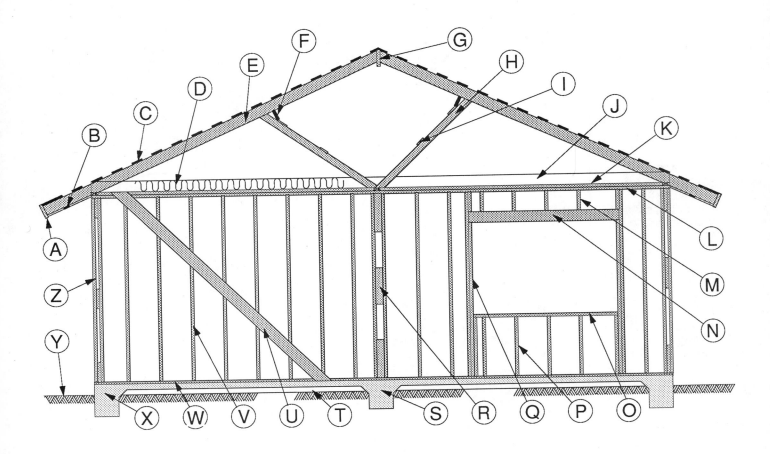

Fig. 25.2 A pictorial framing section on which each member has been called out and defined for your information.

A Fascia Board 2x6, 2x8, or 2x12 inch material nailed into stud ends of the overhanging rafters for trim effect.

B Soffit Eave Vent Continuous ventilating system installed in the under surface of the eave overhang.

C Spaced Roof Sheathing 1 x 4 inch material spaced on 12 inch centers to provide a nailing base for shingles.

D Ceiling Insulation Insulating material placed between the ceiling joists to insulate the ceiling.

E Roof Rafters A series of structural members used to form the skeleton of a roof.

F Purlins, Continuous Timber laid horizontally on the principle rafters for support.

G Ridge Beam Horizontal line of the top edge of a roof where the two sloping sides meet.

H Diagonal Braces 2x4 structural members placed at a 45 degree angle to provide support for roof framing.

I 1x4 Continuous Stiffners Tie roof framing together.

J Ceiling Joist Framing material, usually placed at 24 inch centers, to which ceiling materials are attached.

K Cap Plate Horizontal members nailed to the top plate to tie the walls and partitions together.

L Top Plate The top horizontal member of a framed wall or partition.

M Upper Cripple A 2 x 4 inch framing member cut to fit above a window or a door in a framed opening.

N Header A beam placed above any framed opening. Beam size is determined by the width of the opening.

O Window Sill The bottom member of a framed window.

P Lower Cripple 2 x 4 inch framing member cut to fit beneath a framed window opening.

Q Trimmer 2 x 4 framing member used to support each end of a header.

R Framing Channel Framing method designed to tie interior partitions to exterior walls.

S Interior Bearing Footing Part of a continuous concrete foundation calculated to support the roof load.

T 2 Inch Sand or Gravel Fill Used beneath a concrete slab foundation.

U Let In Brace 1 x 4 inch diagonal brace let into a stud wall to give lateral support.

V Studs Standard 92-1/4 inch framing members placed vertically at 16 inch centers.

W Mud Sill The lowest horizontal member of a framed wall; always of redwood.

X Exterior Footing A continuous concrete footing calculated to support exterior walls.

Y Finish Grade Finished earth grade around building.

Z Framing Corner Framing connection where two framed walls join to form a corner.

WOOD-FRAMING SECTIONS

From Fig. 25.2 you will learn how a framing section is drawn and the name of each framing member. Fig. 25.3 is an exterior wall elevation showing the way windows and doors are framed and how interior partitions are connected to exterior walls. Figure 25.4 is a plan view drawing of the same wall showing stud placement. Note the alternate method shown for framing corners.

DRAWING A WALL-FRAMING SECTION

Figure 25.5 is a framing section view for the book example plan. When drawing the framing section view for your plan, refer to it and also to Fig. 25.20. See the check list is Fig. 25.19 for requirements.

When laying out a framing plan, begin at one corner, placing studs every 16" OC as shown in Figure 25.4. This allows for nailing every 4'. 4' x 8' panels of many types are used for exterior siding.

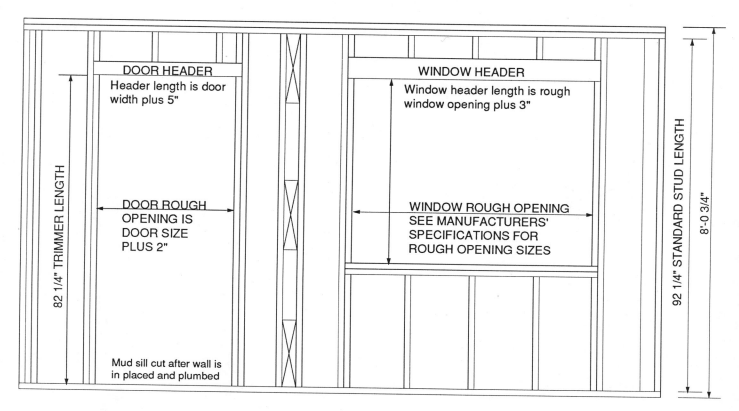

DOOR HEADER
Header length is door width plus 5"

DOOR ROUGH OPENING IS DOOR SIZE PLUS 2"

Mud sill cut after wall is in placed and plumbed

82 1/4" TRIMMER LENGTH

WINDOW HEADER
Window header length is rough window opening plus 3"

WINDOW ROUGH OPENING
SEE MANUFACTURERS' SPECIFICATIONS FOR ROUGH OPENING SIZES

92 1/4" STANDARD STUD LENGTH

8'-0 3/4"

Fig. 25.3 Wall-framing section showing the door and window headers and a framed chanel for an interior partition.

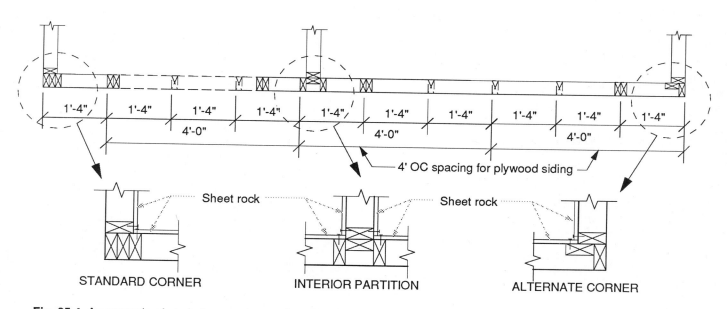

1'-4"   1'-4"   1'-4"   1'-4"   1'-4"   1'-4"   1'-4"   1'-4"   1'-4"   1'-4"

4'-0"   4'-0"   4'-0"

4' OC spacing for plywood siding

Sheet rock   Sheet rock

STANDARD CORNER   INTERIOR PARTITION   ALTERNATE CORNER

Fig. 25.4 An example of stud placement on a plan-view framing layout.

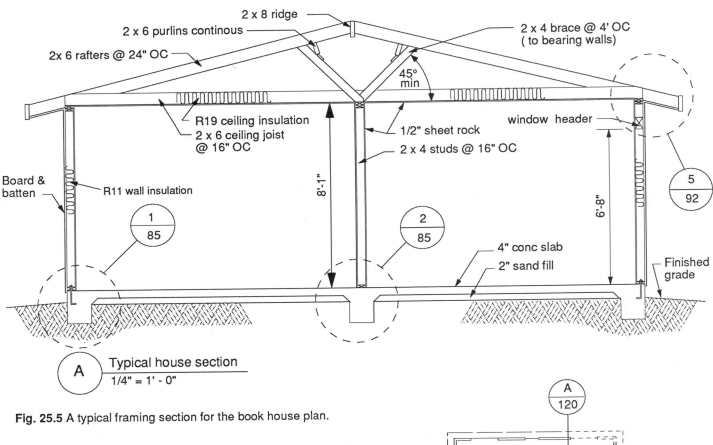

Fig. 25.5 A typical framing section for the book house plan.

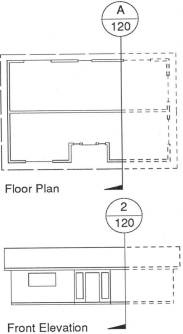

Fig. 25.6 Detail drawing of rain gutters and downspouts for roof eave installation.

Fig. 25.7 A floor-plan and elevation view of a building showing the section-cut location.

GUTTERS AND DOWNSPOUTS

A gutter is a shallow horizontal trough, usually of sheet metal, used to carry rain water off the roof to a downspout. A downspout is a vertical pipe that connects to the gutter and carries the water to the ground. Gutters and downspouts are drawn on the plan as shown in Fig. 25.6 and are also described in a note. In instances where gutters are not used, rain diverters, sheet metal troughs that divert water, are required to be installed over exterior doors.

KEYING TO SECTIONS AND DETAILS

The illustration above shows an imaginary cut through a building. Imagine the dotted area of the drawing removed. From the exposed part of the building, a section view, revealing all construction members, is drawn. The arrow at the end of the symbol always points in the viewing direction.

DOOR AND WINDOW DETAILS

Sizes of all windows and doors are shown on the floor plan. Additional window details, showing the size and location of headers, jambs, and sills or thresholds are also required. Details should show how each window and door opening is to be framed and how doors and windows are to be installed.

Figures 25.8 through 11 are examples of typical door and window framing details. They show such things as the method of construction and the size and kind of materials used. The elevation view in Fig. 25.14 is keyed to the window and door details. The section-cut symbols show the location of each part and where it is cut through.

There are several methods of framing around doors and windows. The drafter must verify details about the types of windows selected and applicable installation procedures.

Manufacturers' literature describing the various types of windows and doors is available. The detail drawings furnished by manufacturers will supply you with clear examples. In many instances, you can simply select applicable details from the literature and trace them or draw enlargements of them.

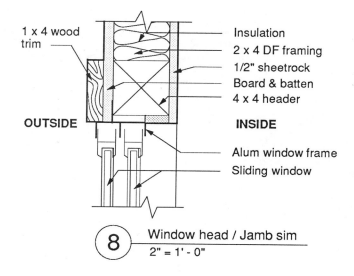

Fig. 25.10

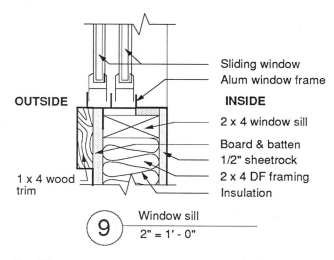

Fig. 25.11

SECTION-CUT SYMBOLS

The section-cut symbols in Fig. 25.14 indicate where the details are cut through. See Unit 21, Dimensions and Notes, for information on drawing section symbols.

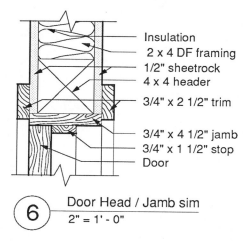

Fig. 25.8

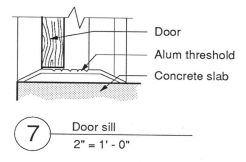

Fig. 25.9

Fig. 25.12 Elevation view showing door and window section-cut locations.

CABINET DETAILS

Manufacturers' literature is available for all types of cabinets. It contains size, style, materials, drawer, and door information. Valuable information can be obtained by studying the drawings provided in this literature. Also refer to Unit 9, Kitchen Layouts.

Cabinetry details are typically shown in plan, section, and/or interior elevation views. (See Figs. 25.13 through 15.) An interior-wall elevation is a vertical view of any given wall area.

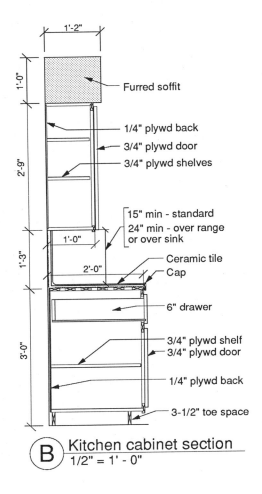

Fig. 25.13 A section view of kitchen cabinetry showing construction methods and measurements.

DRAWING INTERIOR ELEVATIONS

1. From the floor plan, select the wall elevation view you wish to draw and lightly draw a line to represent the floor. Measure the wall width and draw vertical lines representing the two corners. Measure 8' *up* from the floor line and draw the ceiling line.

2. Check door, window, appliance, and/or fixture locations, sizes, and heights. Accurately place doors and windows where required.

3. Referring to the kitchen in your floor plan, draw an elevation view and locate each of the appliances to be placed along the wall. (See Figs. 25.14 and 15, and Unit 9, Kitchen Layouts.)

4. Cover your drawing with tracing paper and plan all the details of the cabinets, taking into consideration the way each cabinet area will be used. Select the best location for drawer units. Plan the most convenient direction for the cabinet doors to swing. Consider how the space would function with cabinet and appliance doors and drawers open. Save your sketches.

5. Measure and draw the base and wall cabinets showing all details including the 3-1/2" toe space.

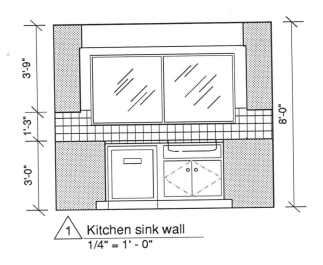

Fig. 25.14 An interior kitchen wall elevation.

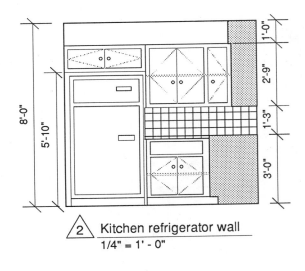

Fig. 25.15 An interior kitchen wall elevation.

FIREPLACE SECTIONS AND DETAILS

A fireplace is shown in plan view on the floor plan, Unit 20, Floor Plans, Fig. 20.3. In a floor-plan drawing it is not possible to show all of the size and construction detail information required. Additional necessary information is provided by drawing fireplace sections and details. (See Figs. 25.16 through 18.) These example drawings depict a standard fireplace. Refer to Unit 16, Fireplaces for additional fireplace information.

Figure 25.16 is an elevation view of a typical fireplace. From this view you can see the finishing material and the height and design of the optional mantel.

Figure 25.17 is a fireplace in plan view with correct fireplace measurements. For your plan, select the size of the firebox and check the accompanying measurement chart for relevant measurements.

Figure 25.18 is a section view of the same fireplace. From this view one can see how the fireplace is to be constructed.

The correct height of the chimney in relationship to the roof is given In Unit 24, Elevations, Fig. 24.15.

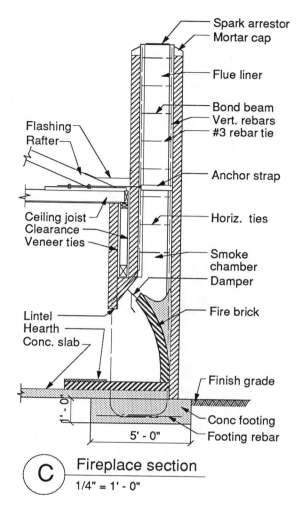

Fireplace section
1/4" = 1' - 0"

Fig. 25.18 A Section view of a standard fireplace showing materials and construction methods.

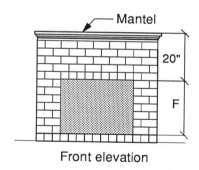

Front elevation

Fig. 25.16 A standard fireplace in elevation view.

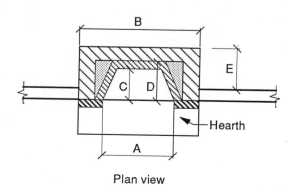

Plan view

Approx. dimensions in inches

A	B	C	D	E	F
24	48	16	20	24	24
30	54	16	20	24	29
36	60	16	20	24	29
48	72	18	22	26	32
60	88	22	27	31	40

Fig. 25.17 An example of a standard fireplace in plan view and an accompanying chart of sizes.

SECTION AND DETAIL-PLAN CHECK LIST

Use this check list when preparing a final section and detail sheet. Many of the typical items which should be on a section and detail sheet are listed below. Some will be applicable to your plan and some will not. Check with your building department to verify local requirements.

Check off each item on this list as follows:

✓___ Completed
X___ Not completed
0___ Doesn't apply

_____ 1. Footing height above grade 6" min.
_____ 2. Foundation vents (wood floor joist)
_____ 3. Fireplace section and details
_____ 4. Show all framing member sizes
_____ 5. Wall framing material
_____ 6. Show all header sizes
_____ 7. Wall spacing, bracing and height
_____ 8. Ceiling height dimension
_____ 9. Rafter span and spacing
_____10. Special framing for beam ceiling
_____11. Ceiling joist spacing and span
_____12. Note size and connections of all post
_____13. Cutting and notching
_____14. Wall and ceiling insulation

_____15. Eve vent
_____16. Fascia board size and material
_____17. Roof pitch
_____18. Collar ties
_____19. Roof trusses manufacture spec.
_____20. Roof material
_____21. Roof sheathing, spacing, and size
_____22. Attic ventilation
_____23. Exterior siding material
_____24. Nailing requirements
_____25. Veneer location height and type
_____26. Foundation bolts, location and size
_____27. Note shear walls
_____28. Section notations with reference to plan

Fig. 25.19 Section and detail-plan check list.

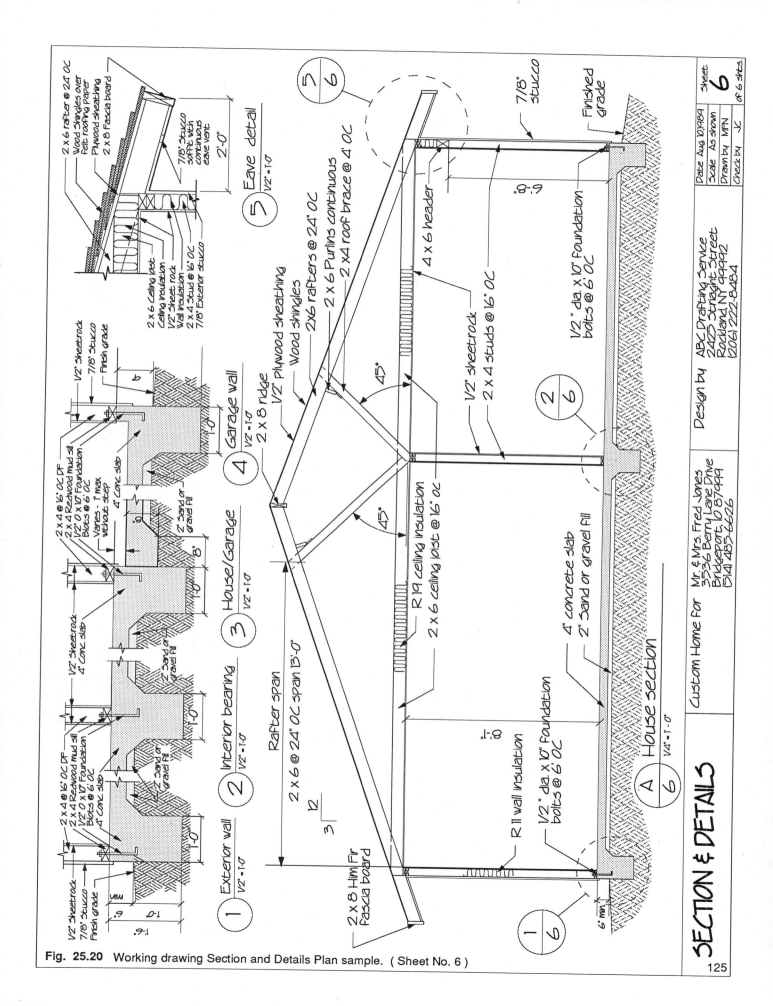

Fig. 25.20 Working drawing Section and Details Plan sample. (Sheet No. 6)

125

PLOT
PLAN

UNIT 26

PLOT PLAN

OBJECTIVE: To learn to draw a complete plan of the building site showing all the details necessary to complete the sheet labeled 1 of the set of working drawings.

WHAT IS A PLOT PLAN?

A plan of a lot is referred to as a plot plan. A plot plan is a drawing of a plot of ground or lot. Visualize a plot plan the same way you would visualize a floor plan. Imagine that you are directly above the lot, looking down on it. Any buildings, trees, or other three-dimensional objects would appear to be flat. The land would also appear to be flat, even if it were sloping or contoured.

PLANNING A NEW HOME ON A PLOT PLAN

A careful study of the use of the entire lot will result in an attractive and convenient arrangement for the house, driveway, car shelter, service, and garden areas.

PLANNING A REMODELING PROJECT ON A PLOT PLAN

A plot plan of the lot, showing all its features, plus the existing house, garage or carport, and driveway, will help you plan for a remodeled home that relates well to the site.

PLANNING AN ADDITION ON A PLOT PLAN

A plot plan of the lot showing the existing house and any other structures on the lot is essential when planning an addition. The plan will reveal available space for the new addition and help you to maximize the use of the lot space. The plot-plan drawing will also be required when application is made for building permits.

SUBDIVISION MAPS

Figure 26.1 is an example of a plot plan for a level lot, rectangular in shape, measuring 70' in width and 100' in depth. This drawing shows lot boundary lines (property lines) only.

The information needed to draw this plot plan was taken from a portion of a subdivision map. A copy of the portion of the subdivision map on which a buyer's lot is located is usually included with the buyer's papers at the time the lot or home is purchased. These maps are quite small and contain limited information; however, you can obtain exact property line locations and dimensions of the lot from them.

DRAW AN EXPERIMENTAL PLOT PLAN

1. Draw a plot plan of a lot on tracing paper fastened over a small sheet of grid paper. Lay it out with the 1/16" scale provided with the book. If you do not have a specific lot in mind, use the sample lot, Fig. 26.1, which is a typical lot size.

2. If your project is remodeling or adding to a home, measure the lot or take the information from the subdivision map.

3. Draw lines representing the property lines of the lot. The lines should be composed of one long dash and two short dashes, as shown in Fig. 26.1.

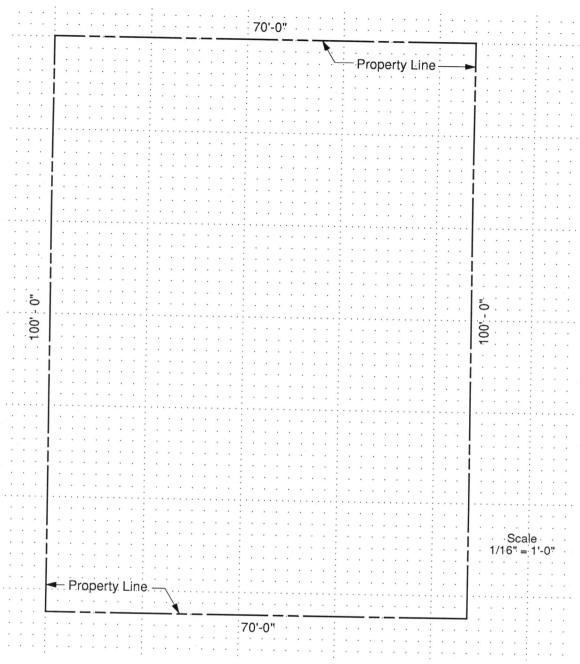

Fig 26.1 An example of a lot drawing (referred to as a plot plan).

SETBACKS

Setbacks are requirements pertaining to the placement of a house on a lot. City or county planning departments in each area require that houses be set back from the property lines a certain distance. Typically, a minimum setback of 15' to 20' is required from the street front property line to the front of the house; 5' is required from each side property line of the lot to each side of the house. A minimum of 15' is required from the back property line to the back of the house. Refer to Fig. 26.2.

> **NOTE:** Setback requirements vary in different communities. It is important to check with your city or county planning department when you are ready to draw a plot plan.

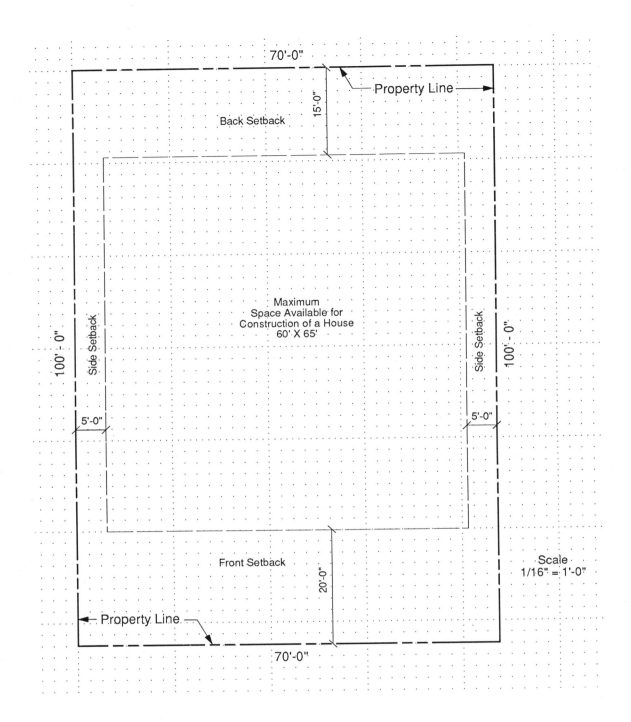

Fig. 26.2 Setbacks, indicated with a dashed line, have been added to the plot plan.

INDICATING SETBACK
REQUIREMENTS ON A PLOT PLAN

1. When you have drawn the lot property lines and verified local setback requirements, indicate setbacks as shown in Fig. 26.2. Copy the short dashed lines used for this purpose.

2. When a plot plan has been drawn with the setbacks lightly indicated, it is easy to visualize the available space for the construction of a house and other facilities or an addition to an existing house.

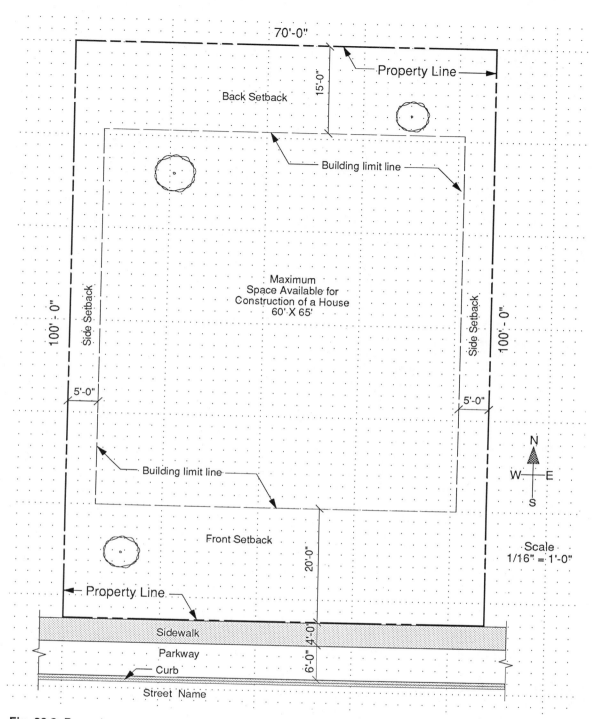

70'-0"

Property Line

15'-0"

Back Setback

Building limit line

100'-0"

Side Setback

5'-0"

Maximum
Space Available for
Construction of a House
60' X 65'

Side Setback

5'-0"

100'-0"

N

W——E

S

Building limit line

Front Setback

20'-0"

Scale
1/16" = 1'-0"

Property Line

Sidewalk

4'-0"

Parkway

6'-0"

Curb

Street Name

Fig. 26.3 Preparing a plot plan.

LOT SPACE YOU CAN BUILD ON

In Fig. 26.2 you see that the maximum width available on the lot, after deducting setbacks, is 60'. Since the lot is 100' deep and the front and back setbacks combined total 35', the remaining lot depth is 65'. There are any number of possibilities for the use of this 60' x 65' space; as described farther along in this chapter.

DRAWING EXISTING FEATURES

1. Draw an arrow to indicate NORTH on the plot plan. Copy its location from the subdivision map. (See Fig. 26.3.)

2. Indicate any trees growing on the lot which are to remain. Trees can be drawn with a symbol as shown, or with a plus mark (+).

3. Note any other existing features or buildings on the lot and their locations. (See Fig. 26.4 for correct symbols.)

4. If you are drawing plans for remodeling or an addition, measure the house and garage and draw them on the lot. Refer to Figs. 26.6 through 10 and Unit 29, Remodeling and Additions.

5. Show existing walks and driveways, as in Fig. 26.5.

6. Locate sidewalks and curbs. (See Fig. 26.5.)

7. Widths of sidewalks vary in each community. If you do not have exact measurements, extend a measurement line beyond the front property line about 10'.

NOTE: The property between the front property line and the curb belongs to the city or county. Curbs, sidewalks and sometimes parkways must be installed in accordance with city or county specifications.

8. Overlay the plot-plan drawing with tracing paper. Placement of the new work such as house, garage, driveway, and walks can now be worked out on tracing paper, leaving the lot drawing intact. Use as many layers of tracing paper as necessary while working out details.

9. Referring to Figs. 26.6 through 10, add any additional concrete work, landscaping, roofed-over areas, etc.

BASIC SHAPES FOR HOUSES AND GARAGES

A house can be any size and shape that you choose to make it, as long as it fits within the limitations of the lot area, allows for convenient arrangement of other facilities and fits within a budget.

The examples of basic house shapes shown in Figs. 26.6 through 10 have been included to introduce you to a few layout possibilities. One of these layouts may serve to guide you in planning your project.

Each illustration shown on the next few pages has unique possibilities for arrangement of interior space and interesting use of lot space.

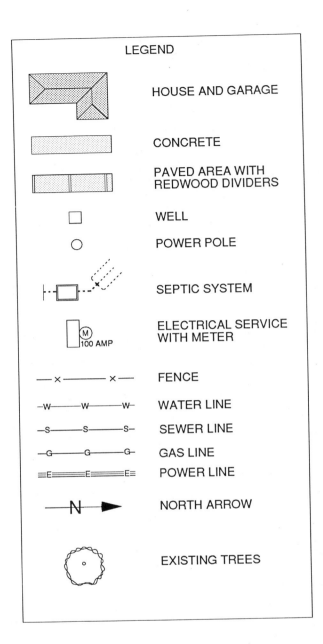

Fig. 26.4 Symbols for use in plot-plan drawing.

STUDYING BASIC HOUSE SHAPES

1. As you study basic house shapes, try to visualize each one on the lot.

2. When you see a shape that is suitable for your project, sketch it on the tracing paper covering your plot plan. This need only be a rough sketch. In this way you can evaluate requirements as you study the basic shapes.

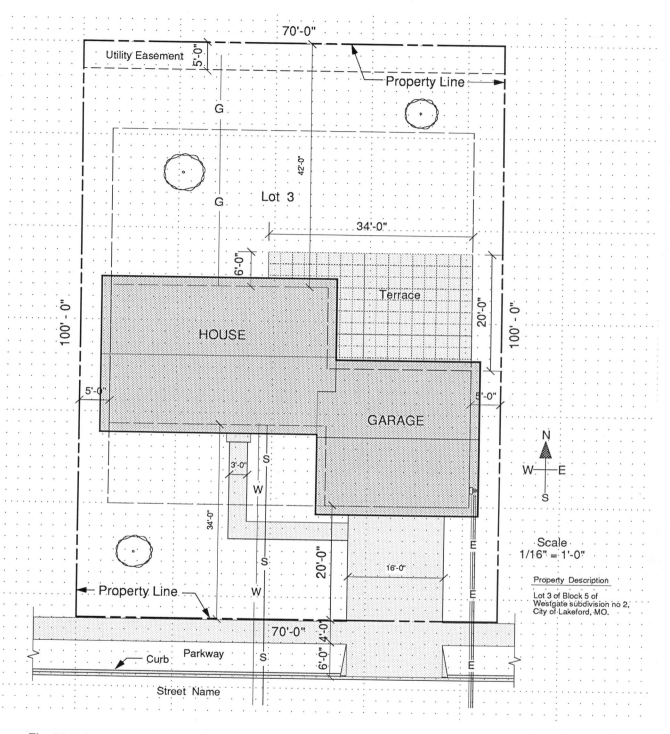

Fig. 26.5 An example of a completed plot plan.

MAKING A PLOT- PLAN WORKING DRAWING

1. Lay out the border and title block on your grid-vellum drawing paper. Title the drawing Plot Plan and number it 1; the order in which it will be bound into the complete set.

2. Referring to your final plot-plan sketches and studies, lay out and draw the lot to a scale of 1/16" = 1'.

3. Refer to Fig. 25.4 for plot plan symbols and designations.

4. Locate and indicate any trees, buildings, fences, or other existing features that are to remain on the lot. Mark them "existing."

5. If you have not verified the setback requirements with your local planning department, this is the time to do so. Draw the house and garage in the chosen location.

6. Draw and identify all concrete work, such as the driveway, walk ways, terraces, patios, porches, etc. These areas should be dimensioned and the designation for concrete used. See Figs. 15.1 and 2 for driveway requirements. During construction, the concrete is usually placed according to the information given on the plot plan.

7. If city facilities are available, indicate the place where water and sewer lines will come onto the property.

8. If a well and/or septic system are to be used, indicate on the plot plan the proposed location for each. Show the septic system, including leaching lines which are part of the system. Requirements can be obtained from your local department of health and sanitation.

9. If natural gas is available, show the location of the line coming onto the property.

10. If other fuel is to be used, such as butane, propane, or oil, show the location of the storage tank and of the fuel line.

11. Check with the electric company for the location of the power source which will serve the proposed home. The closest existing source (pole or underground lead in) is not necessarily the one that will be used to serve the property. Show the location.

12. Check and compare your drawing with Fig. 26.5. This drawing is a completed plot plan for the book sample house.

13. Go over the lines of the drawing with a heavier pressure on your well-pointed pencil.

14. A separate print of the plot plan can be used for planning the landscaping.

15. Subcontractors will need a copy of your completed plot plan.

16. All information should be confirmed with the various building and planning agencies at this time.

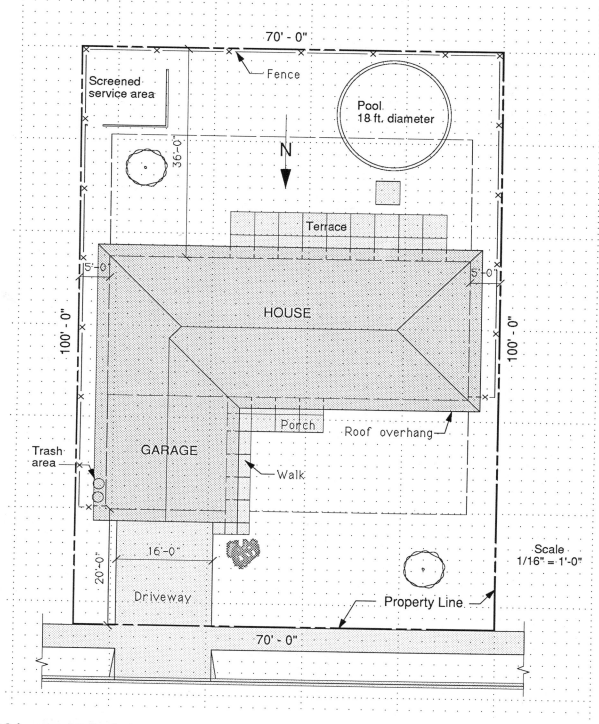

Fig. 26.6 An example of an **L**-shaped house on a 70' x 100' lot.

The **L**-shaped plot-plan layout, Fig. 26.6 is a very functional arrangement of house and garage, and utilizes lot space to the fullest.

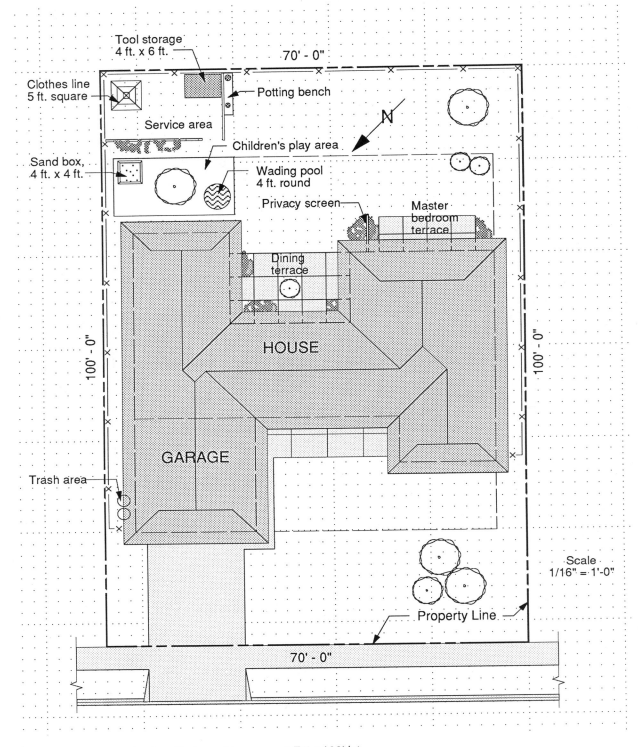

Fig. 26.7 An example of an **H**-shaped house on a 70' x 100' lot.

An **H**-shaped house, Fig. 26.7, has the advantage of sheltered courts or terraces created by the wings of the building. The minimum practical distance between wings, (across courts) is 10'. The total area of this house and garage is 1,904 sq ft.

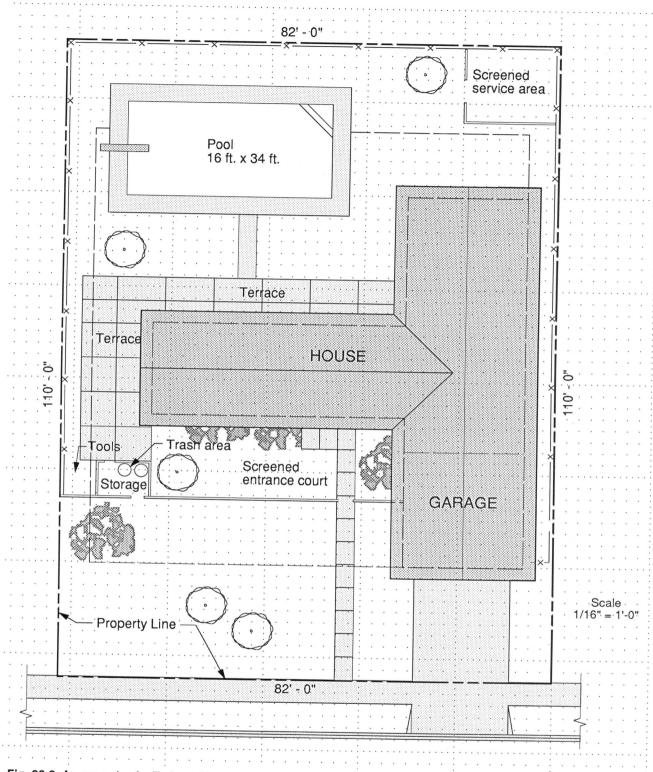

Fig. 26.8 An example of a **T**-shaped house on a 70' x 100' lot.

The **T** shape layout shown in Fig. 26.8 could be positioned in several ways on the lot. This layout might also be a good solution for an irregularly shaped lot. The plan in this illustration is oriented in such a way as to permit maximum sun in the pool area. The total area of the house and garage is 2,072 sq ft.

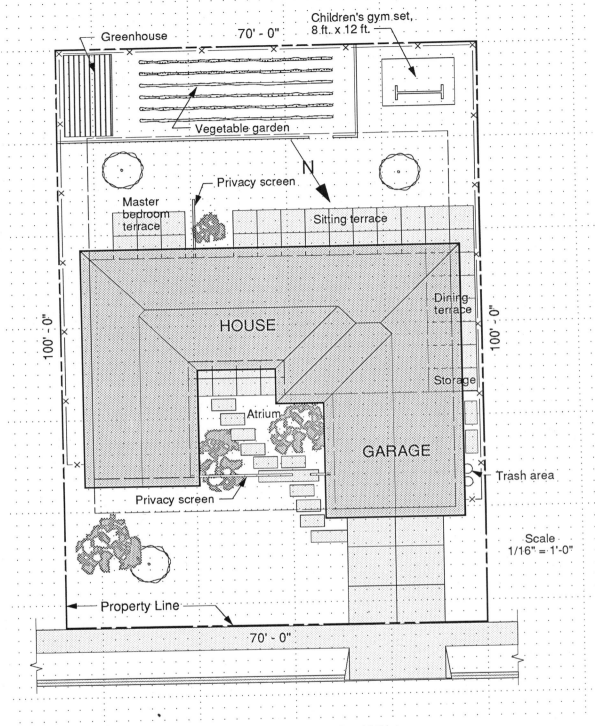

Fig. 26.9 An example of an **ATRIUM** type house on an 82' x 100' lot.

The **ATRIUM OR COURT** in this layout, Fig. 26.9 could also be facing the back garden or either side of the lot. The garden and terrace areas are oriented on the lot in such a way as to obtain morning sun and late afternoon shade in the summertime. The total area of the house and garage is 1,872 sq ft.

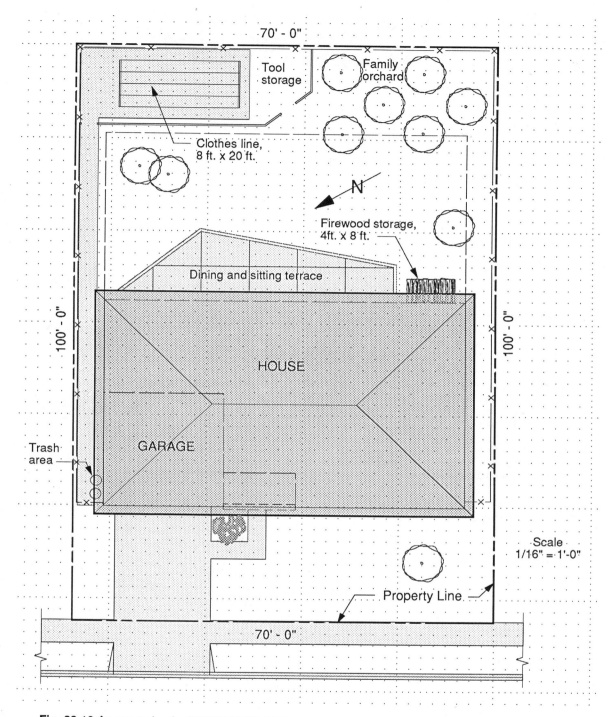

Fig. 26.10 An example of a **RECTANGULAR** house on a 70' x 100' lot.

The **Rectangular** shape in Fig. 26.10 is economical to build and leaves more lot space for outdoor living than is available with the preceding plans. The total area of the house and garage is 2,088 sq ft.

PLOT-PLAN CHECK LIST

Use this check list when preparing a final plot plan. Many of the typical items which should be on a plot plan are listed below. Some will be applicable to your plan and some will not. Check with your building department to verify local requirements.

Check off each item on this list as follows:

√___ Completed
_X___ Not completed
_0___ Doesn't apply

___ 1. Vicinity map
___ 2. North arrow
___ 3. Property lines dimension and bearing
___ 4. Street name and size
___ 5. Sidewalks type, size, and location
___ 6. Driveway size, material, and location
___ 7. Note all existing items to be removed, such as structures or trees
___ 8. Public utilities locations
___ 9. Gas lines location and size
___10. Water lines location and size
___11. Power lines location and size
___12. Sewer lines location and size
___13. Telephone lines, location and size
___14. Show public utilites easement on property
___15. Existing grade
___16. Proposed finish grade
___17. Slope of street and driveway
___18. Finish grade of corner of building
___19. Retaining walls size and material
___20. Driveway aprons

___21. Pool location and size
___22. Splash block or Catch basins
___23. Curbs, size and location
___24. Patio location and size
___25. Concrete walks, size and material
___26. Side yards dimension
___27. Rear yard dimension
___28. Front yard dimension
___29. Street center line
___30. Fence height, material and location
___31. Note floor elevation
___32. Dimension building to property line
___33. Subdivision tract no.
___34. Block no.
___35. Lot no.
___36. Street name and number
___37. City, County and State
___38. Owner's name and address
___39. Drafter's name and address
___40. Scale of drawing
___41. Landscape lighting
___42. Area drain and slope

Fig. 26.11 Plot-plan check list.

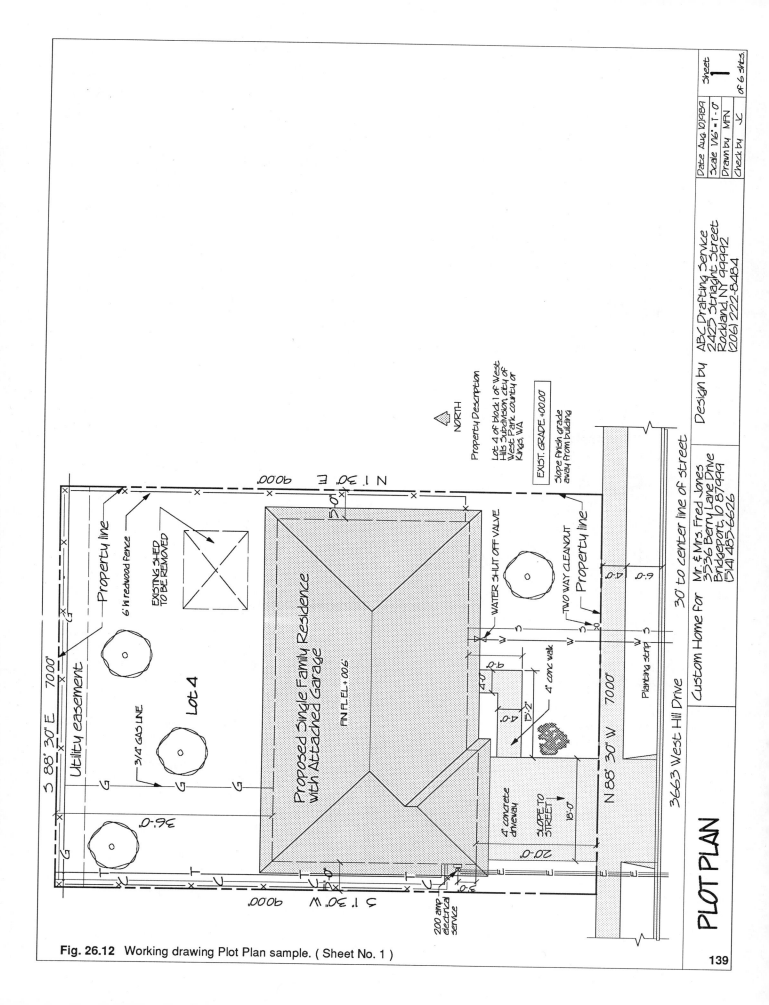

Fig. 26.12 Working drawing Plot Plan sample. (Sheet No. 1)

139

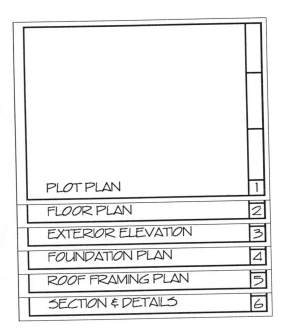

PLOT PLAN	1
FLOOR PLAN	2
EXTERIOR ELEVATION	3
FOUNDATION PLAN	4
ROOF FRAMING PLAN	5
SECTION & DETAILS	6

SECTION 11

UNIT 27

ASSEMBLING WORKING DRAWINGS

Objective: To learn to assemble all the sheets of the set of drawings into a complete set of finalized working drawings.

PREPARING A SET OF WORKING DRAWINGS

1. Review each of the sheets in the set of plans that you have drawn and check sheet numbers. Refer to the check list at the end of each plan sheet unit to verify that all applicable items are included on each sheet. (See Fig. 27.2 for page layout preferences.)

2. Design a cover sheet. Some building departments require that the two sets of plans they receive be bound together with a cover sheet (also called a title sheet). It serves the purpose of protecting the drawings and is a means of immediate identification.

There are no set rules about cover sheets. Some architects and designers place a rendering (perspective illustration) of the building on the cover sheet along with oversize identifying lettering; however clear identifying information is sufficient.

3. The most efficient procedure at this stage of plan development is to have several prints made from each of the sheets you have completed, including the cover sheet. (Refer to Unit 28, Making Prints.)

4. Organize the prints into complete sets by page number and bind them together at the left end by folding the edges over once or twice and stapling.

5. To ensure that you have covered all areas of required mechanical details accurately and to verify specifications, show the set of prints to subcontractors in the fields of heating and air conditioning, electrical work, plumbing, etc. On larger projects, the services of consultants such as an engineer and/or a landscape architect could be required.

6. You would also benefit from talking about your plans with consultants in the fields of interior design, kitchen and bathroom planning, cabinet suppliers and others where applicable.

7. When all of the new information is assembled, you will be in a position to make final decisions regarding all necessary details and to draw them on the plans and/or incorporate them in a list of items (called specifications) typically included with the set of plans.

EVALUATE CONSULTANTS SUGGESTIONS

After each consultant has studied the prints and made suggestions and recommendations, you can begin to finalize the working drawings. Information you obtain will relate to space requirements for such things as: air conditioning units (including the necessary duct work for them) electrical systems and fixtures, plumbing systems and fixtures, and landscaping.

Each person working with the plans will make suggestions for changes. It is advisable to keep an open mind in regard to changes at this point. Try to visualize the changes proposed by others. Some will be necessary if specific equipment is to be used. Many of the ideas gleaned from consultants whose expertise you trust will be valuable.

DESIGN CONTINUITY

Evaluate each suggestion in light of its effect on the plan as a whole. If, after evaluating each suggestion carefully, you decide that a particular change will create a design problem, seek another solution.

Guard against losing sight of the original design concept, thereby letting a hodgepodge of suggestions destroy the continuity and integrity of the plan. Only you, and the individuals for whom you are drafting the plans, understand what the overall goal is. The final decisions must be made after a careful evaluation of all the known facts has been made.

MAKING CHANGES
ON THE WORKING DRAWINGS

1. Most changes can be made on the plans by erasing carefully. Drafting vellum paper is made strong enough to withstand repeated erasures; however, if any of the drawings is becoming smeared and untidy and there are a great many changes to be made, it would be advisable to make a new drawing.

2. Fasten a fresh piece of vellum grid paper over the original drawing and match up the squares. Trace the accurate parts of the drawing and make the changes as you work. Save time by testing changes first on tracing paper overlays.

3. Consider the effect each change will have on other sheets of the working drawings and make a list of things to check for as you work.

ORGANIZING PLAN SHEETS

On larger design projects, the services of one or more design consultants may be required. Professional consultants often provide working drawings consisting of several consecutively numbered sheets. To distinguish one consultant's drawings from the others, each profession has a letter designating their subject area. This letter is placed in the title block on their plan sheet. (See the title block in Fig. 21.5.) The following list shows the standard letters usually used.

A   Architect
C   Civil Engineer
S   Structural Engineer
P   Plumbing
E   Electrical
M   Mechanical
L   Landscaping

VERIFYING PLAN ACCURACY
AFTER MAKING CHANGES

One of the most frequent causes of costly mistakes on drawings is changes. Each thing that is changed will probably effect something else. When your plans have progressed to an advanced stage before changes are made, be sure to check everything you have drawn against your original studies to make certain you have made all relevant changes and to study the effect each change will have on the total project. For example, moving a door or changing the direction it swings could necessitate relocation of a light switch. A window location or size that is changed on a floor plan would also have to be changed on the exterior elevation.

> **NOTE:** *Take the time needed to verify details and catch any errors or omissions in the working drawings. It is much easier and less costly to correct and redraw plans than it is to tear out and make changes during the course of construction.*

PLANNING FOR FUTURE ADDITIONS

If space or items are to be added to the house in the future, it is best not to show that information on the working drawings, but rather to keep it on a separate copy of the plans for your own reference. The only exception to this would be in instances where some work is to be done during construction in order to make later additions possible; for example, pipes in the walls (rough plumbing) for a future bathroom or electrical wiring for an appliance to be added later.

PREPARE A NEW SET OF PRINTS

When you are sure that all details are complete and the plans meet with the approval of all individuals involved, have several sets of plans printed (most building departments require two sets) and staple them together. The plans are now ready for submission to agencies or individuals requiring them.

Fig. 27.1 A set of working drawing prints.

PAGE LAYOUT PREFERENCES

The plan sheets in Fig. 27.2 show typical page layouts for each of the sheets comprising the sample set of plans. The plan sheets you have prepared should be organized numerically, as shown, with a cover sheet on top.

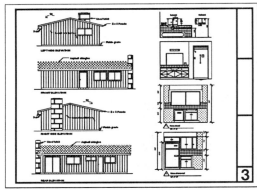

EXTERIOR ELEVATION, UNIT 24

COVER, UNIT 27

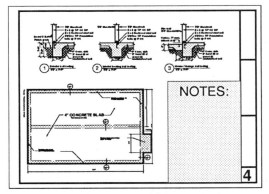

FOUNDATION PLAN, UNIT 22

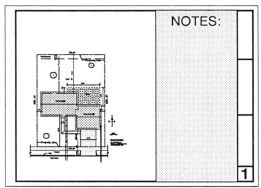

PLOT PLAN, UNIT 26

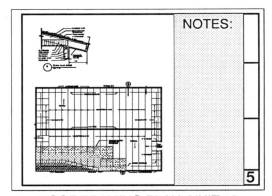

ROOF FRAMING PLAN, UNIT 23

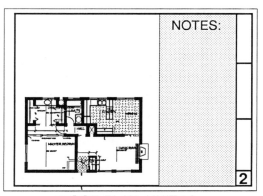

FLOOR PLAN, UNIT 20

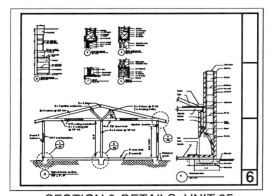

SECTION & DETAILS, UNIT 25

Fig. 27.2 Example of page layout preferences.

Translucent paper makes this task much easier. Second, good quality, inexpensive copies of any size are obtained from drawings produced on translucent paper.

House-plan drawings must be reviewed by the government agencies that will issue permits, lending institutions making construction loans on property, individuals involved with building the house and those who will figure the required building materials. Obviously, one cannot risk having fragile original drawings lost or defaced.

WHERE TO OBTAIN PRINTS

Almost all cities and even most small towns have printers who are equipped to copy your original drawings for a surprisingly low price. Look in the yellow pages of your telephone directory under "Blue Printers."

WHAT ARE BLUEPRINTS?

For many years, blueprinting was the method most commonly used for making prints of architectural drawings. This is a process in which the original drawing is fed into a machine along with a piece of sensitized blueprint paper. After exposure to a light source, the print goes through a wet process. The resulting copy is exactly like the original drawing except that the background is, as its name implies, blue in color. The lines from your original drawing appear on the blueprint as white. It is, in effect, a blue negative print. This type of print is very durable. It can withstand weather and rough handling on the job.

WHAT ARE WHITEPRINTS

Another method of making a print from an original is called whiteprinting. By this process an exact copy is made from an original. A whiteprinter is an uncomplicated machine. The original, along with a piece of sensitized paper, is fed into the machine and exposed to a light source. The print is then passed through a chamber where the image is developed. The resulting print is white. The linework on the original comes out blue on the print. The print is a positive copy of the original. This method is fast and inexpensive. Pencil notations show up clearly on a whiteprint copy. However, when prints are exposed to weather, the blue lines fade. Although white paper with blue lines is most commonly used for house plans, a variety of paper and image colors is available for use in whiteprinters.

SECTION 11
UNIT 28

MAKING PRINTS

Objective: *To learn how prints are made from drawings, and what types of prints are available.*

WHAT IS AN ORIGINAL?

Everything you draw when drafting plans for a home, whether it is a sketch or a carefully detailed and scaled drawing, is considered an original. Originals are always drawn on translucent paper. There are two reasons for this. First, it is frequently necessary to trace through one or more layers of drawings.

OFFICE COPY MACHINES

Office copy machines that reproduce large size drawings are also being used in some architects' and designers' offices. Office copy machines will make good copies from drawings prepared on either translucent or opaque paper. Check prints are often made in this way, and sometimes full sets of prints.

NONREPRODUCIBLE BLUES

Certain shades of blue do not reproduce by either the blueprinting or whiteprinting method of reproduction. The lines on the vellum grid drawing paper have been printed with one of these nonreproducible blues. Consequently, when prints are made from drawings on this type of paper, the blue grid lines do not appear on the print. Grid lines have been printed on drawing paper for convenience in preparing plans only.

Most stationery and drafting supply stores carry a special blue pencil called a *nonrepro* pencil. This pencil is handy for marking notations and calculations on the drawing that are not to appear on the print.

LINEWORK AND REPRODUCTION QUALITY

The appearance and legibility of a print will depend to a certain extent upon the quality of linework on the original drawing. It is suggested that you make a letter-sized sample on vellum grid drawing paper of different line weights drawn in the grades of lead you have been using. It will cost only a few cents to have a print made of this sample. From this experiment, you can tell how well your work reproduces in a print.

HOW SHADED LINES REPRODUCE

The ordinary blue colored pencil, recommended for shading certain areas on your drawing, will reproduce as shading on a print. Include on your sample some shading done with whatever brands of blue pencils you have available; select the best one, as revealed by the print, for all your shading work.

ADDITIONS

The term addition is used when new space of any kind is added to the floor space of an existing house. This space could be in the form of a room enlargement, a new bathroom, kitchen, garage, etc.

REMODELING AND ADDITIONS COMBINED

Remodeling and addition projects often overlap. Frequently new space is added simultaneously with revisions and improvements being made to the existing house.

OVERALL PLANNING
OF HOUSE, LOT, AND ADDITION

When you plan to make a change or an addition to a home, you must make an overall plan. Take into consideration the size and shape of the house, the lot, existing car facilities, space available for an addition, and local building regulations.

THE IMPORTANCE OF A PLOT PLAN

A remodeling project or an addition to a home may be visualized best on a plot plan, where you can clearly see the relationship of the changes and/or additions to the existing house and to the lot. When the existing house is drawn on a plot plan, you can also study the orientation of the house and the proposed addition to neighbor's properties, to the sun and to any special features of the lot. Refer to Unit 7, Sketching and to Unit 26, Plot Plans.

SECTION 12
UNIT 29

REMODELING AND ADDITIONS

Objective: To draw plans for a remodeling project, and/or an addition, which will meet all requirements, maximize use of the available floor space, utilize the lot effectively, and harmonize with the design of the house.

REMODELING

The term remodeling is used to describe changes and improvements being made to an existing house. These changes might include such things as the addition of a new window or door; relocating, repairing and painting walls; or installing new cabinets and countertops.

BEGIN WITH A PLAN
OF THE EXISTING HOUSE

When one is planning a remodeling project, it is essential to begin with a complete plan of the existing house. After you have drawn the house to 1/4" scale, it will be much easier for everyone involved in the project to visualize the desired revisions. When you are working on paper, solutions to space arrangement problems that might not otherwise be evident will occur to you.

MEASURING THE HOUSE

INTERIOR

The procedure for measuring and drawing an individual room in a home is given in Unit 6, Spatial Relationships.

1. On individual pieces of scratch paper attached to a clipboard, make sketches of the interior of each room as shown in Fig. 6.1. Identify each room by name. Measure a corner room first.

2. Measure the thickness of the interior partitions in the house. You will probably find that they are all the same thickness unless there is special treatment on one of the walls, such as brick or paneling.

EXTERIOR

1. Fasten a piece of letter-size paper to a clipboard or other firm, portable surface.

2. Walk around the outside of the house and make a rough sketch of the exterior shape, noting the jogs and offsets. Disregard the windows and doors.

3. Using the longest tape measure you can obtain, measure the exterior of the house and note the measurements on the sketch. When you are measuring, have someone hold the other end of the tape measure and place it on the wall above plants and shrubs where possible.

4. Correct the jogs and offsets as necessary on your sketch, and write in the measurements accurately.

5. Measure the thickness of the exterior wall as revealed in a window or a doorway. Do not include casing or molding thickness. (See Fig. 29.1).

DRAWING A FLOOR PLAN OF THE EXISTING HOUSE

A floor plan of the house, showing the addition, will help you to visualize spatial relationships between the existing and the new areas. New ways to effectively coordinate, integrate, and rearrange space and furnishings within the existing house may also be revealed. Minimum building department requirements include a floor plan showing rooms adjoining the proposed addition. Figure 29.3 shows a remodeling plan for the book sample house. Review Unit 5, Starting to Draw and Unit 20, Floor Plan.

1. Referring to your measurement sketch of the exterior of the house, lay out the exterior walls on vellum grid paper in 1/4" scale, using a 4H lead.

2. With all your measurement sketches in order for convenient reference, proceed to draw the interior partitions. Make notes of room measurements on your plan with a nonreproducible blue pencil, or keep your dimensioned sketches in good order.

3. Tracing from the drawing guides or using a general-purpose template, designate kitchen and bathroom appliances, fixtures, and cabinets on the plan. See Unit 8, Bathroom Layouts and Unit 9, Kitchen Layouts.

4. Designate window and door openings as shown in Figs. 5.2 and 3. Note the size of each.

5. Designate the direction in which the doors swing in each room.

6. It would be a convenience to have the electrical outlets, switches, and light fixtures shown on the plan, especially in areas where revisions are to be made. If you wish to include them, refer to Unit 12, Electrical Work and to Fig. 17.10.

7. When most of the details have been drawn on the plan, go over the wall lines, using a heavier pressure on your pencil. A softer lead, such as a 2H is desirable for this job. All other lines should be heavy enough to be visible through an overlay sheet of tracing paper or vellum. See Unit 2, Lettering and Lines, for recommended lead choices.

8. If the house has two or more stories, you will need a plan of each floor to be remodeled. Use a separate sheet of vellum grid paper for each floor. When drawings are complete, one plan can be placed over the other to check for accuracy of alignment.

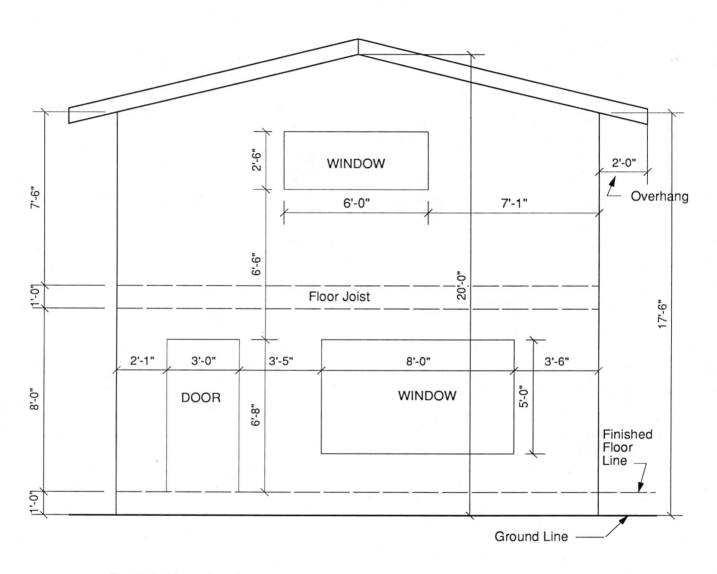

Fig. 29.1 Measuring a house.

SKETCHING REVISIONS FOR REMODELING

1. Study your completed floor plan-drawing carefully and make a list of desired revisions.

2. Tape tracing paper over your floor plan of the existing house and sketch the revisions on the tracing paper in 1/4" scale.

3. Test your revision ideas by placing appliances, fixtures, and furnishings in the new areas and rearranging them in the old. Use drawing-guide cutouts or tracings to facilitate visualization.

4. Verify visually that the new space arrangements you have created on paper are workable by comparing them to similar-size areas in the existing house.

5. Take time with this planning and use as many overlay sheets as necessary. Try different possibilities on paper.

Careful planning at this stage of the project will result in the best possible use of the available space. A good plan can save time and money by preventing needless mistakes and changes.

DEVELOPING THE FLOOR-PLAN DRAWING

1. When you are satisfied with your sketch for the proposed changes, remove the tracing paper.

2. Refer to your sketched changes and lightly mark, for your own reference, any walls that are to be removed.

3. Walls that are to be removed should be dashed on the plan with a heavier pressure on your well-pointed lead. The designation for walls to be removed is shown in Fig. 29.2. See Fig. 29.3 for an example of this designation on a floor plan.

4. Draw in any new walls using a light pressure on your well-pointed lead.

5. Lightly trace the details of cabinetry, fixtures, and appliances that are to remain in the remodeled house.

DESIGNATING NEW WORK

1. With medium weight lines, using a **2H** lead, draw any cabinetry, fixtures and appliances that are to be new. Place them in accordance with your new planning sketch. Units 10 through 18 give symbols and designations for drawing new work.

2. Designate any door openings or windows that are to be new. Refer to Fig. 29.3.

3. Trace the windows and doors that will remain unchanged in the existing house.

4. Go over all the wall lines, old and new, except those to be removed, with a heavier pressure on your pencil, preferably with a softer lead.

5. Shade the walls that are to be new with a colored pencil. Refer to Figures 29.2 through 4.

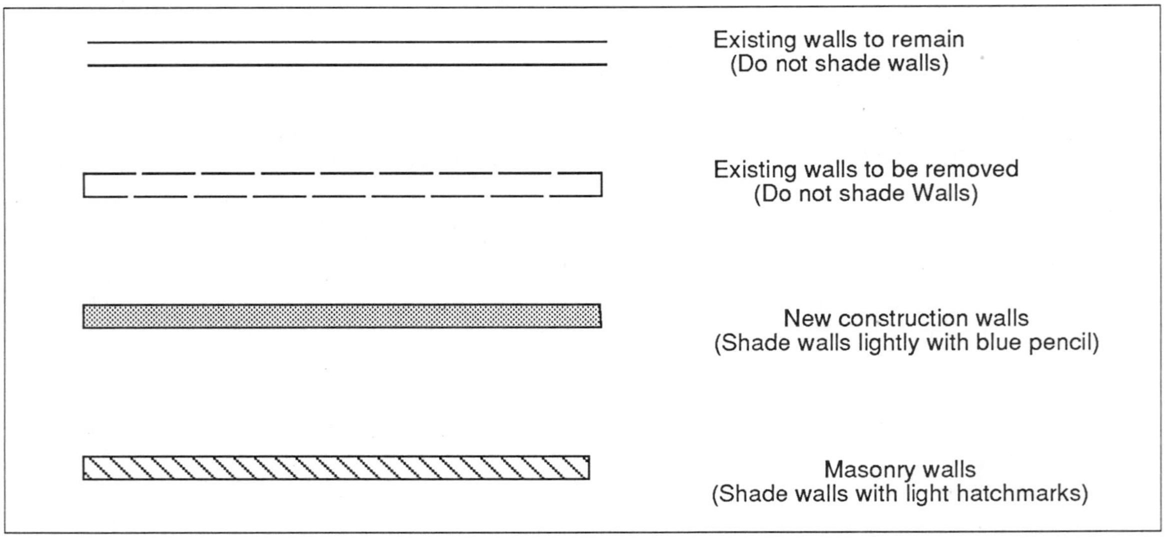

Fig. 29.2 Wall-shading legend.

Existing walls to remain
(Do not shade walls)

Existing walls to be removed
(Do not shade Walls)

New construction walls
(Shade walls lightly with blue pencil)

Masonry walls
(Shade walls with light hatchmarks)

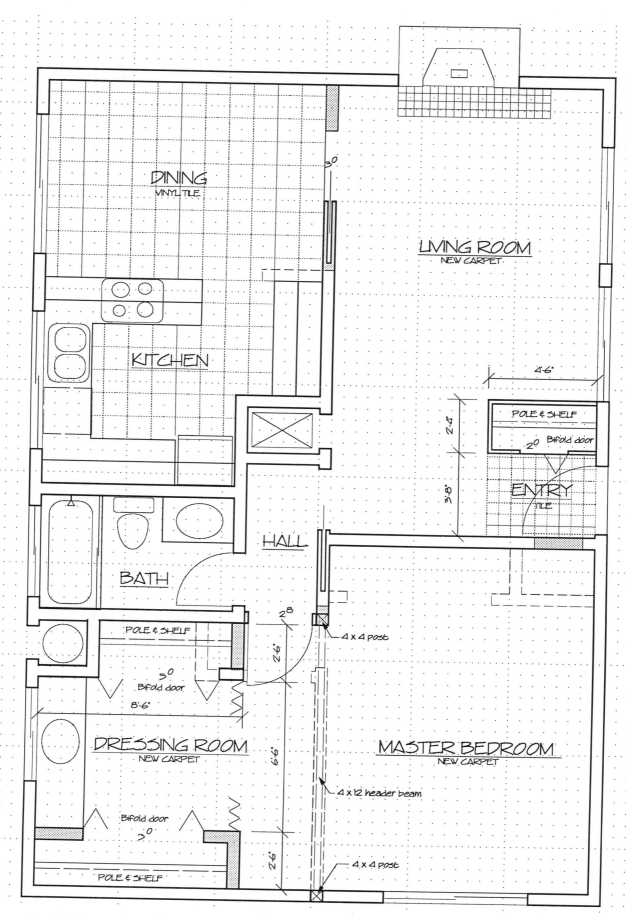

Fig. 29.3 A remodeling plan for the book sample house.

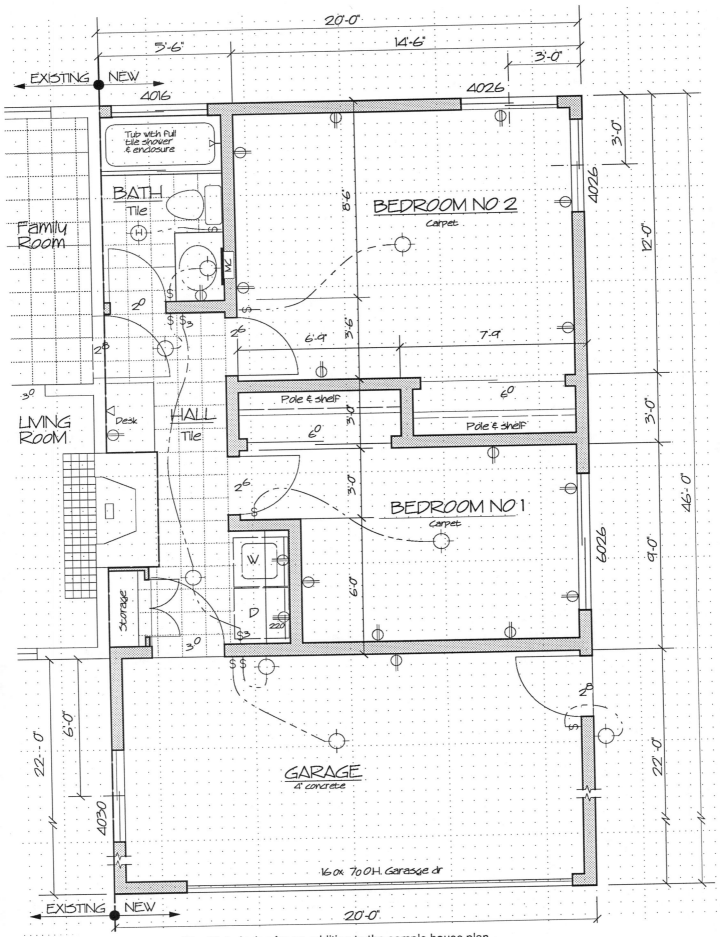

Fig. 29.4 A plan for an addition to the sample house plan.

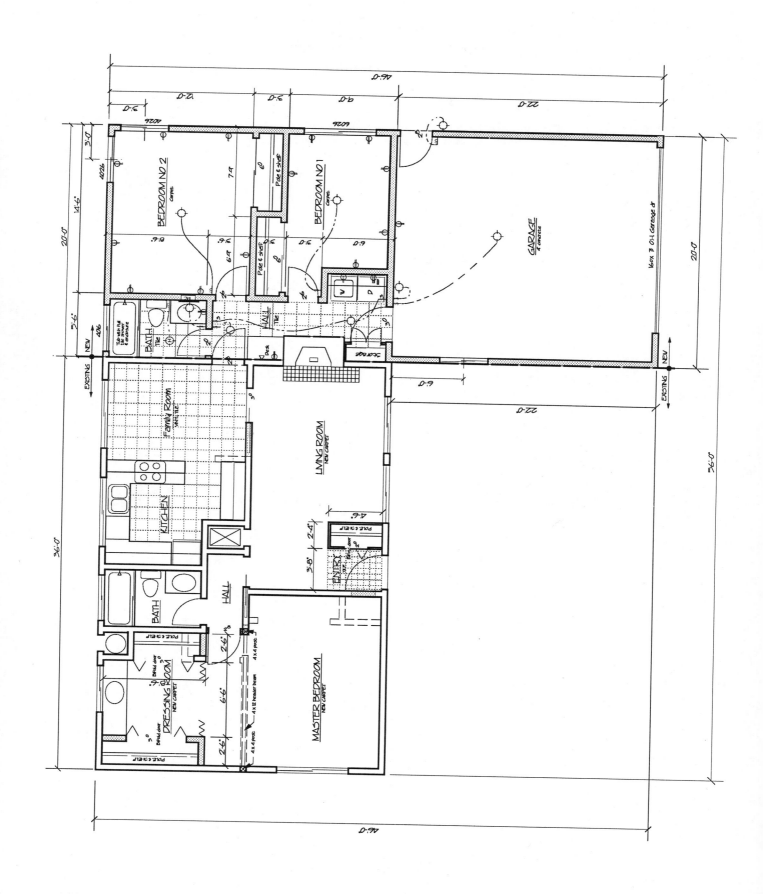

Fig. 29.5 The book sample plan shown with the remodeling and the addition combined. (Reduced to 1/8" scale.)

DRAWING AN EXTERIOR PLAN
FOR A REMODELING PROJECT

In many cases, interior remodeling does not affect the exterior. Sometimes a fresh coat of paint is all that is required. If this is true of the remodeling job you are planning, you will not need plans of the exterior. However, interior remodeling may create a need for new windows and changed door locations. In some cases, complete modernization or restoration of the exterior is desirable.

When alterations are to be made to the exterior, it is advisable to prepare drawings that clearly show the work to be done. Your project will become much more precise and understandable to everyone involved when you have drawings that show the exterior of the house as it will be when the changes are made. Unit 24, Exterior Elevations, explains the procedure to follow for drawing the exterior elevations. Plans for remodeling the exterior are drawn in the same way as drawings for a new home.

DRAWING THE HOUSE AND ADDITION
ON A PLOT PLAN

1. Draw a plot plan of the lot on a sheet of grid paper secured to your drawing surface. Use a light pressure on a well-pointed pencil.

2. Draw the existing house and all other features on the plot plan. Include the garage, driveway, other paving, trees, and garden areas.

3. Go over all the lines with heavier pressure on your pencil when the plot plan has been completed as shown in Fig. 26.11.

4. Add accurate size information. For dimensioning procedures, see Unit 21, Dimensions and Notes.

5. Sketch the addition on a sheet of tracing paper fastened over your completed plot plan.

6. Try several shapes and space arrangements and experiment with all possibilities. Make as many overlays as necessary to achieve an addition that seems to satisfy the requirements and fit within the setback allowances.

7. When you are satisfied with your final sketch, draw the details of the addition carefully on the plot-plan drawing.

NOTE: *If you are not sure about the setback requirements on the lot you are working with, this would be a good time to check with someone in your local planning or building department. You can then draw accurate plans.*

SKETCHING FLOOR PLANS
FOR THE ADDITION

Referring to your plot-plan studies, sketch the addition.

1. Fasten tracing paper securely over the floor plan of the existing house on the drawing surface.

2. Using vellum grid drawing paper, make an overlay of the original drawing. Trace the wall lines of the existing house with a light pressure on your well-pointed pencil.

3. Use dashed lines to represent walls to be removed.

4. Add the lines representing the walls of the addition. Designate any new windows and doors. Lines representing new walls are to be shaded according to the legend in Fig. 29.2.

5. Draw any remaining details, such as kitchen and bathroom fixtures, cabinetry, and the electrical diagram. Refer to Units 8 through 16 for symbols and designations.

NOTE: *Since the addition will be all new work, that portion of the plan will have to be drawn as for new construction. Refer to Unit 20, Floor Plans.*

DRAWING EXTERIOR ELEVATIONS FOR AN ADDITION

It will be helpful to make drawings of the exterior that show how the new work will look. The information given in Unit 24, Exterior Elevations, will show you how to draw elevation views of the house.

1. Begin by Measuring the exterior of the house.

2. Lay out and draw each of the four side views of the exterior of the house. Refer to Unit 24, Exterior Elevations.

SKETCHING THE CHANGES

1. Begin the changes when your drawing of the exterior of the house is complete. Fasten tracing paper over one of the side views that is to be changed in preparation for drawing the revisions.

2. Make as many quick sketches as possible on tracing paper overlays to achieve the best possible solution to design problems.

3. Experiment with several different roof plans and exterior finish materials. (See Figs. 24.15 through 19.) Make as many drawings as necessary to achieve a pleasing effect.

4. Continue to make sketches for each side of the house to be changed.

FINISHING THE DRAWING

1. Draw the new work accurately over the initial elevation drawing of the existing house. The lines used to represent the existing house should be lighter than those representing the addition. (See Fig. 29.5.)

In designing the exterior, avoid a mixture of styles and treatments. Try for continuity of design. In restoration projects, it is important to retain original design concepts and match the new construction materials to the old.

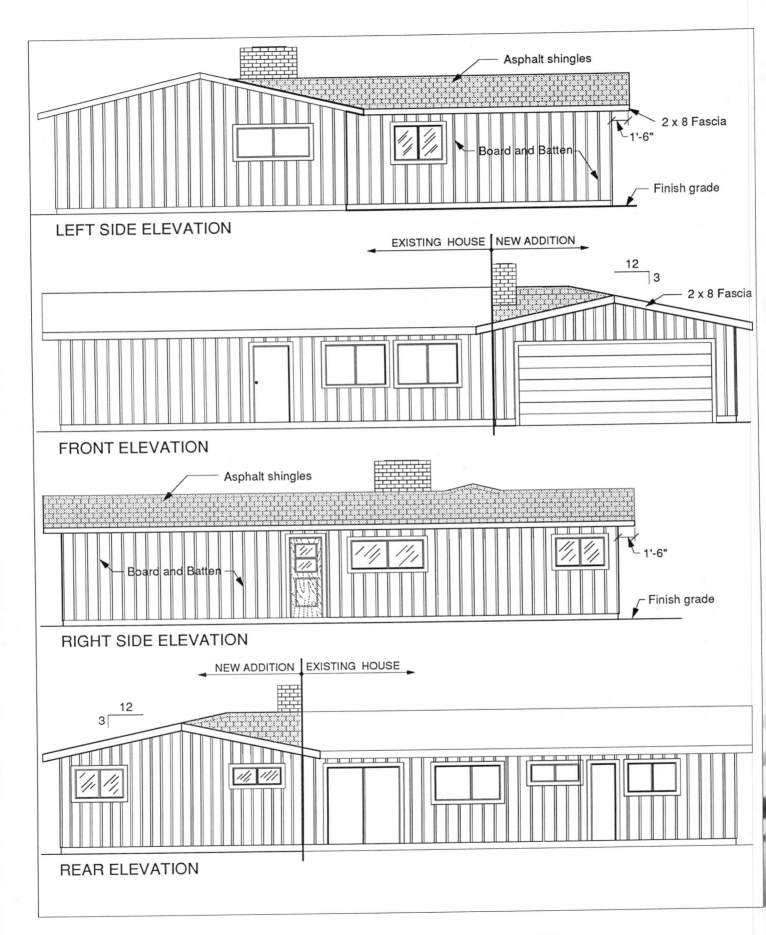

FIG. 29.5 Elevation views of an existing house showing a proposed addition.

BEGIN WITH A SUITABLE FLOOR PLAN

Not all floor plans lend themselves well to changes and additions. The plan selected should require the very minimum number of alterations.

Any plan selected should be studied for suitability of design. The size of the house, as well as the sizes of the individual rooms, is an important consideration, as this influences its ultimate cost.

A major factor that should not be overlooked is the suitability of the plan for the building site and for local weather conditions.

PUT YOUR PLAN TO THE TEST

The only way you can be sure that the right plan has been selected for the purpose is to subject it to the following tests:

1. Make a small-scale drawing of the lot by following the instructions given in Unit 26, Plot Plans.

2. Make the first study of the plan by sketching it on the plot plan, as in Unit 7, Sketching. To do this, fasten tracing paper over the plot-plan drawing and make several quick sketches or bubble diagrams of the plan.

3. Analyze the best use of lot space as explained in Unit 26, Plot Plans.

4. If, as you try different planning arrangements on tracing paper laid over your plot plan, you find that there are problems, such as a poorly located driveway, the sun striking the house on the wrong side, or bedrooms on the noisy side of the lot, try turning over your bubble diagram (which has been drawn on tracing paper), thereby reversing the plan. Lay the reversed plan on the plot plan for study. This will show you how a reversed version of the plan would work on the lot. Reversing a plan often makes a significant difference in the livability of a house. (See Figs. 30.1 and 2.)

SECTION 12

UNIT 30

MODIFYING EXISTING PLANS

Objective: To learn to analyze an existing floor plan and revise, modify, or add to it while retaining all of its attractive and functional features.

MODIFYING PLANS

An existing plan is often selected because of one or two outstanding features that seem particularly suited to the project. However, careful analysis usually reveals several things that must be revised.

If your project is to revise a floor plan, revisions must are made carefully, with skill and thought. The methods and materials provided in this book will help you to make the necessary changes or additions. The revised plan should lose nothing of its
original attractiveness, meets all requirements, and be oriented to advantage on the lot.

DRAWING ROOM STUDIES

It is important that you carefully study each of the rooms in the plan to be sure that they meet requirements and will accommodate the furnishings, appliances, and equipment to be used. Work out the details for each room in the plan. See Unit 17, Room Studies. When you have completed the necessary studies and are sure that the best possible plan for the purpose has been selected, you will be ready to make the required changes.

EXAMPLES OF FLOOR-PLAN CHANGES

Figures 30.3 and 5 are floor-plan examples. Various changes have been made to these plans in Figs. 30.4 and 6. Note that the changes are very simple and have been made without radically changing the design.

ADDING PLUMBING

If extra bathroom facilities are planned, it is often economical to keep areas requiring plumbing as close together as possible. If substantial plumbing changes are required, it would be advisable to consult a plumber about the feasibility of your ideas. Plumbing is one area of construction where cost is often related to the location of fixtures.

DRAWING THE DESIRED CHANGES

1. Fasten the 1/4" scale drawing of the original plan onto the drawing surface.

2. Cover it with an overlay of tracing paper securely fastened to the board.

3. Sketch the desired changes on the tracing paper.

4. Make as many of these sketches as necessary to get the changes exactly as you want them. Consider all aspects carefully and evaluate each change and its effect on the overall plan.

5. Select your final and best sketch and draw a more carefully prepared preliminary drawing, as shown Unit 18, Preliminary Plans.

6. When you are satisfied that your preliminary floor plan reflects the required changes, proceed with the preparation of working drawings. Refer to Units 20 through 26.

CHANGING EXTERIOR ELEVATIONS

1. Trace the 1/4" scale drawings of the exterior elevations lightly on a large sheet of vellum grid drawing paper. See Unit 24, Exterior Elevations.

2. Referring to your floor-plan drawing, make all relevant changes to the elevations.

3. Complete the drawing as shown in Unit 24, Exterior Elevations.

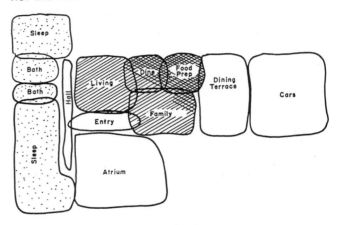

Fig. 30.1 A bubble diagram.

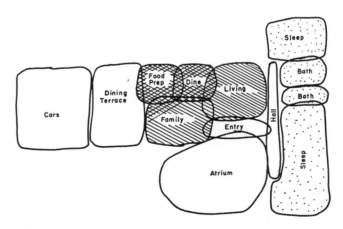

Fig. 30.2 A bubble diagram reversed.

Fig. 30.3 Floor Plan No. 1.

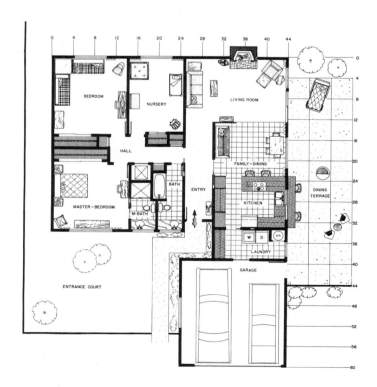

Fig. 30.4 Floor Plan No.1 revised.

Fig. 30.5 Floor plan No. 2.

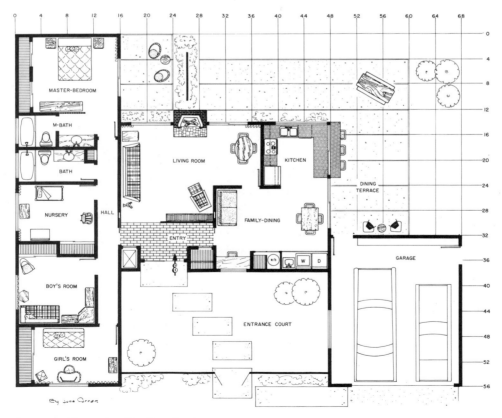

Fig. 30.6 Floor plan No. 2 revised.

A

ATRIUM
An inner court with an open space in the roof.

ATTIC
The space between the ceiling and the roof rafters.

B

BACKING
Backing consists of 2- x 4 inch or 2- x 6 inch lumber nailed horizontally between studs to give solid support for anything that will be attached to finished walls, such as bathroom accessories, drapery rods, etc.

BASEBOARD
A trim board applied after the finish floor has been installed to cover the joint where the floor and wall meet.

BEAM CEILING
A ceiling in which the beams are exposed. Sometimes called an exposed beam ceiling.

BEARING WALLS
Walls structurally capable of supporting the roof load.

BIFOLD DOORS
A door made up of pairs of narrow panels, hinged together.

BLUEPRINTS
Prints made from original translucent drawings.

BOARD AND BAT SIDING
A type of exterior wall finishing for wood-frame houses. Boards or sheets of plywood are applied vertically. The joints are covered with narrow strips of wood called bats. They are usually spaced 16 inches or 24 inches on center.

BUILDING PAPER, ASPHALT IMPREGNATED
A waterproof felt material, available in rolls of various widths and weights. Common applications are on roofs, under shingles or shakes and as an underlayment for built-up roofs. It is also nailed onto the framework of the exterior walls of a wood frame house under stucco or siding.

BUILT-UP ROOF
This is roof treatment consisting of multiple layers of asphalt-impregnated roofing felt, alternately mopped with heated, fluid tar; also called a tar and felt roof.

BUILDING LINES
Dashed lines drawn on a plan of a lot to define the area within which a house or garage may be built; also referred to as setbacks.

BUILT-UP ROOF
A roof treated with layers of felt and asphalt, also called a tar and felt roof.

C

CARPORT
A shelter for a car composed of a roof supported by corner posts. Some carports have storage walls in the end or along one side.

CASING
The visible trim or molding around a door or window.

CL (CENTER LINE)
A line that marks the center of any given space.

CLEANOUT HOLES
In a masonry fireplace, an opening in the bottom course of brick, or in the floor of the firebox; for removal of ashes.

CONCRETE
Concrete is a mixture of sand, gravel and cement used for foundations, floors, patios, driveways,etc.

CRAWL SPACE
The space below the floor of a house usually enclosed by the foundation wall.

CRIPPLE STUD
This is a 2- x 4 inch framing member that has been cut off to fit below or above a framed opening in an exterior or interior wall.

CROSS-SECTION PAPER
Drafting paper on which squares have been printed to indicate scale.

D

DIAGONAL BRACE
A 1" x 4" brace placed diagonally in a framed wall to provide lateral support.

DIAZO PRINTING MACHINE
A machine used to make prints from drawings originally prepared on translucent paper such as vellum.

DIMENSION LINE
A line drawn for the purpose of indicating the distance between two points.

DIMENSIONING SYSTEM
A method of showing actual measurements on scaled drawings.

DIMENSIONS
Figures which indicate actual sizes on scale drawings.

DOWNSPOUT
A vertical pipe that connects to a roof gutter and carries water to the ground.

DUCTS
Round, square, or oval shaped tubes used to conduct cooled or heated air to outlets in individual rooms; usually made of noncombustible material such as sheet metal.

E

EAVE
The underside of that portion of a roof which overhangs or projects beyond exterior walls.

ELEVATIONS, EXTERIOR
Views of the exterior sides of a house or other structure.

ELEVATIONS, WALL
Vertical views of interior walls of a structure.

EXTENSION LINES
Lines which extend from the exterior corners of a building to show the beginning and ending of dimension lines.

F

FACADE
The frontal treatment of a building.

FACE BRICK
Brick used to face a wall for decorative purposes.

FACIA
Facia board, usually 2 x 6, 2 x 8, or 2 x 10 inch lumber, is nailed onto the ends of the overhanging rafters of a roof. The facia is used for trim effect and can be an important element of the design.

FIREBOX
The portion of a fireplace that contains the fire. In masonry fireplaces the firebox is lined with brick that has been hardened and made heat-resistant; called fire brick.

FLOOR SLAB, CONCRETE
A slab of concrete that creates a floor. This slab covers and becomes a part of the footings. Typically, a concrete floor slab is 4 inches thick and is poured over 4 inches of gravel, a vapor barrier, and steel mesh reinforcing. When a floor slab is used, the ground is graded to slope away from the house to drain water away from the foundation.

FOOTINGS
The concrete supporting base of the foundation wall. Footings are placed in undisturbed ground and extend to a depth below the frost line. Their purpose is to support the house and prevent settling.

FOUNDATION, CRAWL-SPACE
In instances where a floor-joist system is to be used, a wall is constructed on top of the footings. It can be of concrete and poured at the same time as the footings, or of cement block or brick. The average foundation wall is installed so that there is 18 inches of crawl space between the bottom of the floor joists and the ground. With this system, pipes for plumbing and heating and cooling ducts can be installed beneath the floor.

G

GLASS, INSULATING
Windows which are glazed with two pieces of glass spaced apart, about one quarter of an inch and sealed to form a single unit with an air space between. This process is also called double glazing.

GLASS, LAMINATED OR SHATTER RESISTANT
A layer of clear plastic is fused between two sheets of glass to prevent shattering.

GLASS, OBSCURE
Opaque, decorative glass usually used for privacy in bathroom windows and other areas requiring privacy.

GLASS, PATTERN
A variety of patterns, designs, and colors are used to make glass decorative, create privacy or diffuse light.

GLASS, PLATE
Polished glass that is without the waves characteristic of sheet glass, varies in thickness from 1/8 to 1-1/4 inches thick.

GLASS, SAFETY
Laminated, tempered and wire glass are all preferred for safety characteristics.

GLASS, SHEET
Sheet glass has a characteristic waviness. It comes in single strength (3/32 inches thick), double strength (1/8 inches thick) and heavy (3/16, 7/32 and 1/4 inches.)

GLASS, TEMPERED
Glass which has been heat strengthened.

GRAPH PAPER
Drafting paper marked off in squares for use in scale drawing.

GUTTERS AND DOWN-SPOUTS
Troughs and pipes that carry rain water off the roof and away from a house or other structure.

H

HEADER
A beam placed above a framed opening for a window, door, closet, fireplace, etc. The header size is determined by the width of the opening and the weight that it will carry.

HEARTH
The noncombustible floor area in front of a fireplace.

HEAT LOSS (OR GAIN) CALCULATIONS
Calculations made to determine the amount of heat transmission through exterior walls, windows, roof, or floors.

HOSE BIB
A water faucet, located on the outside of a house, with a fitting to which a hose can be attached.

I

INSULATION
Material used in walls and ceilings to prevent heat from penetrating or escaping from ceiling or exterior walls.

J

JOISTS
Beams used in a floor-joist system to support the floors.

L

LEACHING LINES
Part of a leaching system consisting of a series of perforated pipes which allow the effluent from a septic tank to leach into the soil.

LOT BOUNDARY LINE
The survey line around the perimeter of a piece of property that indicates the legal boundaries.

M

MASONRY
Stone, brick, block, tiles, or concrete, used to form the walls or other parts of a structure.

MECHANICAL PENCIL
A pencil made especially for drafting consisting of a metal or plastic holder into which separate leads are inserted. Leads of various grades are interchangeable in this type of pencil.

MOLDING
Decoratively shaped trim, usually of wood, used to finish joints such as those in wall finishes, at the ceiling line, or to trim openings such as doors, windows, etc.

N

NORTH ARROW
An arrow drawn on a plot to indicate the direction of north.

O

ON CENTER
The words "on center," abbreviated OC when used in reference to wood framing, mean that measurements are given from the center of one framing member to the center of the next. For example, framing studs are usually spaced at 16 inches OC.

OPAQUE PAPER
Paper you cannot see pencil lines through when tracing.

ORIENTATION
The way the house is placed on the lot in relationship to the sun.

OVERHANG
That portion of the roof, second story, or deck that projects beyond the exterior walls.

OVERLAY
Translucent tracing paper laid over a drawing for the purpose of revising the first drawing.

P

PLATES
There are three framing members described as plates: (a) Bottom Plate: The bottom horizontal member of a framed wall or partition (sometimes called a sole plate). (b) Top Plate: The top horizontal member of a framed wall or partition. (c) Cap Plate: After the framed walls and partitions are in place, the cap plate is installed. It is nailed to the top plate in such a way as to tie all wall and partition framing together.

PLOT PLAN
A plan of a lot showing the existing features and the proposed new construction.

PRELIMINARY PLAN
A sketch representing first ideas for the shape of a house and the arrangement for rooms.

PLYWOOD
A sheet of laminated wood, usually 4' x 8', but available in other lengths. It is made of three or more layers of veneer (thin wood) laminated (glued) together. It is available in several thicknesses and in a tongue-and-groove pattern. It is used as sheathing on roofs and over floor joists as subflooring. It is also used in some instances on exterior walls as sheathing and for shear panels.

R

RAIN DIVERTERS
Sheet metal troughs placed over entrances to divert water.

RAFTERS
Framing members used to form the skeleton of a roof.

RIDGE
The horizontal line of the top edge of a roof where the two sloping sides meet.

ROOF GUTTER
A shallow horizontal trough, usually of sheet metal, used to carry water off a roof to a down spout.

ROOF PITCH
The rise or slope of a roof.

ROOF SHEATHING
When plywood is nailed over roof framing, it is called roof sheathing. Roofing materials are applied over it.

ROOF TRUSS
Prefabricated roof framing.

ROUGH-IN PLUMBING
Permanent, concealed parts of piping, usually in the framed wall.

ROUGH SILL
The horizontal framing member at the bottom of a window opening is the rough sill.

RUNNING BOND
A masonry pattern, also called 1/2 bond.

S

SCALE
A line length used to represent a unit of measure (as a quarter of an inch to a foot). Also a measuring instrument.

SCHEMATIC DIAGRAM
A bubble diagram.

SETBACK
Space requirements regarding the placement of a house on a lot. City or county planning departments usually require that houses be set back from the lot boundary lines a certain distance. These requirements vary and must be verified with local planning or building departments.

SHAKES
Shake roofing material, usually of cedar or redwood, is similar to shingles, but shakes are thicker and longer. Shakes are available in medium and heavy weights and give a massive rustic look to a house.

SHINGLES

Shingles are uniformly shaped, individual pieces of roofing material that are nailed to the roof sheathing (either strips of wood called skip sheathing or solid plywood) in overlapping rows. The term is used to cover a wide variety of types of roofing materials, such as wood, asphalt, slate, ceramic, asbestos, etc. Shingles of various types are also used as siding for special effects.

SIDING

Most materials, other than stucco or masonry, which are used to cover the outside walls of a wood framed house are called siding. Materials commonly used are various types of wood, manufactured in sheets measuring 4 ft. in width by 8, 9, or 12 ft. in length, or boards to be installed either horizontally, vertically or diagonally. Aluminum or vinyl products and various types of shingles are also suitable siding materials.

SOLID-CORE DOOR

A door with a core that is solid as opposed to one that is hollow.

SPECIFICATIONS

Descriptions of materials, equipment, construction methods, standards and workmanship requirements. Included as part of the plan and the construction contract.

SQUARE FOOTAGE

A unit of measurement used to define the floor area of a house.

STACKED BOND

A masonry pattern

STUDS

Studs in wood framing are usually 2 in. x 4 in. They are used to frame exterior walls and interior partitions. Studs are usually spaced at 16" OC, which means they are spaced 16" apart when measuring from the center of one stud to the center of the next. In some areas building codes approve 24" OC spacing in residential frame construction.

SUBDIVISION MAP

A map of the subdivision in which subject property is located. Usually prepared by the developer and approved by city or county planners.

SUBFLOOR

A floor nailed on top of the floor joists to form a rigid base for finish flooring such as asphalt, vinyl tile or carpet. T & G (tongue-and- groove) plywood is often used for this purpose.

T

TEMPERED GLASS

Heat strengthened glass used where safety glass is required.

TONGUE AND GROOVE

Tongue-and-groove is abbreviated T & G. Some plywood, planking, siding, and insulation boards are finished on the long side so that they will fit together. There is a tongue on one edge which fits into a corresponding groove on the adjoining sheet.

TRAFFIC PATHS

The paths through a house where people are most apt to walk from one area or room to another.

TRIMMER STUDS

Trimmer studs are the short 2- x 4 inch framing members which support each end of a header.

V

VAPOR BARRIER

Sheet plastic or polyurethane are usually used when a vapor barrier is required beneath a concrete floor slab.

VELLUM

Translucent paper suitable for drafting purpose.

W

WALLBOARD

Wall finishing material, usually of gypsum or wood paneling that is nailed to framing studs and finished in a variety of ways.

WEATHERSTRIP

Metal, rubber, vinyl, or fabric used around doors and windows to make them as airtight as possible.

WHITEPRINTING

A method of making prints from original translucent drawings.

WINDOW SASH

The wood or metal surrounding the glass in any type of window.

WING

A part of a building extending out from the main structure.

These housing code requirements have been excerpted from the Uniform Building Code. A copy of the housing code requirements, as adopted by each city or county, can be obtained from local building departments.

TITLE SHEET

1. Indicate on the title sheet of the plans, the names of the legal owners and of the person responsible for the preparation of the plans.

2. Specify on the title sheet of the plans the gross floor area of each element of this project including dwelling, garage, carport, patio, deck, and balcony.

PLOT PLAN

1. Submit a fully dimensioned plot plan drawn to scale showing the north arrow. Include the location, size, and use of all existing and proposed structures on the lot. Identify property lines and show lot dimensions and all easements. Show distances between all structures, proposed and existing, and property lines.

2. Projections, including eaves, may not extend more than 12 inches into the required setback from the property lines. Eaves over required windows shall be not less than 30 inches from the side and rear property lines.

3. Note on the plan that surface water will drain away from the building and show the drainage pattern.

4. Show the lot and finish floor elevations.

FLOOR PLAN

1. All rooms to be identified as to use. Show dimensions of all rooms.

2. Superficial floor area: Every dwelling unit shall have not less than 150 square feet of superficial floor area. Every room which is used for both cooking and living or both living and sleeping purposes shall have not less than 150 square feet of superficial floor area. Other habitable rooms shall have an area of not less than 70 square feet. Where more than two persons occupy a room used for sleeping purposes, the required superficial floor area shall be increased at the rate of 50 square feet for each occupant in excess of two. Other habitable rooms, except kitchens, shall have not less than 70 square feet with the

least dimension not less than 7 feet. Superficial floor area is defined as clear floor space exclusive of fixed or built-in cabinets or appliances.

3. Habitable rooms, other than kitchens, shall contain at least 70 square feet of floor area with no dimension less than 7 feet.

4. Window area must be at least 1/10 of the floor area with a minimum of 10 square feet in all habitable rooms.

5. Openable window area in habitable rooms must be 1/20 of the floor area and a minimum of 5 square feet. In bathrooms, laundry rooms, and similar rooms, 1/20 of the area is required and the minimum is 1.5 square feet.

6. If light and ventilation are being supplied from an adjacent room, at least 1/2 of the common wall must be open and have an opening of not less than 25 square feet.

7. Required windows shall not open into a roofed porch unless the ceiling of the porch is at least 7 feet high and the longer side is at least 65% open.

8. Provide mechanical ventilation capable of providing five air changes per hour in bathrooms, water closet compartments, laundry rooms, and similar rooms if required openable windows are not provided.

9. Sleeping rooms shall have a window or exterior door for emergency exit. Sill height shall not exceed 44 inches above the floor. The window must have an openable area of at least 5.7 square feet with the minimum openable width of 20 inches and a minimum openable height of 24 inches.

10. For habitable rooms, show that ceiling height is a minimum of 7' - 6". Show that the ceiling height for laundry rooms, hallways, corridors and bathrooms is a minimum of 7 feet.

11. Walls and soffits of enclosed usable space under interior stairs shall be protected on the enclosed side as required for one-hour fire-resistive construction. Detail 16 inches maximum spacing of framing members supporting gypsum board.

12. For wood-framed floor joist systems, show minimum under floor access of 18" x 24".

13. Provide a floor plan of rooms adjoining proposed addition. Indicate any window or doors which are affected by the addition.

14. Show location of attic access with minimum size 22" x 30". Detail how the access opening is to be framed if rafters or trusses do not provide adequate space.

15. A door may open inward at the top step of a stairway provided top step is not more than 7 1/2" lower than the floor level.

16. Garage requires one-hour fire protection on the garage side of walls and ceiling common to the dwelling. Detail 16 inches maximum spacing of ceiling framing members supporting gypsum board. Walls supporting ceiling require equivalent fire protection.

17. Show 1 3/8" solid core self-closing door for openings between garage and dwelling.

18. All elements supporting floor above garage, including walls supporting floor joists, to have one-hour, fire-resistive protection on the garage side.

19. A garage is not permitted to open into a room used for sleeping purposes.

20. Doors may open into the garage only if the floor or landing in the garage is not more than 1/2" lower than the door threshold.

21. Provide an 18" raised platform for any FAU, water heater, or other device in the garage which may generate a flame or spark.

22 Show the locations of the water heater and heating/cooling appliances.

23. Show the source of combustion air to furnace/water heater.

24. Furnace and/or water heater shall not be installed in any bedroom, bathroom or in a closet or confined space with access only through such room, unless specified as direct vent appliance, enclosed furnace or electric heating appliance.

25. Show I.C.B.O. approval number for prefab fireplace.

26. Show location of permanently wired smoke detector, centrally located in corridor leading to sleeping rooms or above stairs if sleeping rooms are on upper level.

27. Show on the plan the amperage of the electrical service, the location of the service panel and the location of any subpanels. If residence exceeds 1800 square feet, provide 200 amp service or provide service sizing calculation on attached form.

28. Show location of all electrical receptacles, switches and fixtures.

29. Note convenience outlets in bathroom, outdoors and in garage and basements (other than for laundry and similar equipment) shall be GFI protected.

30. Dimension on the plans, the 30 inch clear width for water closet compartments and 24 inch clearance in from of water closet.

31. Show T and P Value on water heater and show route of discharge line to exterior.

32. Provide dryer vent to outside.

33. Note on the plan that the hose bibbs and lawn sprinkler system shall have approved backflow prevention devices.

FOUNDATION PLAN

1. Note on plans that wood shall be 6 inches minimum above finish grade.

2. Dimension foundation per U.B.C.

Floor supported	Stemwall	Width	Depth*
1	6"	12"	12"
2	8"	15"	18"

Provide two #4 reinforcing bars in all footings.
*Depth is below undisturbed soil.

3. Show foundation sills (mudsills) to be pressure treated or equal.

4. Show foundation bolt size and spacing.

5. Where applicable, show concrete pier size 14" x 14" or 16 square foot - spacing - and depth into undisturbed soil.

6. If holddowns are required, note on plan that holddown anchors must be tied in place prior to foundation inspection.

7. Provide continuous reinforced footings beneath all interior bearing walls.

8. For floor-joist systems, show minimum underfloor ventilation equal to 1 square foot for each 150 square feet of under-floor area. Openings shall be as close to corners as practicable and shall provide cross ventilation on at least two approximately opposite sides.

FRAMING PLANS AND SECTIONS

1. For floor-joist systems, show minimum 18 inches clearance from grade to bottom of floor joists and minimum 12 inches clearance to bottom of girders.

2. Show garage framing section, size of header over garage door opening, lateral cross bracing at plate line, method of bracing garage front, and holddowns if required.

3. Provide roof framing, ceiling-joist framing and, where a floor-joist system is used, floor-framing plans.

4. Show solid blocking at ridge line and at exterior walls on trussed roofs.

5. Show rafter purlin braces to be not less than 45 degrees to the horizontal.

6. Show that purlins are to be no smaller than the rafters supported.

7. Show rafter ties. Rafter ties shall be spaced not more than 4 feet on center and be just above the ceiling joists, where rafters and ceiling joists are not parallel.

8. Show 1/2 inches minimum clearance between top plate of interior partitions and bottom chord of trusses and truss clips typical.

9. Specify roof slope.

10. Roof slope must be adequate for roof type specified.

11. Specify roof material and application. Show weight of felt.

12. Where applicable, provide skylight details.

13. Plastic skylights must be separated from each other by at least 4 feet.

14. Show attic ventilation. Minimum required vent area is 1/150 of attic area or 1/300 of attic area if at least 50% of the required vent is at least 3 feet above eave vents or cornice vents. Show required area and area provided.

15. Note cross bridging or blocking. Floor joists and rafters 12 inches or more in depth shall be supported laterally by bridging at intervals not exceeding 8 feet, unless both edges are held in line.

16. When using a floor-joist system, floor joists shall be double under bearing partitions running parallel with the joists.

17. Bearing partition, perpendicular to joists, shall not be offset from supporting girders, beams, walls or partitions, more than the depth of the joist.

18. Show wall bracing. Every exterior wood stud wall and main cross partition shall be braced at each end at least every 25 feet of length with 1 x 4 diagonal let-in brace or equivalent.

19. Show wall-framing section. Indicate interior and exterior wall covering and insulation R value.

20. Show double top plate with minimum 48 inch lap splice.

21. Show that nailing will be in compliance with code.

22. Show stud size and spacing. Maximum allowable stud heights; bearing wall: 2 x 4 and 2 x 6 maximum 10 feet; non-bearing: 2 x 4 maximum 14', 2 x 6 maximum 20 feet.

23. Specify all header sizes for opening over 4' wide.

24. Specify plywood grade and panel identification index.

25. When roof pitch is less than 3:12, design ridge as a beam.

26. Show or note fire-stop at the following locations per code.

   a. At all interconnections between concealed vertical and horizontal spaces such as occur at soffits, drop ceilings and cove ceilings.

   b. In concealed spaces between stair stringers at the top and bottom of the run and between studs along and in line with the run of stairs if the walls under the stairs are unfinished; and

   c. In openings around vents, pipes, ducts, chimneys, fireplaces, and similar openings which afford a passage for fire at ceiling and floor levels, with noncombustible materials.

27. When trusses are used, provide truss details, calculations, and lay out plan.

28. Columns and posts located on concrete or masonry floors or decks exposed to the weather or to water splash or in basements and which support permanent structures shall be supported by concrete piers or metal pedestals projecting above floors unless approved wood of natural resistance to decay or treated wood is used.

29. Show plywood sheathing over exposed eaves, or other weather-exposed area, to be Exterior Exposure I or C-C plugged 30. Ridges, hips, and valleys shall be at least one size larger than supported rafters.

30. In open beam construction, provide strap ties across the beams at the ridge support and provide ties at wall plates.

31. Detail all post-to-beam and post-to-footing connections and reference the detail to the plan.

32. Provide calculations for lateral loads, shear panels, shear transfer, and related.

MISCELLANEOUS DETAILS

1. Show a weep screed at the foundation plate line on all exterior and stud walls to be stuccoed.

2. Provide fireplace construction details or note construction to be per attached fireplace standard drawing.

3. Provide 36 inches high protective railings for porches, balconies, and open sides of stair landings. Openings between railings shall be less than 6 inches.

4. Provide stairway and landing details.

   a. Maximum rise 8 inches and minimum run 9 inches.

   b. Minimum headroom is 6 feet 6 inches.

   c. Minimum width is 30 inches.

5. All handrails shall satisfy the following:

   a. Provide handrail for stairways with four or more risers.

   b. Handrail shall be 30 inches to 34 inches above the nosing of treds.

   c. The handgrip portion of handrail shall be not less than 1 1/4 inches nor more than 2 inches in cross-sectional dimension.

6. Provide four elevations.

ENERGY CONSERVATION

Each state has specific Energy Conservation Regulations that all house plans must comply with. Obtain a copy of these requirements for your state, and include the required information with the set of plans being submitted to the building department.

APPENDIX C

JOIST SPAN

JOIST SIZE	FLOOR JOIST		CEILING JOIST	
	SPACING	MAX SPAN	SPACING	MAX SPAN
2 X 4			12" OC 16" OC 24" OC	11' - 0" 10' - 0" 8' - 9"
2 X 6	12" OC 16" OC 24" OC	10' - 11" 9' - 8" 7' - 10"	12" OC 16" OC 24" OC	17' - 4" 15' - 9" 13' - 3"
2 X 8	12" OC 16" OC 24" OC	14' - 4" 12' - 9" 10' - 4"	12" OC 16" OC 24" OC	22' - 10" 20' - 9" 18' - 1"
2 X 10	12" OC 16" OC 24" OC	18' - 4" 16' - 3" 13' - 3"	12" OC 16" OC 24" OC	29' - 2" 26' - 2" 23' - 1"
2 X 12	12" OC 16" OC 24" OC	22' - 4" 19' - 9" 16' - 1"		

CEILING JOIST USING VISUAL GRADED LUMBER WITH DRYWALL CEILING
FLOOR JOIST USING VISUAL GRADED LUMBER WITH OR WITHOUT DRYWALL CEILING
SEE UNIFORM BUILDING CODE

RAFTER SPAN

RAFTER SIZE	SLOPE LESS THAN 4:12		SLOPE 4:12 OR GREATER	
	SPACING	MAX SPAN	SPACING	MAX SPAN
2 X 4	12" OC 16" OC 24" OC	8' - 9" 7' - 11" 6' - 11"	12" OC 16" OC 24" OC	9' - 4" 8' - 6" 7' - 5"
2 X 6	12" OC 16" OC 24" OC	13' - 9" 12' - 6" 10' - 11"	12" OC 16" OC 24" OC	14' - 10" 13' - 5" 11' - 9"
2 X 8	12" OC 16" OC 24" OC	18' - 1" 16' - 6" 14' - 4"	12" OC 16" OC 24" OC	19' - 6" 17' - 9" 15' - 6"
2 X 10	12" OC 16" OC 24" OC	23' - 1" 21' - 0" 18' - 4"	12" OC 16" OC 24" OC	24' - 11" 22' - 8" 19' - 9"
2 X 12	12" OC 16" OC 24" OC	28' - 1" 25' - 7" 22' - 4"		

ROOF RAFTERS USING VISUAL GRADED LUMBER WITH OR WITHOUT
DRYWALL CEILING
SEE UNIFORM BUILDING CODE

A

Access	ACC
Access panel	AP
Acoustical	AC
Acoustical plaster	ACPL
Acoustical tile	ACT
Acrylic plastic	ACR
Addendum	ADD
Adhesive	ADH
Adjacent	ADJ
Adjustable	ADJT
Aggregate	AGG
Air conditioning	A/C
Aluminum	AL
American Institute of Architects	AIA
Amount	AMT
Ampere	AMP
Anchor bolt	AB
Anchor, anchorage	ANC
Approximate	APX
Architect (ural)	ARCH
Area	A
Asphalt	ASPH
At	@
Average	AVG

B

Balcony	BALC
Basement	BSMT
Bathroom	B
Bathtub with shower	BTS
Batten	BATT
Beam	BM
Bearing	BRG
Bedroom	BR
Below	BEL
Bench mark	BM
Beveled	BVL
Bidet	BDT
Block	BLK
Blocking	BLKG
Board	BD
Board feet	BD FT
Bottom	BOT
Bracket	BRKT
Brick	BRK
British thermal unit	BTU
Broom closet	BC
Building	BLDG
Building line	BL
Built-up roofing	BUR
Built-in	BLT-IN
Built-up	BU
Button	BUT
Buzzer	BUZ

C

Cabinet	CAB
Carpet (ed)	CPT
Casement	CSMT
Cast iron	CI
Catch basin	CB
Caulking	CLKG
Ceiling	CLG
Ceiling height	CHT
Cement	CEM
Center	CTR
Center line	CL
Center to center	C to C
Ceramic	CER
Ceramic tile	CT
Channel (structural)	C
Check	CHK
Circle	CIR
Circuit breaker	CIR BKR
Circumference	CIRC
Cleanout	CO
Clear (ance)	CLR
Closet	CLO
Closure	CLS
Cold water	CW
Column	COL
Combination	COMB
Compartment	COMPT
Composition (composite)	COMPO
Concrete	CONC
Connection	CX
Construction	CONST
Continuous or continue	CONT
Contract (or)	CONTR
Copper	CPR
Corrugated	CORR
Counter	CTR
Countersink	CS
Course (s)	CRS
Cover	COV
Cross grain	CRG
Cubic feet per minute	CFM
Cubic foot	CFT
Cubic yard	CYD

D

Damper	DPR
Dampproofing	DP
Dead load	DL
Deep, depth	DP
Degree	DEG
Demolish, demolition	DEM
Depressed	DEP
Detail	DTL
Diagonal	DIAG
Diagram	DIAG
Diameter	DIAM
Dimension	DIM
Dining room	DIN RM
Direct current	DC
Dishwasher	DW
Dispenser	DPR
Disposal	DISPL
Distance	DIST
Ditto	DO
Door	DR
Double	DBL
Double hung	DH
Double-strength (glass)	DS
Douglas fir	DF
Downspout	DS
Drain	D
Drain tile	DT
Drainboard	DRB
Drawer	DWR
Drawing	DWG
Drinking fountain	DF
Dryer	D
Dumbwaiter	DW

E

East	E
Electric (al)	ELEC
Electric water cooler	EWC
Electrical panelboard	EP

Elevation	EL	Galvanized pipe	GP
Elevator	ELEV	General contract (or)	GC
Emergency	EMER	Glass, glazing	GL
Enclose (ure)	ENC	Glazed structural tile	GST
Engineer	ENGR	Grab bar	GB
Entrance	ENT	Grade beam	GB
Equipment	EQP	Grade	GR
Estimate	EST	Gravel	GVL
Excavate	EXCA	Grille	GR
Exhaust	EXH	Ground	GRND
Existing	EXG	Grout	GT
Expansion bolt	EB	Gypsum lath	GPL
Expansion joint	EXP JT	Gypsum plaster	GPPL
Exposed	EXP		
Extension	EXT	**H**	
Exterior	EXT	Hall	H
Exterior grade	EXT GR	Hardboard	HBD
		Hardware	HDW
F		Hardwood	HWD
Fabricate	FAB	Head	HD
Face brick	FB	Header	HDR
Face of concrete	FOC	Heating	HTG
Face of finish	FOF	Heavy duty	HD
Face of masonry	FOM	Height	HT
Face of studs	FOS	Hollow core	HC
Factory finish	FF	Hook (s)	HK
Fahrenheit	F	Horizontal	HORIZ
Family room	FAM R	Horsepower	HP
Fasten, fastener	FAS	Hose bib	HB
Feet	FT	Hot water heater	HWH
Feet per minute	FPM	Hour	HR
Fence	FN	House	HSE
Fiberboard	FBD	Hundred	C
Fiberglass	FGL		
Figure	FIG	**I**	
Finish (ed)	FIN	Illuminate	ILLUM
Finished floor elevation	FFE	Incandescent	INCAND
Finished floor line	FFL	Incinerator	NCIN
Finished opening	FO	include (d), (ing)	INCL
Fire alarm	FA	Inflammable	INFL
Fire brick	FBRK	Inside diameter	ID
Fire extinguisher	FE	Inside face	IF
Fire-retardant	FRT	Inspection	INSP
Fireplace	FPL	Install	INST
Fireproof	FP	Insulate (d), (ion)	INS
Fitting	FTG	Interior grade	INTGR
Fixture	FIX	Interior	INT
Flammable	FLAM	Interlock	ILK
Flashing	FLG	Iron pipe size	IPS
Flexible	FLX		
Floor (ing)	FLR	**J**	
Floor cleanout	FLCO	Jamb	JMB
Floor drain	FD	Joint	JT
Floor plate	FPL	Joist	J
Flooring	FLG	Junction box	J-BOX
Fluorescent	FLUR		
Flush joint	FJT	**K**	
Folding	FLDG	Kickplate	KPL
Foot	FT	Kiln dried	KD
Footing	FTG	Kilowatt	KW
Forward	FWD	Kitchen cabinet	KCAB
Foundation	FND	Kitchen	KIT
Four-way	4-W	Kitchen sink	KSK
Frame (d), (ing)	FR	Knockout	KO
Fresh air	FRA		
Front	FR	**L**	
Full size	FS	Label	LBL
Furnace	FURN	Lag bolt	LB
Furnished by others	FBO	Laminate (d)	LAM
Furred (ing)	FUR	Landing	LDG
		Latitude	LAT
G		Laundry	LAU
Gallon	GL	Lavatory	LAV
Galvanized	GV	Leader	LDR
Galvanized iron	GI	Left	L

Length	L	Preformed	PRF
Level	LEV	Perimeter	PERI
Light	LT	Perpendicular	PERP
Lightweight	LW	Piece	PC
Limestone	LMS	Plan	PLN
Linear feet	LIN FT	Plaster	PLAS
Linen closet	L CL	Plasterboard	PL BD
Linoleum	LINO	Plastic laminate	PLAM
Lintel	LTL	Plastic	PLAS
Live load	LL	Plastic tile	PLAS T
Living room	LR	Plate glass	PG
Location	LOC	Plate	PL
Louver	LVR	Platform	PLAT
Lumber	LBR	Plumbing	PLMB
		Plywood	PWD
M		Polished	POL
Manufacture (er)	MFR	Polyethylene	POLY
Marble	MRB	Porcelain enamel	PE
Masonry	MAS	Position	POS
Material	MTL	Pounds per cubic foot	PCF
Maximum	MAX	Pounds per lineal foot	PLF
Mechanic (al)	MECH	Pounds per square foot	PSF
Medicine cabinet	MC	Pounds per square inch	PSI
Medium	MED	Prefabricate (d)	PFB
Membrane	MMB	Prefinished	PFN
Metal threshold	MTHR	Preliminary	PRELIM
Millwork	MWK	Premolded	PRMLD
Minimum	MIN	Property	PROP
Mirror	MIR	Property line	PL
Miscellaneous	MISC	Pull chain	PC
Modular	MOD	Pushbutton	PB
Molding, moulding	MLD		
Mount (ed), (ing)	MT	**Q**	
Movable	MOV	Quarry tile	QT
Mullion	MULL		
		R	
N		Rabbet	RBT
Natural grade	NAT GR	Radius	RAD
Natural	NAT	Rail (ing)	RL
Noise reduction	NR	Rainwater conductor	RWC
Nominal	NOM	Range	R
Nonmetallic	NMT	Receptacle	RECP
North	N	Recessed	REC
Not in contract	NIC	Redwood	RDWD
Not to scale	NTS	Reference	REF
Number	NO	Refrigerator	REGR
		Register	REG
O		Reinforce	REINF
Oak	O	Reinforcing bar	REBAR
Obscure	OBS	Remove	REM
Office	OFF	Required	REQ
On center	OC	Resilient	RES
One-way	1-W	Return air	RA
Opaque	OP	Return	RET
Opening	OPG	Revision (s), revised	REV
Opposite	OPP	Revolutions per minute	RPM
Outside diameter	OD	Right hand	RH
Outside face of concrete	OFC	Right of way	ROW
Outside face of stud	OFS	Right	R
Overall	OA	Riser	R
Overhead	OH	Roof drain	RD
		Roof	RF
P		Roofing	RFG
Paint	PNT	Room	RM
Painted	PTD	Rough opening	RO
Pair	PR	Rough	RGH
Panel	PNL	Rubber base	RB
Parallel	PAR	Rubber tile	RBT
Parking	PK		
Particle board	PBD	**S**	
Partition	PTN	Safety glass	SFGL
Pave (ing)	PV	Schedule	SCH
Pavement	PVMT	Screen	SCN
Pedestal	PED	Sealant	SNT
Per	/	Seating	STG
Percent	%		

Second	SEC	Tread	T
Section	SEC	Typical	TYP
Select	SEL		
Select structural	SS	**U**	
Self-closing	SC	Undercut	UC
Service	SERV	Underwriters' Laboratories	U.L.
Service sink	SSK	Unfinished	UNF
Sewer	SEW	Urinal	UR
Sheathing	SHTH		
Sheet metal	SM	**V**	
Sheet	SHT	V-joint (ed)	VJ
Shelf, shelving	SH	Vanity	VAN
Shower	SH	Vapor barrier	VB
Siding	SDG	Varnish	VAR
Similar	SIM	Veneer	VNR
Single-hung	SH	Vent stack	VS
Single-strength (glass)	SS	Vent through roof	VTR
Sink	SK	Ventilation	VENT
Skylight	SKL	Ventilator	V
Socket	SOC	Vermiculite	VRM
Soil pipe	SP	Vertical grain	VG
Solid core	SC	Vertical	VERT
Soundproof	SP	Vinyl base	VB
South	S	Vinyl fabric	VF
Spacer	SPC	Vinyl tile	VT
Speaker	SPK	Vinyl	VIN
Special	SPL	Vinyl wall covering	VWC
Specification (s)	SPEC	Vitreous clay tile	VCT
Square feet	SQ FT	Volt	V
Square inches	SQ IN	Volume	VOL
Square	SQ		
Stainless steel	SST	**W**	
Stairs	ST	Wainscot	WSCT
Stand pipe	ST P	Wall cabinet	WCAB
Standard	STD	Wall hung	WH
Steel	ST	Wall to wall	WTW
Stock	STK	Wall vent	WV
Storage	STO	Waste stack	WS
Storm drain	SD	Water closet	WC
Street	St	Water heater	WH
Structural	STR	Water repellent	WR
Substitute	SUB	Water	W
Supply	SUP	Waterproof	WP
Surface four sides	S4S	Waterstop	WS
Surface	SUR	Watt	W
Surface two edges	S2E	Weatherproof	WP
Suspended	SUS	Weephole	WH
Switch	SW	Weight	WT
Symbol	SYM	Welded wire fabric	WWF
Synthetic	SYN	West	W
System	SYS	Wet Bulb	WB
		Wheel bumper	WHB
T		White pine	WP
Tackboard	TKBD	Width, wide	W
Tackstrip	TKS	Window	WIN
Tangent	TAN	Wire mesh	WM
Tar and gravel	T & G	Wired glass	WG
Technical	TECH	With	W/
Telephone	TEL	Without	WO
Television	TV	Wood base	WB
Temperature	TEMP	Wood	WD
Temporary	TEMP	Working point	WPT
Terra-cotta	TC	Wrought iron	WI
Terrazzo	TZ		
Thermostat	THERMO	**Y**	
Thick (ness)	THK	Yard	YD
Thousand board feet	MBD FT	Yellow pine	YP
Thousand	M		
Three-way	3-W	**Z**	
Threshold	THR	Zinc	ZN
Toilet	TOL		
Tolerance	TOL		
Tongue and groove	T&G		
Top of slab	TSL		
Top of wall	TW		
Towel bar	TB		
Transom	TR		

INDEX

1/4"

1/8"

1/16"

GUIDE LINES FOR LETTERING PRACTICE

GRID-PAPER GUIDE

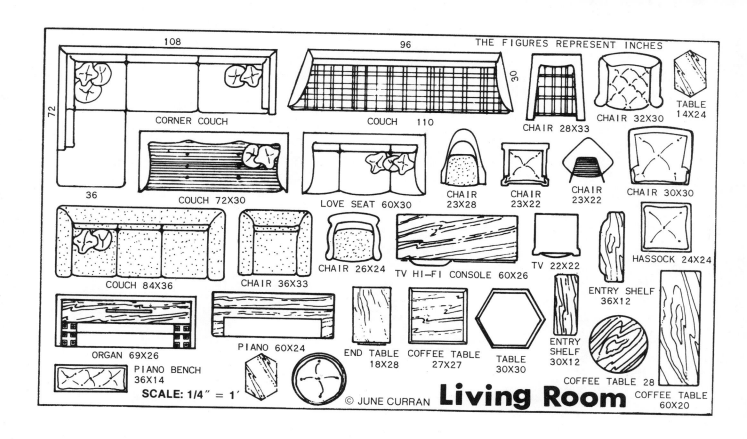

THE FIGURES REPRESENT INCHES

108

CORNER COUCH

72

36

96

30

COUCH 110

CHAIR 28X33

CHAIR 32X30

TABLE 14X24

COUCH 72X30

LOVE SEAT 60X30

CHAIR 23X28

CHAIR 23X22

CHAIR 23X22

CHAIR 30X30

COUCH 84X36

CHAIR 36X33

CHAIR 26X24

TV HI-FI CONSOLE 60X26

TV 22X22

HASSOCK 24X24

ENTRY SHELF 36X12

ORGAN 69X26

PIANO 60X24

END TABLE 18X28

COFFEE TABLE 27X27

TABLE 30X30

ENTRY SHELF 30X12

COFFEE TABLE 28

PIANO BENCH 36X14

SCALE: 1/4" = 1'

© JUNE CURRAN

COFFEE TABLE 60X20

Living Room

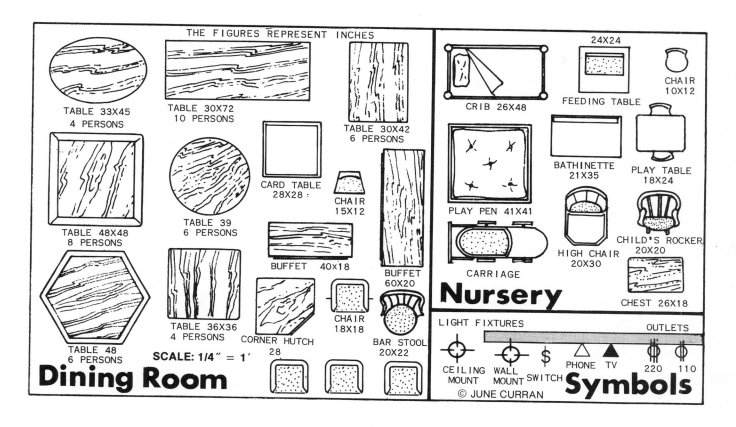

THE FIGURES REPRESENT INCHES

TABLE 33X45 4 PERSONS

TABLE 30X72 10 PERSONS

TABLE 30X42 6 PERSONS

TABLE 48X48 8 PERSONS

TABLE 39 6 PERSONS

CARD TABLE 28X28

CHAIR 15X12

BUFFET 40X18

BUFFET 60X20

TABLE 48 6 PERSONS

TABLE 36X36 4 PERSONS

CORNER HUTCH 28

CHAIR 18X18

BAR STOOL 20X22

SCALE: 1/4" = 1'

Dining Room

CRIB 26X48

24X24

FEEDING TABLE

CHAIR 10X12

BATHINETTE 21X35

PLAY TABLE 18X24

PLAY PEN 41X41

HIGH CHAIR 20X30

CHILD'S ROCKER 20X20

CARRIAGE

CHEST 26X18

Nursery

LIGHT FIXTURES   OUTLETS

CEILING MOUNT   WALL MOUNT   SWITCH   PHONE   TV   220   110

© JUNE CURRAN

Symbols

CUT-OUTS AND TRACING GUIDES

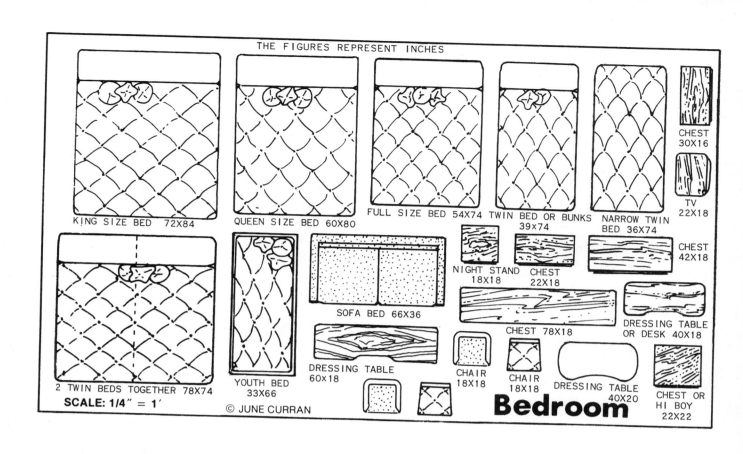

THE FIGURES REPRESENT INCHES

KING SIZE BED 72X84

QUEEN SIZE BED 60X80

FULL SIZE BED 54X74

TWIN BED OR BUNKS 39x74

NARROW TWIN BED 36X74

CHEST 30X16

TV 22X18

NIGHT STAND 18X18

CHEST 22X18

CHEST 42X18

SOFA BED 66X36

CHEST 78X18

DRESSING TABLE OR DESK 40X18

DRESSING TABLE 60x18

CHAIR 18X18

CHAIR 18X18

DRESSING TABLE 40X20

CHEST OR HI BOY 22X22

2 TWIN BEDS TOGETHER 78X74

SCALE: 1/4" = 1'

YOUTH BED 33X66

© JUNE CURRAN

Bedroom

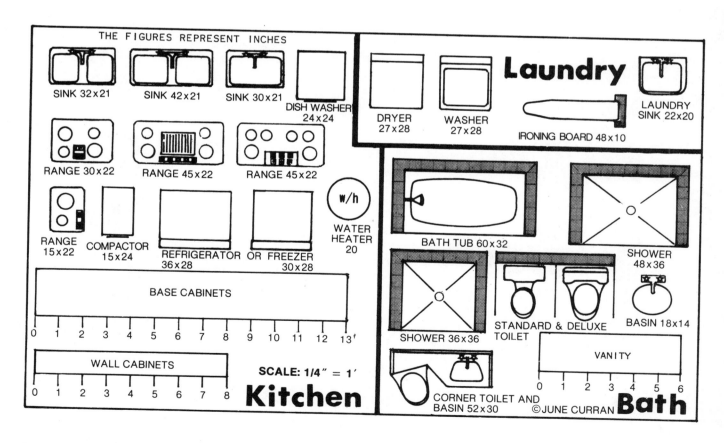

THE FIGURES REPRESENT INCHES

SINK 32x21

SINK 42x21

SINK 30x21

DISH WASHER 24x24

RANGE 30x22

RANGE 45x22

RANGE 45x22

RANGE 15x22

COMPACTOR 15x24

REFRIGERATOR 36x28

OR FREEZER 30x28

WATER HEATER 20

BASE CABINETS

0 1 2 3 4 5 6 7 8 9 10 11 12 13'

WALL CABINETS

0 1 2 3 4 5 6 7 8

SCALE: 1/4" = 1'

Kitchen

Laundry

DRYER 27x28

WASHER 27x28

IRONING BOARD 48x10

LAUNDRY SINK 22x20

BATH TUB 60x32

SHOWER 48x36

SHOWER 36x36

STANDARD & DELUXE TOILET

BASIN 18x14

VANITY

0 1 2 3 4 5 6

CORNER TOILET AND BASIN 52x30

©JUNE CURRAN

Bath

CUT-OUTS AND TRACING GUIDES

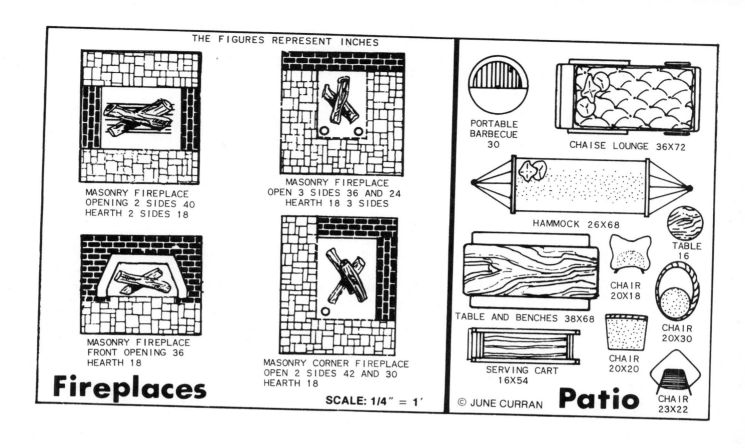

THE FIGURES REPRESENT INCHES

MASONRY FIREPLACE
OPENING 2 SIDES 40
HEARTH 2 SIDES 18

MASONRY FIREPLACE
OPEN 3 SIDES 36 AND 24
HEARTH 18 3 SIDES

MASONRY FIREPLACE
FRONT OPENING 36
HEARTH 18

MASONRY CORNER FIREPLACE
OPEN 2 SIDES 42 AND 30
HEARTH 18

Fireplaces

SCALE: 1/4″ = 1′

PORTABLE
BARBECUE
30

CHAISE LOUNGE 36X72

HAMMOCK 26X68

TABLE
16

CHAIR
20X18

TABLE AND BENCHES 38X68

CHAIR
20X30

SERVING CART
16X54

CHAIR
20X20

Patio

CHAIR
23X22

© JUNE CURRAN

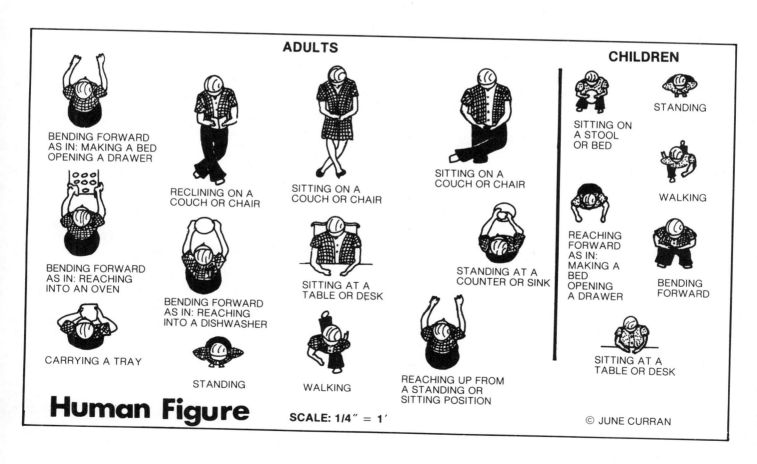

ADULTS

CHILDREN

BENDING FORWARD
AS IN: MAKING A BED
OPENING A DRAWER

RECLINING ON A
COUCH OR CHAIR

SITTING ON A
COUCH OR CHAIR

SITTING ON A
COUCH OR CHAIR

SITTING ON
A STOOL
OR BED

STANDING

BENDING FORWARD
AS IN: REACHING
INTO AN OVEN

BENDING FORWARD
AS IN: REACHING
INTO A DISHWASHER

SITTING AT A
TABLE OR DESK

STANDING AT A
COUNTER OR SINK

REACHING
FORWARD
AS IN:
MAKING A
BED
OPENING
A DRAWER

WALKING

BENDING
FORWARD

CARRYING A TRAY

STANDING

WALKING

REACHING UP FROM
A STANDING OR
SITTING POSITION

SITTING AT A
TABLE OR DESK

Human Figure

SCALE: 1/4″ = 1′

© JUNE CURRAN

CUT-OUTS AND TRACING GUIDES

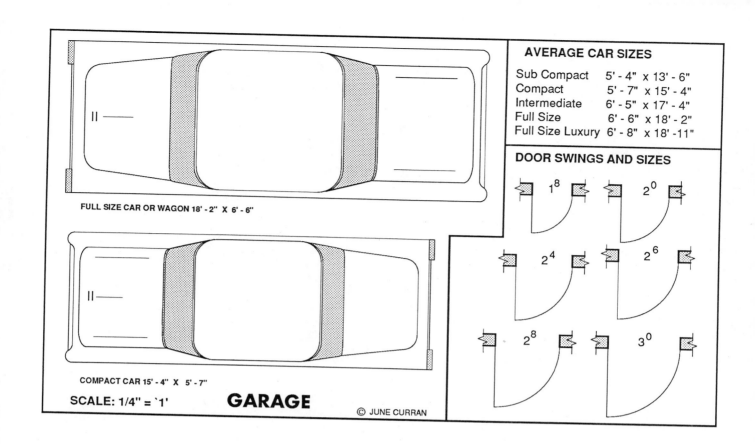

FULL SIZE CAR OR WAGON 18' - 2" X 6' - 6"

COMPACT CAR 15' - 4" X 5' - 7"

SCALE: 1/4" = `1'   **GARAGE**   © JUNE CURRAN

AVERAGE CAR SIZES

Sub Compact	5' - 4" x 13' - 6"
Compact	5' - 7" x 15' - 4"
Intermediate	6' - 5" x 17' - 4"
Full Size	6' - 6" x 18' - 2"
Full Size Luxury	6' - 8" x 18' -11"

DOOR SWINGS AND SIZES

1^8 2^0

2^4 2^6

2^8 3^0

CUT-OUTS AND TRACING GUIDES

SCALE: 1/4 INCH = 1 FOOT

0 6 1 2 3 4 5 6 7 8 9 10 11 12 13 14 15 16 17 18 19 20 21 22 23 24 25 26 27 28 29 30 31 32 33 34 35 36

SCALE: 1/8 INCH = 1 FOOT

0 1 2 4 6 8 10 12 14 16 18 20 22 24 26 28 30 32 34 36 38 40 42 44 46 48 50 52 54 56 58 60 62 64 66 68 70 72

SCALE: 1/16 INCH = 1 FOOT

0 2 4 8 12 16 20 24 28 32 36 40 44 48 52 56 60 64 68 72 76 80 84 88 92 96 100 104 108 112 116 120 124 128 132 136 140 144